ARGUMENT AND ARGUMENTATION

Jean Saindon
York University

THOMSON

NELSON

Australia Canada Mexico Singapore Spain United Kingdom United States

THOMSON

NELSON

Argument and Argumentation
by Jean Saindon

**Associate Vice President,
Editorial Director:**
Evelyn Veitch

**Editor-in-Chief,
Higher Education:**
Anne Williams

Acquisitions Editor:
Bram Sepers

Marketing Manager:
Shelley Collacutt Miller

Developmental Editor:
James Polley

**Content Production
Manager:**
Jamie Larson

Production Service:
International Typesetting
and Composition

Copy Editor:
Cathy Witlox

**Manufacturing
Coordinator:**
Ferial Suleman

Design Director:
Ken Phipps

**Interior Design
Modifications:**
Katherine Strain

Cover Design:
Johanna Liburd

Cover Image:
© M. Thomson/Zefal
Corbis

Compositor:
International Typesetting
and Composition

**Photo/Permissions
Researcher:**
Kristiina Bowering

Printer:
Thomson West

**Library and Archives Canada
Cataloguing in Publication**

Saindon, Jean Emmett
   Argument and argumentation /
Jean Saindon.

Includes index.

ISBN-13: 978-0-17-610316-3
ISBN-10: 0-17-610316-3

1. Reasoning—Textbooks. I. Title.

BC177.S18 2007   168
C2006-906691-4

CONTENTS

MODULE 2 CLARIFYING MEANING 14

MODULE 4 ASSESSING DEDUCTIVE ARGUMENTS   57

MODULE 7 FALLACIES 115

MODULE 8 ANALYZING AND ASSESSING EXTENDED ARGUMENTS   153

MODULE 12 WRITTEN ARGUMENTATION   249

PREFACE

AUDIENCE AND USES

This text is designed for a first-year course in informal logic, critical reasoning, fallacies, argument essay writing, and argument and argumentation. It can also be used as a secondary text for upper-level courses that focus on argumentation, the analysis of arguments, issue analysis, conceptual analysis, argument essay writing, and philosophy.

The module format of *Argument and Argumentation* allows instructors the flexibility to use the text in a variety of ways, for a range of audiences and classes. Some modules or parts of modules can be used independently of one another to meet instructors' individual teaching needs. Typical informal logic courses may focus on Modules 1 through 8. Courses devoted to the study of fallacies can concentrate on Modules 1 through 3 and then focus heavily on Module 7. Instructors focusing on argumentation may move selectively through Modules 1 to 3 and then concentrate on Modules 10 and 11. Those who wish to emphasize developing written arguments can focus on Module 12.

This text is designed to be used in conjunction with the accompanying Student Manual, which provides answers to the Quick Quizzes and additional exercises.

UNIQUE FEATURES OF THE TEXT

Focusing on argumentation, this book places the traditional components of critical reasoning texts within the broader context of argumentation and reasoning with reasoners. While incorporating the established elements of critical reasoning — identifying, analyzing, and assessing arguments — it explores topics, issues, positions, and considerations; the dynamics of argumentation; and the presenting, challenging, and defending of arguments.

In addition to discussing the core elements of argument analysis and critique, *Argument and Argumentation* addresses topics not commonly covered in critical thinking texts, including conceptual analysis, issues analysis, the development and defending of arguments, and written argumentation. Its unique treatment of some standard topics, such as methods for neutralizing fallacies, identifying look-alikes, and incorporating challenges and responses as part of argument analysis, distinguishes it from other works in the field.

A Canadian text, *Argument and Argumentation* uses examples that address situations that interest and challenge Canadian students. Contemporary controversial issues developed throughout the text in different analysis and critique contexts offer students relevant examples of how to apply the skills they learn. Recognizing that students embarking on the study of logic and philosophy often lack the background for dealing with important issues, the text focuses on a number of key topics and begins to build that background. Exploring modern-day concerns such as the right to euthanasia, the legalization of gay marriage, and the societal impact of pornography, the text lays the foundation for both a deeper understanding of today's issues and rich, enlightening classroom conversation. Through examples and exercises on these recurrent themes, *Argument and Argumentation* emphasizes that reasoning is often about concerns of general significance, and not just isolated arguments. This focus on real-world contentious issues impresses upon students that the study of argumentation is not abstract or purely theoretical but important and practical in both academic life and beyond.

The text draws substantially on student experience. Many examples are sourced from student arguments or student comments on arguments in the public arena. Rather than trying to provide ideal analyses of issues from a privileged point of view, the text contains composites of those written by students. For example, the analyses of the gay marriage passage (Module 8), euthanasia (Module 9), *The Adventures of Huckleberry Finn* (Modules 1 and 10) are all derived from student analyses. This reflects the basic assumption of the text that argumentation is an ongoing process involving reasoners.

The Quick Quizzes throughout the text (and their answers in the Student Manual) offer students a means of testing their understanding. The expectation is that students, having studied the relevant material, will take the Quick Quizzes, then check their answers to assess where they need to concentrate more effort. The Student Manual also provides additional exercises for the student to work through.

ACKNOWLEDGMENTS

To the scholars who reviewed this text, for your thoughtful, helpful, and stimulating comments, thank you.

To my copy editor, Cathy Witlox, who not only clarified my prose but taught me in the process, thank you.

To all of my students in Modes of Reasoning, for whom this text is written, for your challenges and inspiring enthusiasm for the material, thank you.

To Dr. John King, for your editorial assistance and especially for your challenges, provocations, and conversations over the years, thank you, my friend.

To those who have sustained, nurtured, and encouraged me and been inspirations in life and critical thinking, Kate Krug and Valda Leightheizer, Richard Dickinson and Chris Doran, Geon van der Wyst and Aleksander Antonijevich, Joe Rudyk and Angela Korwan, Chris Johnston, Rob Gentry, and Alycia Chambers, thank you, my friends.

Finally, to Kathie Conlin-Saindon, without whom this project would not have been possible, for being an inspired educator, practitioner, and living exemplar of critical thinking, who has sustained, supported, inspired, and challenged me, and been my lifeline to the world for the past ten years, thank you. *Ensemble d'avantage*—"together we are more"— our motto, a fitting adage for argumentation and for life.

INTRODUCTION

1.1 LEARNING OBJECTIVES

After completing this module, you should be able to

1. explain how argument and argumentation are forms of critical reasoning;
2. explain the difference between argument and argumentation;
3. explain and use key concepts, including argument, argumentation, reason, premise, conclusion, and issue;
4. explain the difference and be able to distinguish between mere opinion, reasoned opinion, and evidential claims;
5. explain the concept of constitutive rules of argumentation and how the specific rules function in argumentation; and
6. explain the difference and be able to distinguish between a topic, an issue, a position, and the reasons for that position.

1.2 CRITICAL REASONING AND ARGUMENTATION

Many aspects of our lives involve **reasoning,** the process of connecting and assessing ideas. We reason, for example, every time we formulate or solve a problem, make a decision, draw an inference, connect or synthesize two ideas, analyze, make a prediction, evaluate, make a judgment, explain an event, apply an idea or thought to a new situation, generalize from experience, interpret an event or work of literature, or follow or give directions.

We are all intuitive reasoners, reasoning constantly, usually without reflecting on it. Sometimes we follow patterns of reasoning or use ideas we have been exposed to in our environments — through parents, school, peers, and society. Although many of these patterns may "work" much of the time, they can also lead us astray at critical times. As intuitive reasoners, we tend to generalize, making determinations based on a small number of cases or from atypical cases if they are vivid or catch our attention.

This is why we need critical reasoning. **Critical reasoning** involves reflecting on our reasoning, analyzing it, evaluating it according to standards or criteria, and assessing the standards we use in evaluation — in other words, making our reasoning explicit and being critical about it. To help us improve our reasoning, we must develop standards and apply them to both our reasoning and that of others.

We can develop critical reasoning skills in any area in which we reason — in observing the world, problem-solving, interpreting actions and literature, or arguing. This text focuses on the critical reasoning skills involved in argument and argumentation.

We often confuse two senses of the term **argue.**

> I had an argument with my brother. He got angry and left.

In this sense of *argue,* we are saying we had a confrontation, a dispute that involved raised voices and heightened emotions. Here, *argue* and *argument* mean to disagree, to yell and scream, to engage in a heated dispute.

Argue can also mean giving reasons for a claim.

My brother's argument convinced me that we should buy the car together.

My brother has given me reasons for us to buy a car together. And I have been convinced by those reasons.

Having a good argument and being convinced by that argument are two distinct things. My brother may have a good argument, but I may not be convinced by it. I may have a better argument, or I may require something other than a good argument to sway me.

This text focuses on the second notion of argument — the giving of reasons for a claim. Our primary goal here is to help the reader develop the critical skills for analyzing, assessing, challenging, and defending reasoning involving arguments.

We use arguments in all kinds of reasoning — in defending a position we have taken, in evaluating a course of action, in urging a course of action for others, in justifying, in explaining, in predicting, in making a decision about what to do. We offer reasons for claims we have made. Lawyers marshal evidence and arguments to make their case; accountants provide arguments to support their financial recommendations; wives use arguments to convince their husbands to redecorate the kitchen; politicians use arguments to get the electorate to accept their policies and elect them; students give arguments for better grades. We use arguments to negotiate a deal, establish social policy, convince a friend where to go for supper. Using arguments is one of our most basic skills.

We can use arguments for many underlying purposes,

- to find out the truth about an issue;
- to persuade;
- to inquire;
- to prove something; or
- to examine a line of reasoning.

They can also be used

- to intimidate;
- to legitimize;
- to justify;
- to rationalize;
- to impress; and
- for a host of other functions.

Critical thinking involving arguments requires developing tools — and skills in the use of those tools — for analyzing, evaluating, creating, challenging, and responding to challenges.

Argument refers to a set of claims, one of which is offered in support of another claim. That is, an argument occurs when one or more claims — the **reasons,** or **premises**— are offered as justifications, evidence, or support for another claim, called the **conclusion of the argument.** The term *argument*, in this sense, refers to the claims, both reasons and conclusions, taken together.

In everyday use, people often use *argument* to refer to a position or stand they have taken — in essence, the conclusion of an argument. For example, someone will say, "My argument is that Canada should not be involved in the war in Afghanistan." This is not how we use the term in this text. Without stating reasons, such a statement is simply an **unsupported claim.** Only when we add the reasons that support the claim does it become an argument.

A **claim** is a statement that can be either true or false. A question, such as "Should Canada be involved in the war in Afghanistan?" is not a claim; however, the answer to a question may be.

"Canada should be involved in the war in Afghanistan" is a claim and, therefore, may be either true or false. A phrase or sentence fragment is not a claim either. For example, "Involved in the war in Afghanistan" is not a claim, but we can turn it into one by making it into a complete sentence. Only complete sentences can be claims. (Kinds of claims are further discussed in Module 6.) The following are claims:

- AIDS is a serious disease.
- Creationism should not be taught in the science classroom.
- Mandatory drug testing violates individuals' rights.

None of these is yet an argument. An argument consists of at least two related claims, one of which is offered as justification, evidence, or support for the other. The claim being justified is called the conclusion; the claim providing the evidence, the supporting claim, is called the reason or the premise. The following are arguments:

- AIDS is a serious disease, because over half of those who have contracted the virus have died.
- Creationism should not be taught in the science classroom because it is not scientific.
- The right to privacy is a basic human right. Mandatory drug testing violates the right to privacy. Therefore, mandatory drug testing violates basic human rights.

Each of the claims in the first set has been transformed into the conclusion of an argument in the second. One or more reasons have been offered in support of each of the conclusions. An argument does not have to be good to be considered an argument. It merely has to have a conclusion and one or more reasons for that conclusion. The reason(s) offered may or may not be good; it (or they) may or may not adequately support the conclusion; there might be better reasons and support possible for the conclusion. Nonetheless, in each case above, a reason has been offered in support of the claim that is the conclusion. An argument has been given.

QUICK QUIZ 1.1   Identifying Arguments

Identify which, if any, of the following are arguments.

1. Mary lied when she said that she had attended the conference.
2. Mary did not attend the conference but submitted an expense claim for the conference.
3. Mary lied because she claimed to have attended the conference although she hadn't.

Answers for all Quick Quizzes in this text are provided in the Student Manual. After doing the Quick Quizzes, consult the Student Manual to check your understanding of the material.

1.3 WHY GIVE ARGUMENTS?

Why should we give reasons for the claims we make? Aren't reasons just **opinion,** and isn't everyone entitled to his or her own? Don't reasons differ from person to person? Isn't all reasoning subjective? These are common objections to the giving of reasons and arguments. These objections partially rest on a false set of assumptions about what arguing can do and partially involve poor reasoning.

Let us examine these objections one by one: *Reasons are just opinion. And reasoning is purely subjective.* If "just opinion" in this objection means that different people have different beliefs and that the truth of a belief is simply a matter of one's point of view, then the claim is both contradictory and false. I may believe that Paul Bernardo was not the Scarborough rapist, that the world is flat, or that gold has an atomic number of 237. Others may believe something different. Our believing these claims does not make them true or false. They are **evidential claims** — claims about the world for which evidence that is independent of my beliefs is relevant. And my beliefs are false, given the available evidence. Evidence and argument are relevant to establishing such claims. The evidence goes beyond what I believe to what the world is actually like independent of my beliefs about it. Not all of the evidence may be available at a given point in time, or we may disagree about what the evidence is or its implications, but that makes the claim unresolved, not simply a matter of opinion.

Sometimes we have **simple opinions;** that is, beliefs for which we have no reasons. The Beatles are better than the Rolling Stones. I may have no reasons for this opinion other than I prefer the music of one to the other. But asked why the Beatles are better than the Stones, I might be able to give reasons. Once I give reasons, my simple opinion becomes a **reasoned opinion,** and we can engage in an argument over it. Most of us have simple opinions about many things; however, that does not prevent us from turning them into reasoned opinions.

Some issues seem to be ones on which we will never reach an agreement on. Is abortion morally justifiable? The differences on this issue run deep. That does not mean, however, that arguing about it is futile or that reasons have no function. By articulating my reasons for and probing the argument I use to support my position on abortion, I can discover something about the beliefs to which I am committed and better understand what I believe. Understanding my fundamental commitments on an issue can lead to my changing them.

Probing your arguments, I can learn something about you and about your commitments. I may even discover grounds to change my mind on the issue. Even if I don't, I gain a better understanding of you and your position and myself and my own position.

We give reasons, not simply to persuade others nor simply to defend ourselves. We give reasons because we are interested in seeking the truth about an issue, in basing our beliefs and actions on the best available evidence and premises for those beliefs and actions. By probing the reasons behind beliefs, we can identify what we and others are really committed to, resolve conflicts between our various beliefs and values, understand ourselves and others better, and make better decisions.

The claim that reasoning is subjective, or that we all have different reasons for the beliefs we hold and therefore should not challenge the beliefs of others, rests on a form of misplaced tolerance. **Tolerance** is the idea that we recognize and respect the beliefs and practices of others. However, this does not mean that we accept all reasons and all beliefs as equally legitimate. Not all reasoning and not all reasons are good ones. We make errors in reasoning, use false and irrelevant claims as reasons, commit fallacies. If I choose to study computer science because I believe that everyone who graduates with a computer science degree gets a high-paying job, and if in reality the market for people with computer science degrees is poor, I am basing my actions on a false assumption about the world. I have a reason for my decision, but it is faulty. Someone who respects me and does not want me to make a costly mistake would likely point out the error of my reasoning rather than "tolerate" my mistaken belief.

Respecting others and their ideas does not mean that we cannot or should not challenge their ideas and beliefs when we think those ideas are wrong or misguided. Through argument we cannot force others to accept our challenges and change their minds. However, we can try to show the weakness of the claims and arguments presented and leave it up to each person to decide what he or she will do about the problems in the reasoning. We thereby help others to better understand their ideas and what those ideas commit them to. Some people may change their beliefs. Others may take the critique as a challenge to find better reasons for their positions. We show greater respect for someone's ideas by engaging in rational argumentation about those ideas than by simply tolerating whatever the person says.

Reasoning and using arguments help us examine what we believe and what our beliefs commit us to, help us make better choices about our actions, help us understand the world, and help us interact with others. Reasoning matters in society in general. After all, it is better to base social policy on reason than on an alternative option.

QUICK QUIZ 1.2 Distinguishing Simple Opinion, Reasoned Opinion, and Evidential Claims

Identify which of the following are simple opinions and which are reasoned opinions. If there is an argument, identify the reason and the conclusion, and determine whether the main conclusion is the kind of claim that can be based on objective evidence.

1. Abortion is wrong.
2. Abortion is wrong because it ends a human life.
3. I can't stand *American Idol*.
4. *American Idol* represents the best in contemporary television programming. It appeals to a large audience, has high production values, and gives the audience something they can identify with.
5. Broccoli is good for you; it is high in calcium and some essential vitamins as well as being high in fibre.

1.4 ARGUMENT AND ARGUMENTATION

When we "give an argument," we present reasons for a claim we want to justify or support. An argument is a set of claims — the conclusion we are supporting or defending and the reasons we offer for that conclusion. The critical analysis and evaluation of arguments involve

1. clarifying meaning and paraphrasing the key claims;
2. identifying the parts of an argument (reason and conclusion) and portraying the structure of the argument, relating the reason to the conclusion;
3. evaluating whether the reason supports the conclusion;
4. evaluating the truth of the reason;
5. evaluating presuppositions and implications; and
6. evaluating the argument for fallacies (errors in reasoning).

The criteria for evaluating arguments are based on the central purpose of arguments. Good arguments seek to establish the truth of the conclusion by showing that the conclusion follows from, or is justified by, true premises. The reasons provide us with grounds for accepting the conclusion, which is often in doubt or controversial. The usual study of argument focuses on the claims made within an argument, the meaning and truth of the claims, and the relationship of the claims to one another. Although this is effective for analyzing static texts and arguments, it does not capture the fluid process by which reasoners construct and defend their positions over the course of an interaction, nor does it capture the additional rules needed to ensure that the argument stays on track. **Argumentation** does that.

Argumentation is a form of discourse in which we use arguments to seek the truth about an issue. It involves the dynamic process of reasoning with others — of constructing arguments, presenting those arguments, and challenging and responding to the challenges of others. One person makes a claim or takes a position; another person responds to it by asking for elaboration or challenging what is said. The first speaker defends his original argument with further reasons. The second speaker makes another challenge. Argumentation refers to this dynamic process of reasoning between reasoners. This allows us to focus on the idea that arguments are given and analyzed in contexts in which we try to create and recreate rational meaning, to persuade and influence, and to engage rationally, not only with an issue but also with one or more other human beings, in the attempt to discover the truth about an issue.

The process of argumentation can occur without another reasoner being present. When we analyze a text, construct our own argument, or write a paper, we can engage in argumentation by considering how other possible reasoners might respond to our arguments. We can even enter into a dialogue with ourselves, taking on the roles of both the presenter and the challenger of the argument.

Argumentation involves three major components — the content (the arguments), the people engaged in the argumentation, and the process.

1. The **content** includes the substance of what is being argued — the issues, positions, and claims produced through the practice of arguing.
2. The **people** are the parties engaging in the practice of arguing — those who are giving, critiquing, and revising arguments. There are minimally two roles taken in argumentation — the **presenter,** or **defender,** of the argument and the **challenger,** or **critic.** Both are called **arguers.** Each of these roles has a unique set of functions and expectations; however, an individual may switch roles in a given interaction, or an individual, when examining his or her own work, may assume both roles in turn.

     Understanding the people can involve understanding not just their arguments but also their emotions, commitments, interests, immediate role in context, and purpose for giving an argument.
3. The **process** is how the participants in an argument interact with one another. This includes both (a) the actual practices and behaviours — what people are doing — and (b) the normative rules that define the ideal of effective argumentation.

Individuals involved in argumentation engage in various behaviours and practices. Some of these may further the aims of argumentation; others may hinder them. People who claim to be engaging in argumentation but knowingly use false information, force, or modes of reasoning that they know are misleading undermine the basic aims and purposes of argumentation. Although they are employing some of the tools of argument and argumentation, they are not using them in the pursuit of truth and understanding. These behaviours thwart the arguer's aim.

Just as argument critique involves a set of criteria for evaluating, so, too, does argumentation. While argumentation uses the normative criteria for good reasoning found in the analysis and evaluation of arguments, it extends those to the dynamic nature of arguments and includes principles for such things as listening, challenging and responding, and resolving an encounter.

We use arguments, usually for persuasion or rational persuasion, in many kinds of discourse, including advertising, political speeches, policy documents, as well as everyday life. **Discourse** means any form of conversation, discussion, or presentation of ideas with an audience in mind.

Different forms of discourse suit different purposes. The purpose of **persuasion** (as opposed to **rational persuasion,** defined below) is to convince someone of something. Argument is simply one tool that can be used to achieve this aim. It is not the only tool. We can use appeals to emotion, group membership, or common practice, which are all means of nonrational, or faulty, persuasion, and may be useful when the aim of discovering the truth about something is secondary. For example, the goal of defence attorneys is not to seek the truth but to get acquittals for their clients. The goal of advertisers is to entice consumers to buy their products. The truth may get in the way of these aims. Rational persuasion, by contrast, is the process of using good (that is, rational) arguments to convince someone.

Each form of discourse is defined by its end or purpose. This end establishes normative expectations and principles that define what the interaction is and how it proceeds. These normative principles are the **constitutive rules** that define the basic parameters and conduct of an activity. For example, one of the constitutive rules of intimacy is a mutual sharing of personal experiences and emotions. Breaking the constitutive rules means that one is interacting poorly or not doing it at all; bending the constitutive rules means that one is doing some kind of counterfeit of the interaction or is engaged in a different activity altogether. So in our example, if one person in an intimate exchange gives a fictitious account of his or her experiences and emotions, the two parties have not engaged in an intimate disclosure. One party has merely pretended.

The **end** or **purpose of argumentation** is **rational inquiry**— that is, the rational pursuit of truth about an issue through reasoned discussion using argument, and the rational appreciation of difference through reasoned discussion using argument. Although related to other forms of communication, such as negotiation, conflict management/resolution, problem solving, and empathetic communication, argumentation is distinguished by the focus on reasoned discussion using argument.

What differentiates argumentation from activities like negotiation, where the goal is arriving at a mutual agreement to resolve conflicting interests; conflict management, where the goal is the resolution (or management) of conflict; and politics, where the goal is the exercise of power, is a commitment to the aim of rational inquiry, and the principle that issues should be resolved solely by an appeal to the evidence and reasoning about those issues as reflected through arguments.

1.5 THE CONSTITUTIVE RULES OF ARGUMENTATION[1]

Some of the basic constitutive rules of argumentation include the following:

1. **The *truth-seeking principle*.** The parties involved in argumentation are committed to searching for the truth or the most rationally defensible position about the issues about which they are arguing. This means that the parties should be willing to examine alternative positions, look for the insights in the positions of others, and encourage other participants to present arguments for alternate positions or raise objections to any position with regard to any disputed issue. Violation of this subverts the very purpose of argumentation.

   If we reject the idea that we are searching for truth about an issue, then we are engaged in some other kind of activity — persuasion, negotiation, or conflict management.

---

[1] van Eemeren, Frans H., and Rob Grootendorst. *Argumentation, Communication and Fallacies: A Pragma-Dialectical Perspective.* Hillsdale, N.J.: L. Erlbaum, 1994 and T. Edward Damer, *Attacking Faulty Reasoning: A Practical Guide to Fallacy-Free Arguments,* Fifth Edition. Belmont, California: Wadsworth Publishing Company, 2005.

2. **The *respect principle*.** The participants agree to distinguish between the individual advancing a position and the positions and arguments that the person is presenting. This principle recognizes that individuals may hold positions for a variety of reasons and may change their positions with argument. It commits the participants in argumentation to being "hard" (rigorous) on the arguments, positions, and issues yet "soft" (receptive) on the individual as a person and as a reasoner. It demands that participants respect the integrity and personhood of the other(s) engaged in the argumentation while at the same time challenging the arguments and positions as strongly as they can. It also entails that all parties have an equal right to present their own arguments and their challenges to the arguments of others.

   Dismissing someone's arguments out of hand, attacking the person rather than his or her arguments, using threats or force to get someone to do what we want all violate this principle. Strenuously challenging our argument partner's arguments, however, is actually an application of the principle.

3. **The *argument principle*.** Any position one takes must be established either by agreement of the parties or by argument. Establishing a position by argument involves giving reasons that are true and that both parties accept as relevant and sufficient to justify the conclusion. Establishing a position by agreement is only tentative. Two arguers may agree "for the sake of argument" on a given starting position or claim in order to see where that claim leads. However, either partner can withdraw the agreement and challenge the claim. A challenge to an agreed-upon starting point requires that it be defended. In principle, any claim can be challenged and must be capable of being established by argument, even if a given claim in a given argument is not. A requirement of the argument principle is that individuals try to offer the best reason or make the strongest case for their position and put up the strongest challenges to dispute their partners' arguments.

   Committing to the argument principle means that the dispute partners use the following criteria for posing the best arguments possible:

   a. present their positions, claims, and challenges clearly;
   b. give reasons and challenges that are relevant;
   c. give reasons that are true or mutually acceptable; and
   d. give reasons that are sufficient to justify the conclusion.

   In short, arguers should strive to give what we will later call *sound arguments*, and both arguers should acknowledge that they can make mistakes.

   Someone who knowingly uses false evidence, refuses to provide evidence for his or her claims, or shifts the burden of proof violates this principle.

4. **The *fallibility principle*.** Each argument partner acknowledges that he or she could be wrong. Believing that certain claims are beyond proof or disproof and that evidence is irrelevant would violate this principle.

5. **The *listening principle*.** The arguers have an obligation to listen to and attempt to understand the arguments of their argument partners. By extension, participants are obliged to present the arguments of their dispute partners fairly, while (1) remaining consistent with the original claims, (2) remaining consistent with the intentions of the arguer, or (3) giving the strongest possible argument for the position. (These are listed from weakest to strongest.) If there is any doubt about the intention of or the implicit claims within the argument, the arguer should be given the benefit of the doubt in any reformulation. This is sometimes called the **principle of charity in interpretation.**

   Misrepresenting or distorting dispute partners' positions or attributing to them claims they have not made violates this principle.

6. **The *burden of proof principle*.** The burden of proof for any position rests on the participant who advances the position. If and when a challenger asks, the defender of a position has an obligation to provide an argument for that position.

   Refusing to provide evidence for one's claims or insisting that one's partner disprove them rather than offering proof is a violation of this principle.

7. **The *principle of challenge and response*.** Each participant has the right to challenge the claims and arguments of the others in the dialogue. Indeed, each has an obligation to challenge the claims and arguments of the others, even if he or she personally agrees with them. The challenge must be relevant to the position or argument advanced and defended by the presenter. Anyone whose claims or arguments are challenged is obligated to respond to the challenge in an appropriate way, presenting reasons that are directly relevant to the position and argument at issue.

   Dismissing a challenge to one's argument and, in some cases, refusing to challenge an argument violates this principle.

8. **The *resolution principle*.** An issue will be considered resolved if the proponent for one of the positions (1) successfully defends that position by presenting an argument that uses acceptable and relevant premises that provide sufficient grounds to support the conclusion and (2) provides an effective rebuttal to all serious challenges to the argument or position at issue. Unless an arguer can demonstrate that these conditions have not been met, he or she should accept the conclusion of the successful argument and consider the issues, for all practical purposes, to be settled. In the absence of a successful argument for any alternative position, the arguers are obligated to accept the position that is supported by the best of the arguments presented. If a participant does not accept the best-supported position, that participant is obligated to develop challenges to the position and better arguments for his or her own position.

9. **The *suspension of judgment principle*.** If no position comes close to being successfully defended, or if two or more positions seem to be defended with equal strength, the participants should, in most cases, suspend judgment about the issue. If practical considerations require an immediate decision, they should instead weigh the relative risks of gain or loss connected with the consequences of suspending judgment and decide the issue on these grounds.

10. **The *reconsideration principle*.** If a successful, or at least good, argument for a position is subsequently found by any participant to be flawed in any way that raises new doubts about the merit of the conclusion, that participant is obligated to reopen the issue for further consideration.

QUICK QUIZ 1.3   Applying the Constitutive Rules of Argumentation

Each of the following is a move or response in an argumentation. Explain whether the individuals engaged in the interaction are adhering to the basic principles of argumentation. Identify which constitutive rules are violated, if any.

1. I don't care what your objection is. I know what I believe and I'm not going to change my mind on the issue.
2. So far, your objections haven't undermined my argument. Until they do, I'm not agreeing with you on this.
3. That's just a typical feminist argument. And you know I don't agree with feminists on anything.

QUICK QUIZ 1.4   Using the Constitutive Rules

Examine each of the following lines of dialogue from an argument exchange. Identify which constitutive rule the line of dialogue follows or violates and explain why.

1. You have challenged my claim that the government is hiding the remains of a crashed UFO at a secret air base. I admit I don't know where it is. But how do you know they're not hiding one?
2. We have been going at this for two hours. I think we have made some progress and we've both refined our positions and reasons. However, we haven't reached consensus on this. I suggest we go away and think about it.
3. You know, Fred, we reached agreement on that issue yesterday. I was thinking about it overnight and realized that one of the arguments you used to persuade me just doesn't work. Do you have some time now for me to run my challenge by you?

1.6 BASIC DYNAMICS OF ARGUMENTATION

The constitutive rules define the basic framework, the ground rules, within which argumentation occurs. They do not provide us with a model for the dynamics and possible moves and countermoves within an argumentative encounter, but a model of argumentation dynamics does.

Outline of a Basic Argumentation Dynamic

An *argumentation dynamic*—the give and take that occurs within a discussion involving argumentation — can be complex. The following identifies some key features of that dynamic.

1. At least two people are involved in the argumentation. Each takes one of two roles, defender and challenger. Those roles may alternate as the discussion progresses.
2. The defender makes a claim.
3. The challenger asks for reasons.
4. The defender provides reasons.
5. The challenger restates his or her understanding of the argument, asks for clarification, probes the position, or challenges the reasons.
6. The defender responds to the challenge by defending the reasons. If the challenger has presented a good challenge, the defender may modify his or her own reasons, introduce a new line of reasoning, or modify his or her position.
7. The challenger continues with further probing and posing of challenges to the position until a resolution is reached or the two parties agree to suspend judgment.

Throughout the encounter, both sides use various communication skills (active listening, restating, providing feedback to clarify) and argument skills (developing cogent arguments, defending claims, providing counterexamples and responding to them, clarifying meaning, challenging and defending claims) to further the aim of rational inquiry.

The process of an actual encounter is likely to be both more complex than this and far messier. There are nearly as many possibilities for how an argumentation can play out as there are argumentations and arguers. Throughout the process, a participant can make any number of possible moves — some that advance the inquiry; others that hinder it. Basic skills for conducting an effective argumentation include paraphrasing, formulating and critiquing arguments, supplying implicit premises, examining presuppositions, using counterexamples, defending claims, clarifying meaning, and identifying and avoiding fallacies. We will explore these in Module 11.

Topics, Issues, Positions, and Arguments

Argumentation typically occurs about topics or issues on which people take positions. Arguments are given for their positions. Focusing solely on arguments — claims, reasons, conclusions — ignores the fact that arguments function in the larger context of topics and issues.

A *topic* is the subject of concern of an inquiry or dispute. It is normally stated in one or two words or a phrase. "Pornography" is a topic; so is "degrading." "The evolution of humankind," "abortion," "Frankenstein as an anti-science novel," and "the development of civilization" are all topics. They can play the role of the central subject of a discussion.

An *issue* is a point of contention within a given context and between at least two disputants, inquirers, or points of view. It is a matter that elicits disagreement about acceptability or truth, or a problem that elicits disagreement about the correct or appropriate solution. An issue is a central point on which a debate or inquiry hinges. An issue on the topic of abortion might be formulated as follows: "Should there be laws regarding abortion in Canada?" A subsidiary issue might be "Should the state accord legal rights to the fetus at any stage of development?" Another issue on the topic of abortion might be "Is abortion immoral?" Any topic may have multiple issues.

Issues are commonly phrased as questions, and there are usually differing opinions about the answer. By phrasing an issue as a question, we can distinguish issues from positions. "Is abortion ever morally justified?" is an issue, but "Abortion should be illegal" is a position.

There may be a variety of issues about a topic or in a dispute or inquiry. The *main issue* is the one we are trying to resolve in the given dispute. However, other issues may also be central. An issue is central to a dispute or inquiry when its resolution is critical to resolving the dispute or inquiry. "Is abortion ever morally justified?" may be the main issue in a given context. However, the issue "Is the fetus a moral and legal person?" is central in resolving the dispute over whether abortion is morally justified. If the fetus is not a moral or legal person, then it is not entitled to moral or legal protection.

A well-formed issue

- is precise;
- is controversial;
- involves one central idea; and
- is stated in neutral terms.

A *position* is a stand taken on an issue. In the abortion issue, above, one position might be "Yes, there should be laws regarding abortion in Canada." This is a relatively ambiguous position, since it could mean that we should have laws allowing abortion or it could mean that we should have laws criminalizing abortion. This statement of the position is *ambiguous*— that is, it has at least two alternative meanings and, from the context, we are unable to determine which of those meanings is intended.

If no reasons are given for a position, it is an **undefended position.** Once reasons are given for a position, the reasons and the claim that states the position together become an argument and the position becomes the conclusion of the argument. It is now a *defended position.*

We will explore the topics model in more detail in Module 10, after we have focused on identifying and structuring arguments.

A Simple Argumentation Dialogue

Context:
The university student council has proposed a referendum on a supplemental health levy to pay for certain items not paid for by provincial health insurance. This includes some prescription drugs, physiotherapy, and chiropractic services. The levy will also provide basic health care for foreign students who are not covered by the provincial health care scheme. Two students are discussing the issue.

A: I don't think we should support the supplemental health care levy.

B: Why not?

A: Because most people don't need it.

B: So you're saying that since only a few might need supplemental health insurance, we shouldn't support it.

A: Yeah.

B.   How do you know only a few need supplemental health insurance?

A: Because most students are covered by their parents' health insurance.

B: How do you know that?

A: I just assumed it.

B: I have some doubts, but let's suppose for the moment that that is true. So what you are saying is that the only reason to support the additional health levy is if most students don't have supplemental health insurance coverage.

A: Yes.

B: So you don't think drivers in the province should have to support public transit since the majority of residents don't use it and don't need it?

A: I wouldn't agree with that.

B: What's the difference?

QUICK QUIZ 1.5   Identifying Topics, Issues, Positions, and Arguments

For the simple example of argumentation above, identify

1. the topic;
2. the issue;
3. the position taken by A;
4. A's reason(s) for that position; and
5. B's position in this dialogue, if he takes one.

Examine each turn taken by A and B in the dialogue and, using the outline of a basic argumentation dynamic on page 10, identify the purpose of each turn in the dialogue—does it identify a position, state a reason, reformulate, challenge, or perform some other function?

MODULE SUMMARY

Reasoning involves the connecting and working through of ideas. Critical reasoning involves the critical reflective examination of our reasoning. One form of critical reasoning is the critical evaluation of arguments. Arguments involve the giving of reasons for claims we make. Argumentation is the dynamic process of giving, challenging, and responding to challenges to our reasoning. This text develops the tools for analyzing and evaluating arguments and argumentation. To analyze an argument, we identify its main features (premises and conclusions) and their relation to one another. To assess an argument, we clarify its meaning, determining the truth of the reasons and whether the reasons support the conclusion. The dynamic process of argumentation is based on the constitutive rules—normative rules that define good and bad argumentation.

KEY TERMS

ambiguous
argue (two senses)
arguers
argument
argument principle
argumentation
argumentation dynamic
burden of proof principle
challenger/critic
claim
conclusion of the argument
constitutive rules
content
critical reasoning
defended position
discourse
end/purpose

evidential claims
fallibility principle
issue
listening principle
main issue
opinion
people
persuasion
position
premises
presenter/defender
principle of challenge and
    response
principle of charity in
    interpretation
process
rational inquiry

rational persuasion
reasons
reasoned opinion
reasoning
reconsideration principle
resolution principle
respect principle
simple opinions
suspension of judgment
    principle
tolerance
topic
truth-seeking principle
undefended position
unsupported claim

CLARIFYING MEANING

2.1 LEARNING OBJECTIVES

After completing this module, you should be able to

1. explain how language functions in reasoning;
2. explain how the misuse of language can mislead in reasoning;
3. explain the difference between a word (term), a concept, and a thing;
4. explain the difference between meaning (sense), referent, and connotation;
5. explain the role of context in determining meaning;
6. identify and neutralize common problems of meaning, including vagueness, ambiguity, loaded language, and doublespeak;
7. explain the different kinds of definitions, when to use them, and the strengths and weaknesses of each;
8. identify and be able to use the criteria for a good definition; and
9. identify, differentiate, and be able to construct and use the different kinds of definitions appropriately.

2.2 INTRODUCTION

To be effective in argumentation, we need to (1) be clear in expressing our own arguments and claims and (2) be able to understand and help clarify our argument partner's arguments and claims. After all, if we aren't sure of what our fellow arguer means, we can't know whether we agree or disagree.

> Anitha: Justice requires that we treat people with special needs differently.
>
> Philippe: That's not justice. You can't be just if you are treating people differently.

If Anitha and Philippe do not clarify what they each mean by *justice*, they are likely to engage in a frustrating dialogue. Effective argumentation requires that we understand precisely what our argument partner is claiming. Asking what is meant, identifying examples (referents) of "justice," and defining the term would all help here.

Read the following:

> Obfuscation International and Corporate Mismanagement Enterprises announce a multiphasic strategic integrative alliance to leverage the functionality of their collaborative management solutions for a global win–win solution. The new cross-platform product initiatives will provide 24/7/365 distributed, dynamic, innovative methodologies in a rapidly growing global economy in order to initialize new interactive opportunity structures, orchestrate mission-critical content, and incentivize holistic and compelling utilities for recontextualized multiphasic intermediate users and end users.

This passage does not communicate clearly. Rather than expressing the ideas simply, the author has hidden behind jargon and big words. Though perhaps intended as a contribution to argumentation, it violates the truth-seeking and respect principles, as well as the unstated principle of clarity — that we seek to present our positions as clearly as we can — a corollary of the truth-seeking principle.

Whenever we use language that hides (obfuscates) our meaning or use terms imprecisely or without clearly defining them, we are undermining effective argumentation. Argumentation requires the clear expression of claims and arguments.

A related difficulty involves the use of code words — words used with special meaning in a particular context:

> Civilian contractors were employed to soften up the detainees.

Without knowing the precise meaning of the terms within that context, we don't know whether to accept this as true or challenge it. In the context of the United States' involvement in Iraq, it takes on quite a specific meaning, but it is in a form of code — the terms are used in special ways to hide the meaning of what is being said. Decoded, the statement says that mercenaries tortured the prisoners, which, although perhaps the case, may not be how the author wants the audience to interpret it. Some familiar contemporary terms that serve the purpose of masking a statement's meaning include *collateral damage, disanimate,* and *misspoke.* By using general terms that are more ambiguous than plain language, the speaker can hide the reality of what is being said. This thwarts the aim of clear communication. Not understanding the claims of our argument partners or of the texts we are reading prevents us from engaging effectively in dialogue and, thereby, argumentation.

2.3 THE VARIOUS FUNCTIONS OF LANGUAGE

We use language for many purposes:

- to inform and describe

  "Victoria is separated from Vancouver by a large body of water called the Strait of Georgia."
  "The genetic revolution started with Gregor Mendel."

- to question

  "How do I get to Victoria from Vancouver in a hurry?"
  "Why do you say that the genetic revolution started with Gregor Mendel?"

- to direct

  "Insert Tab A in Slot B."
  "Make sure your essay has a thesis and a bibliography."
  "Take a seaplane from downtown Victoria to downtown Vancouver."

- to perform (a performative utterance is one that simply by its utterance makes something happen)

  "I pronounce you man and wife."
  "I sentence you to ten years of hard labour."

- to evaluate

"*That was a well-written play but poorly acted.*"

"*The quickest way of getting from Victoria to Vancouver is by seaplane.*"

"*Stealing is wrong.*"

The function of language can usually be identified through grammatical form. Providing information is done with declarative sentences; asking questions is done with interrogative sentences and often involve changes in intonation; and giving direction is done with imperative sentences. Other functions of language may not be associated with particular speech or grammatical forms. Language can be used to express or arouse emotions, establish bonds (even intimate ones), or sever them. It can both create and resolve conflict. And it can entertain us through stories, jokes, poetry, or drama. This is not an exhaustive list, nor are the functions mutually exclusive. Storytelling, for example, can simultaneously arouse emotions, provide information, build solidarity with others, and create conflict with yet others.

Our concern is with the informative and evaluative uses of language, since these are what we use for argument and argumentation. The informative use of language conveys information through **statements,** which are claims that can be true or false. Evaluative language, on the other hand, expresses judgment or point of view. The qualities desired in both are clarity and precision, using the most appropriate terms and defining any unfamiliar, contentious, or key terms.

QUICK QUIZ 2.1   The Functions of Language

What is the function of each of the following sentences?

1. I'm elated that Canadian women won the gold in hockey.
2. That is a job well done.
3. Wow!
4. Not one of the women on the team is a professional, but they all played like professionals.

Answers for all Quick Quizzes in this text are provided in the Student Manual. After doing the Quick Quizzes, consult the Student Manual to check your understanding of the material.

2.4 *HOW* WORDS MEAN: WORDS, CONCEPTS, AND REFERENTS

A language is a symbol system, composed of words (sometimes called "terms") organized into meaningful structures (in English, sentences). *Cat, sat,* and *mat* organized into a well-formed sentence might result in "The cat sat on the mat." (In this text, italics are used to indicate that we are talking about the word itself, not about its meaning or referent — the object represented by the term.) For the informative use of language, structures are intended to convey information about the world we experience.

Words— sounds or their representation in writing — stand for a group of objects. The term *cat* is itself not a cat; it signifies one of a group of objects we identify as cats.

Most words stand for or represent **concepts,** ideas we have of things. We can express a concept in a word ("cat"), a phrase ("Chicago blues"), a sentence ("Justice involves both fairness and equality"), or a set of sentences.

Concepts are our basic means for making sense of the "buzzing, blooming confusion" we encounter in this life. They provide us with categories for interpreting and organizing our experiences and relating their parts to one another. Different concepts provide us with various ways of thinking. For example, calling someone a *detainee* rather than a *prisoner of war* involves choosing one concept rather than another. Although we are talking about the same person, the meanings of the terms differ considerably. The concept *prisoner of war* is tied to other ideas and therefore connects to the world in a different way than the concept *detainee*.

Sometimes disputes arise over which concept applies in a given situation. Labelling someone a *terrorist* invokes a set of categories that may blind us to other options for addressing such a person. It may also put our argument partner on the defensive. We may end up fighting over what labels to attach to the situation rather than over the situation itself.

Using the components of a concept — meaning and referent — can help us address such issues. A concept normally has these two components but may also have a third: connotation.

The **meaning,** or **sense,** of a concept is derived from a set of shared expectations for rules of use that members of a language community have about a given concept, often enshrined in a definition. Assigning a meaning to a concept is an attempt to fix the rules for its use. The meanings of some concepts are relatively invariant; others differ between social groups or change over time.

The **referent** of a concept is the object (thing, process, activity) symbolized by the concept. The referent of the concept *cat* is each and every walking, meowing, furry creature that we identify as a cat. A referent may be (this is not an exhaustive list)

- a single object — a cat, a plant, a bicycle
- a process — applying for a passport
- a relationship — brother
- a property of something — red, tall, bald
- an action — voting
- an individual — Mary
- an abstract property — justice

Some words do not represent concepts but instead help demonstrate the relationship between concepts. For example, *the, of, very, and,* and *about* have no referents. Such terms have a function in the language — they help us construct grammatically correct sentences — but they have neither a meaning in the usual sense nor a referent.

Because meanings are based on the way a term is used in the language, meaning is essentially contextual. Groups of language users may use a term and its related concept differently. An individual might also use the same term differently in various contexts, as in Anitha's and Philippe's uses of *justice*. To illustrate further, *cat* can refer solely to a domestic feline; any member of the family Felidae, including the lynx, panther, lion, and tiger; a jazz musician or aficionado of jazz; anyone we think is cool; a type of boat (catamaran); the process of hoisting an anchor; the search for sexual partners (catting around); a spiteful woman; or malice (cattiness).

Which concept is being used and how it is being used depend on the context of the utterance, the speaker, and the audience. Normally, the context alerts the listener to which of the possible meanings is intended. When my partner asks me to let the cat out for the night, I don't release the mooring lines on the boat and cast it adrift.

In some cases, we may agree on the meaning of a concept — for example, *to steal* means "to take something that is someone else's property without that person's permission"— but disagree on what within the world that identifies (the referent). Two people who agree on the meaning of stealing and agree that taking a CD from a record store without paying constitutes stealing may disagree on whether downloading a song through a peer-to-peer network without paying is also stealing. They agree on the concept and its abstract meaning but not on its application in specific contexts. We often develop concepts in one context (e.g., property rights for physical entities); when confronted with a new context, however (e.g., information and the Internet), we may apply the existing rules for the use of the concept in quite different ways, even though we agree on the concept's meaning and its original application. The issue here is whether we should apply the concept of property, developed in one context, to a new referent.

Alternatively, we may agree on a referent yet disagree on the concept that should be applied to describe it. Is taking something without permission always stealing?

QUICK QUIZ 2.2   The Role of Context

Consider possible alternate meanings for the statements below. Explain how the context might affect the meanings of the key terms or claims. How could they be interpreted in different contexts?

1. Meet me by the bank.
2. The president is a man of utmost honour, lives by the highest ethical standards, and tells only the truth.
3. We will ensure that all children have access to child care.
4. Liberals are free-spending and irresponsible.

Abstract terms, adjectives, and adverbs often don't have a solitary, independent referent. Justice, truth, and integrity are not concrete individual things in the world, although they do refer to states of being. I can point to a woman of integrity, a just act, a truthful document, although I cannot point to a separate entity that is integrity, truth, or justice. Similarly, "boring" is not a specific concrete thing. Rather, it describes (and evaluates) the way in which something is done.

We often use abstract terms such as *justice, pornography, family values, torture,* or *insurgent* without clearly understanding either the meaning or the referent. By identifying concrete situations in which we would use such terms, we can start to understand the meaning of a given concept as it is applied in a particular context — the reality behind the label (i.e., word). By using more concrete terms, identifying the referent of those terms, and providing definitions of the concepts we use, we can clarify our intent.

The third component of concepts is **connotation.** The connotation is not part of the concept itself or the criteria for identifying it but rather the subjective and emotional associations we make with the concept. The **literal meaning** of *democracy* is "a form of government in which political authority is ultimately held by those who are governed." Since in Western nations this is considered a good thing, the term has a positive connotation.

Some terms have positive connotations universally (e.g., *friend, justice, freedom*); others have negative connotations universally (e.g., *oppression, pornography, terrorist*); yet others have neutral connotations (e.g., *sidewalk, bicycle, lamp*). Some terms' connotations vary depending on the audience (e.g., *liberal, socialist, feminist, fundamentalist, pro-choice*).

Connotations may be personal — having been savaged by a dog, someone may break out in a sweat just hearing the word *dog* — or they may be shared, like *democracy* or *justice*. Some connotations are common to most members of a language community; others are much more specific to small groups or even individuals.

QUICK QUIZ 2.3   Words, Concepts, Referents, and Connotations

Identify the possible referents and meanings for the key concepts and explain the meaning of the claim in each of the following. Where different referents and meanings are possible, identify these and show how the claims' meanings may be affected.

1. *Comment made during the Sponsorgate (Liberal advertising) scandal:* The Liberals are corrupt.
2. Bikers are members of criminal organizations.
3. Intelligence is genetic.

When dealing with terms that have strong connotations, one way of avoiding the inferences they can lead to is to separate such terms into one claim that identifies the literal meaning and another that identifies the emotive component.

> Fundamentalist Christians are trying to force their beliefs about evolution on others.

Fundamentalists and *force their beliefs on others* have strong connotations. For those who are not fundamentalist Christians, the word *fundamentalist* can raise a red flag. For many Christians, the term *fundamentalist* can be offensive.

The connotation can be neutralized by finding language that is less loaded and more neutral, and then identifying separately the emotive force of the claim. A **neutral claim** is a claim with the strong emotional connotations removed. The **emotive force** identifies the emotional nature (positive or negative) within the connotation and explains how it operates in the original claim.

> Neutral claim: People with strong, conservative Christian religious convictions are trying to get others to adopt their views about evolution.
>
> Emotive force: The emotive force of this claim is strongly negative. Fundamentalists are expressing their opinions in a manner that the author of this claim thinks involves force or coercion or is in some other way unjustified.

Both *fundamentalist* and *force* have negative connotations.

In trying to get the audience to accept the neutral claim, emotionally laden elements are used, in effect, as the reason or justification for acceptance.

By distinguishing between the claim and the connotations, we can more easily understand and assess what the claim is and are less likely to be taken in by the connotation of the terms.

Consider another example:

> The terrorists in Afghanistan want to take the country back to the Dark Ages.

Loaded terms include *terrorists* and *take the country back to the Dark Ages.*

> Neutral claim: Those resisting the occupation of Afghanistan by Allied forces want to bring about a more conservative society based on fundamentalist Islamic religious principles.

> Emotive force: These people are bad people, and their agenda is bad for the people of Afghanistan.

Fundamentalist, as it is used here, may also be emotionally laden and may need neutralizing.

This is not a simple paraphrase of the claim. Rather, it is an analysis of the claim that focuses on the meaning of what is being said and the referent, and distinguishes the informative content (neutral claim) from the connotative elements (emotive force). With the terms neutralized, the listener or reader can examine the claims to see if the emotive force provides any reason for accepting the literal claim. Usually it doesn't.

The *fallacy of prejudicial language* involves using loaded or emotional terms to influence the audience to think or do something based solely on the emotional content of the claims rather than on valid reasons. Prejudicial language can be either positive or negative. That is, it can strive to get the audience to accept or reject a claim or position.

> Context: Several medical doctors are indicted for fraud for charging the provincial health ministry for services they have not done.

> Headline: Quacks charged with fraud.

The same technique used for neutralizing connotations can be used to neutralize prejudicial language: translating a prejudicial claim into a neutral claim and presenting the emotional or prejudicial language as a separate claim. The above could be translated into

> Neutral claim: Some medical doctors are being charged with fraud.

> Emotive force: These medical doctors were poor physicians (quacks). Referring to a physician as a quack is a way of dismissing the individual.

QUICK QUIZ 2.4   Neutralizing Connotations and Prejudicial Language

In each of the following, identify whether there are terms or claims with strong connotations. If so, neutralize the connotation by dividing the claims into the literal meaning and the emotive force.

1. The anti-choice terrorists have prevented abortion providers from doing their legal work. They have bombed their offices, killed them, and stalked their employees. These enemies of freedom need to be stopped.
2. *Spoken by a U.S. commentator:* Those spineless cowards who oppose the valiant U.S. efforts in Iraq are soft on terror and encouraging the murder of our brave fighting men.
3. We should be wary of legalizing gay marriage. If we change the definition of marriage to include same-sex marriage, then there appear to be no grounds for limiting marriage to two people or prohibiting it between near relatives. The move to change the nature of marriage could result in legalizing polygamy and incest.

2.5 SOME COMMON PITFALLS IN THE USE OF LANGUAGE

Although our communicative goal in argumentation is to express ourselves in clear, accurate language, this does not always come readily. Sometimes we fail to speak precisely, we falter in presenting our ideas, or we are simply unaware that we aren't using language well. This section identifies some common mistakes and how to correct them.

Vagueness

A concept or claim is **vague** when its meaning or application is unclear, fuzzy, or inexact in the context. In the case of a vague concept, the listener cannot determine with certainty how or when the concept would be applied. With a vague claim, the listener cannot determine precisely what the claim means and, hence, under what conditions it would be true or false.

The police have issued a bulletin to be on the lookout for a bald white male, age about 35. *Bald* is vague in the context. There are clear cases of people who are bald. A person with no hair on his head, such as Howie Mandel or Captain Jean-Luc Picard, is bald. We can also identify clear cases of people who are not bald, such as Brad Pitt. If we were to gradually add one hair at a time to Captain Picard, at what point would he stop being bald? Is a man who has only a fringe of hair about the ears bald? There is no precise answer to this. Do I as a citizen turn in every white male over 30 who is follicularly challenged or only those with absolutely no hair on their heads? "Bald" is a vague concept in the context of the police bulletin.

Much of English involves some degree of vagueness. Whether this is a problem depends on the context and the degree of precision needed within that context.

> Warning on pesticide container:
>
> Do not use near livestock or humans.

This warning is vague. How near is *near*? A metre? Two metres? Ten metres? Half a kilometre? Without more precise instructions, I could harm myself or the livestock. I'm also not told whether it is safe to use in the vicinity of other kinds of animals — for example, cats and dogs. After all, technically, they are not livestock.

When a concept is vague, we don't know what it means or refers to in certain contexts. As a result, we can't assess or act on the claim. Consider the following:

> A job hunter in an interview is asked about his experiences in teamwork. He answers, "I learned many valuable lessons from teamwork."

Without elaboration, this answer is vague. If the job hunter elaborates by providing specific examples and instances, then it is simply a poor introduction to a better answer.

The following are principles that will help in making statements that are clear and precise and that avoid vagueness:

1. **Be clear about what you are trying to express.** If you don't know what you are trying to say, you are more likely to be vague.
2. **Select the precise terms to express your meaning.** Vague and sloppy language results when you simply use whatever words are at hand rather than trying to find the words that express your meaning exactly.
3. **Use concrete rather than general terms.** Instead of describing a vehicle as "roomy," state that it seats five adults comfortably.

4. **When you do use general terms, provide examples.** The job hunter above could briefly describe an experience he had as a part of a team and explain how it influenced his approach to teamwork.

5. **Use precise quantifiers rather than indefinite quantifying terms.** Indefinite quantifying terms include *some, a few, many, near, far, young,* and *old.* The pesticide instructions could be improved using this method: "Do not use within 25 feet of where humans, livestock, or other animals travel."

QUICK QUIZ 2.5   Vagueness

Given the context, which of the following concepts or claims are vague? Explain why and how the vagueness could be corrected. Use the principles for addressing vagueness to make the claims more precise.

1. *A police constable, having pulled over a motorist, asks the motorist if he has had anything to drink.* The motorist answers, "Just a couple of beers."
2. *A paper comparing the anatomy of various primates:* "A gorilla has long arms."
3. *Astrological profile:* "You have a strong need to be liked but are fiercely independent. You are strong-willed with a drive for achievement, yet you take time to stop and smell the flowers."

The Missing Quantifier/Qualifier

A particular kind of vagueness arises from the **missing quantifier** or **qualifier.** An unquantified or unqualified claim is assumed to apply to all members of the group that the claim is about when, at best, it is true of only some members or subgroups within the whole.

> Drug users resort to crime to support their habit, so they are a threat to society.

This claim suggests "all drug users" are threats to society, yet, if pressed, the arguer will likely be able to support only that "some users of some illicit drugs" are. "Some drug users" would quantify the claim, although not very precisely. "Heroine users" would qualify the claim. *Quantifiers* supply numbers; *qualifiers* restrict claims by limiting them to kinds of things. Missing quantifiers and qualifiers lead the arguer and the audience to believe that all members of the group are relatively homogenous and that they all have the property attributed to them. It hides the diversity and variation within the class being referred to.

In the debate over a Danish newspaper's publishing of cartoons depicting the prophet Muhammad, claims such as the following were made:

> Muslims oppose free speech.

Subsequent discussions tended to treat all Muslims as one undifferentiated mass. People making such claims failed to see or acknowledge the differences among individual Muslims or the various Muslim sects and communities. The missing quantifier often reflects a crude stereotyping of the group being discussed.

A universal claim (one that applies to all) is sometimes used instead of a more restrictive claim when referring to a general tendency or feature that characterizes a large number or the majority of a group.

> Men leave child care up to women.

In such cases, it would be more accurate and less misleading to formulate the claim more precisely, indicating the range of scope of the claim.

> Most men leave the majority of child care responsibilities to women.

Without knowing the details, this may be as precise as we can get. For a better argument, it would be advisable to get accurate numbers.

The best way of avoiding problems with missing quantifiers is to recognize the differences within groups and formulate the claims in a much more restrictive way by providing an appropriate quantifier.

QUICK QUIZ 2.6   Missing Quantifiers and Qualifiers

In the following, identify claims that have missing quantifiers and qualifiers, suggest possible differences and variations among the referents, and provide a more restrictive claim. If there are strong connotations, neutralize them.

1. Universities need to clean up their act. All I read about are students getting out of control, having sex parties, posing for *Playboy*, drinking, and uttering racist remarks. The police regularly have to be called to homecoming at Queen's, and McGill was just voted one of the leading "party schools" in North America. What ever happened to going to university to learn?
2. Scientists defending evolution are opposed to religion.
3. *Said by one university faculty member to another:* "Students are getting worse. My recently assigned papers were so badly written, I had to hand them back for rewriting. And the incidence of plagiarism is at epidemic proportions."

Ambiguity

Ambiguity occurs when a term, phrase, or sentence has two or more distinct meanings, both make sense in the given context, and it is not clear which one is intended in that context. The difference between vagueness and ambiguity is that with ambiguous terms and claims, there are two or more clear meanings, but we cannot be sure from the context which is meant, whereas with vague terms and claims, there is no clear and precise meaning.

Former U.S. President Bill Clinton's claim "I did not have sexual relations with that woman" had a convenient ambiguity in the meaning of the term *sexual relations*. The term can mean "sexual intercourse" (in the narrow sense), or it can mean "any kind of sexual activity" (in the broader sense). President Clinton was using the term in the narrow sense, denying that he and Monica Lewinsky had had sexual intercourse, while most of his audience interpreted what he said as a denial of having engaged in any sexual activity in the broader sense of the term.

A sociologist in a lecture identifies a particular religious group as a cult. A student who is a member of that religious group takes offence and challenges his claim. The instructor replies that her religious group is precisely what he means by a cult. The instructor is likely using *cult* in a specialized sociological sense to refer to an independent religious group in a context where there are a number of religious bodies and no one of them dominates, whereas the student is using *cult* in the more ordinary sense, meaning a breakaway religious group often led by a messianic leader and assumed to be extremist in some way.

When confronted with a situation in which a claim seems obviously or unnecessarily controversial and one side does not consider it as such, examine the passage to determine if one or more of the key terms is being used ambiguously. Try substituting alternate meanings to see if the claim can be made more acceptable.

QUICK QUIZ 2.7   Ambiguity

In each of the following, find any terms that are used ambiguously and identify their alternate meanings.

1. The theory of evolution is just a theory. And theories are not factual, just speculative. So the theory of evolution is just a speculation.
2. How can the doctor say that my mother is dead? With the respirator, she is still breathing.
3. Mathematics is a science. After all, it is taught in the faculty of science.

Words That Conceal: Euphemisms, Doublespeak, and Code Words

Some uses of language intentionally hide what is being said and the underlying reality. Euphemisms and code words involve using imprecise terms or phrases or substituting less than fully precise language to mask a claim's meaning.

A *euphemism* is a vague term or phrase used in place of a concrete term. Euphemisms are used to avoid offending or to disguise what is being talked about. We use euphemisms (1) for things considered unpleasant or potentially offensive — death (e.g., *passed on, is now with God,* or *didn't make it* instead of *died*), sex, excretion; (2) for things considered too sacred to be uttered (e.g., the name of the supreme being — itself a euphemism — cannot be uttered in some religions); or (3) to cover up what it is we are referring to (e.g., *collateral damage*).

A particular kind of euphemism is *doublespeak,* which involves using an abstract or indirect term or phrase in place of a direct one with the intent of concealing what is being said. Bureaucratese, a form of doublespeak, is composed of inflated language —*administrative assistant* for *secretary; sanitary engineer* for *janitor; sunshine units* for *radiation leaked from an improperly functioning nuclear power plant.* Bureaucratese is well-known for its use in hiding the unpleasant truth of firing employees: They are *laid off, downsized, right-sized, realigned.* And then workers who have no protection against this are described as a *flexible work force.*

Military and political communications, where the function is to neutralize or distance oneself from what is being said, are full of doublespeak: *Collateral damage* replaces *unintended civilian casualties; disanimate* replaces *kill; effect regime change* replaces *overthrow the existing government.* The neutral language of doublespeak results in a *death squad* becoming a *public safety unit;* a *body bag* (originally, *flexible coffin*) becoming a *human remains pouch; off-target bombs* becoming *incontinent ordinance* (as though they were errant puppies peeing on the couch); an *air attack* becoming a *protective reaction strike.* In the sentence "The president misspoke," does *misspoke* mean he intentionally lied, unintentionally misstated something, or something else altogether? In this case, the doublespeak has created an unresolved ambiguity.

Code words are terms that have one meaning to the public at large but have a special meaning to a particular target audience. In hotly contested political issues, a speaker will often use code words to address his or her supporters without having to be specific and thereby inciting controversy. This is sometimes called "dog-whistle phrasing," a reference to the high-frequency whistle heard only by dogs. Only the target audience hears what's actually being said.

A social conservative speaking of "a return to family values" is using a dog-whistle phrase that sounds harmless to the public but has specific meaning to his conservative audience. "Traditional family values" is code for conventional gender roles in which women are subservient to men; the restriction of marriage and child-rearing to heterosexual couples; and opposition to abortion, single-parent families, divorce, sex education, and contraception. Since the term is not sharply defined, listeners can apply those parts of the meaning they consider relevant and with which they agree. As the phrase makes no overt claims, it cannot be challenged.

Euphemisms, doublespeak, and code words contribute to a lack of clarity and understanding in language. The best way of handling these is to identify the referent and to translate the term, phrase, or claim into simple language.

QUICK QUIZ 2.8   Words That Conceal

Translate the following into plain language.

1. *Military:* We made a preemptive reaction strike to neutralize the enemy. However, there was some civilian collateral damage. Several of the coalition forces succumbed to friendly fire.
2. The municipal government is committed to revenue-enhancement measures through cost recovery for nonessential programs.
3. *Corporate e-mail announcement:* George Footloose has left the company, effective immediately.

Hypostatization

Hypostatization (also called *reification* — literally, making a thing of a concept) involves ascribing existence to abstract or conceptual entities and treating them as though they are real entities with the properties of real entities.

> Nature has dictated that the sole purpose of sex is reproduction. Any other purpose goes against the wishes of nature.

This is an example of a hypostatization because *nature,* an abstract term referring to a variety of processes and activities, is being used as if it were a word denoting a person who has intentions and can make pronouncements about those intentions.

> We all have an obligation to society.

Society is being hypostatized. It is not a single entity. Rather, society is the totality of individuals and their relationships to one another. It is easy, though, to think of society as a concrete entity that makes demands and to whom we have collective obligations.

Not all uses of abstract or general terms result in hypostatization. Sometimes we use general terms as a form of shorthand for a more complex statement, writing or speaking **elliptically** to convey a much fuller meaning in an extremely condensed form. This can often lead to misunderstanding.

The above claim about nature could mean that the sole function of sexual intercourse in the biological world is reproduction. This is a partial translation of the initial statement, and, therefore, it is elliptical. It does not personify nature — so there is no hypostatization — nor does it carry the evaluative and normative overtones of the original statement. Hypostatization usually does not occur when we are speaking in a form of shorthand; it does occur when we interpret the general term as a concrete entity and ascribe properties and characteristics to that hypothetical entity. In any given context, it can be difficult to determine whether a term is being used elliptically or is being hypostatized.

Almost any abstract entity—art, history, love, society, the state, science, women, men, religion, specific religions, the university—can be hypostatized.

One way of handling a hypostatization is to translate the concept or claim into one that does not reify any terms (i.e., turn them into things). If that can be done, then the original claim is elliptical. The above statement about society could be translated into a claim or set of claims that does not reify society. It might mean the following:

> Everyone who is a member of a social group has obligations not only to specific other members but to all members of the group by virtue of being a member of that group.

This does not reify society, so we can conclude that the original statement was an example of elliptical shorthand, rather than a reification, or hypostatization.

Such translations clarify the meaning and may also identify what is contentious about the claim.

Hypostatized terms are often ambiguous. They may refer to a nonexistent abstract entity as a concrete thing, or they may be an elliptical way of saying something else. We have to examine the context to determine which is the case.

QUICK QUIZ 2.9   Hypostatization

In each of the following, determine if any terms are being hypostatized. If so, identify the term, explain how it is being hypostatized, and state the possible problems that could result because of the hypostatization. If it is possible to treat the terms elliptically, provide an elliptical translation of the claim.

1. Poverty is stalking our nation's children.
2. The male gender believes that women are inferior and seeks to dominate and control them.
3. The nation demands that every citizen rally behind the war effort.
4. The gay community is trying to impose its views about marriage on the rest of society.

Metaphors

A *metaphor* is a figure of speech in which two dissimilar things are compared. A word or phrase referring to one thing is applied to another to suggest a similarity between them.

> A tidal wave of illegal immigrants is flooding across the border.

The metaphors in the above statement compare the number of illegal immigrants crossing the border to a tidal wave, a destructive, uncontrollable force. Metaphors often create vivid images and draw connections through the similarities without making the claims and connections explicit.

While we have no difficulty understanding such a metaphor, the language fails to answer a crucial question: Just how many immigrants are crossing the border? What constitutes a "tidal wave" of immigrants?

Metaphors can make our language come alive. They can, however, also short-circuit (note that *short-circuit* is also a metaphor) critical reasoning and argumentation. Using the metaphor of a tidal wave when speaking about illegal immigrants suggests a very large problem. It does not clearly identify the size or complexity of that problem. A metaphor may be used to illustrate a point, but if it replaces the reasoning and evidence required to support that point, then it becomes a problem.

Metaphors and analogies are similar. Whereas a metaphor makes an implicit comparison between two things, an **analogy** draws an explicit comparison. "The influx of illegal immigrants is like a tidal wave" is an analogy. The statement is now an explicit comparison.

Metaphors are so deeply ingrained in our language that we often don't notice that we are using them. We talk of couch potatoes, short-circuiting thought (see above), seeing through someone, the lawyer grilling the witness, the Canucks being toast this season, their goose being cooked, the government's strategy for the war in Afghanistan being a recipe for disaster, the Habs' farm team, adding fuel to the fire, being burned up, out of touch, hot for someone.

Metaphors are incredibly valuable. Not only do they enrich and enliven our language; they often enable us to see an issue more creatively and vividly. Problems arise when they obscure the reasoning, when we mistake the metaphor for the reality, or when the metaphors lead us to draw inferences. A classic example of this is in the application of economic metaphors to war and genetics. We talk about whether the war in Afghanistan is "worth it," whether we are "too heavily invested," and what the long term "payoffs" will be. The use of such metaphors encourages us to think in terms of a certain framework drawn from economics and can distract us from other frameworks — for example, ethical issues about the war. Some geneticists talk about "competition" between genes, the different "investment strategies" of eggs and sperm, and their "payoffs." Sports, war, and evolutionary metaphors ("survival of the fittest") abound in business. Yet business is not simply a game, nor is it war, nor is it an evolutionary process. The problem arises when we reduce the complexities of the term being compared to the concept with which we are comparing it.

We can deal with metaphors in two related ways. But before getting to that point, we have to identify that metaphors are being used. We do this by isolating the item under discussion and determining what it is being compared to:

Item under discussion: immigrants crossing our borders

Is being compared to: a tidal wave, a flood

To deal with the metaphor, we can then translate the statement into language that does not contain metaphors:

A large number of illegal immigrants are crossing our borders.

The clear language enables us to examine the claim more critically. For example, this translation highlights the lack of precision in this particular claim. How many is "a large number?"

A second way to address metaphors is to generate a different one. It can help us see the same thing in a different light.

Our country is becoming a haven for hundreds of thousands of economic refugees.

This metaphor likens illegal immigrants to refugees and suggests that the country is a "haven." This conjures up quite a different image. Calling them *economic refugees* rather then *illegal immigrants* reframes the image and can lead us to question which, if either, is a more accurate portrayal.

These common pitfalls of language usage can give way to faulty reasoning if we base our reasoning on them. Ambiguity, for example, can lead to the fallacy of equivocation. Improper use of metaphor and analogy can lead to the fallacy of faulty analogy. For more on fallacies, see Module 7.

QUICK QUIZ 2.10   Metaphors

Identify the metaphors in the following statements and translate them into neutral language. Determine what is under discussion and what it is being compared to. Indicate whether or not the metaphors in each passage are likely to mislead. Explain.

1. *Politician during an election campaign:* Canadians are staggering under a massive tax burden. If elected, we will relieve the weight borne by the ordinary taxpayer.
2. There's a hole in that theory.
3. He spends his time wisely.

2.6 CLARIFYING MEANING THROUGH DEFINITIONS

Definitions establish a common meaning for and a common understanding about a concept. They have various functions. Understanding the different kinds of definitions, their purposes, and the criteria for good definitions can help us choose which kind to choose in a specific situation.

Ostensive Definitions

An *ostensive definition* is one that defines a concept by providing examples of it, rather than outlining the criteria for the use of the concept. Pointing to a cat, I could say, "That is a cat," in effect identifying the referent, or a set of referents, for the term. This does not, however, tell you what the meaning of the concept is or what makes something a cat and not a dog. To clarify an ostensive definition further, I can use contrast to show what it is not: "That is a cat," pointing to a cat, "and that is not," pointing to a dog.

This kind of definition is useful in introducing someone to a new concept and in providing the basis for developing other kinds of definitions. When used in conjunction with another kind of definition, the example serves as an illustration, rather than as a definition.

Operational Definitions

An *operational definition* defines a concept by describing a procedure or operation one goes through. The result of the procedure is the concept being defined. This type of definition is most commonly found in science and social science studies, policy studies, and organizational and governmental regulations. "Intelligence is defined as the score achieved on a standardized IQ test." "Relationship power in this study is defined as marital decision-making as determined by responses to a standardized questionnaire on marital decision-making." "A voting member is defined as someone who has been a member of the union for three months."

Operational definitions typically provide technical criteria that are easy to measure. The advantage of a good operational definition is that it can ensure the same procedure is used across different populations in a study so that results are comparable.

There are some difficulties with such definitions. Because they are relative to a given study, they may not correspond to the way the terms are used by others. Also, there may be more to *relationship power* or *intelligence* than the operations measure, not to mention that the operational definition may not measure what we normally mean by *power* or *intelligence*. There is also the problem of whether the operations actually capture a useful sense of the concept.

Finally, different operational definitions are used for the same term from one study to the next. This means that one cannot easily or confidently compare the results of separate studies. If one study defines an occasional smoker as "someone who smokes ten cigarettes a week," and another defines an occasional smoker as "someone who smokes ten cigarettes a month," the two operational definitions are measuring different things but using the same name for them. Recognizing this can be important in reading scientific and governmental studies. How researchers define such things as poverty (an income of less than x, where x varies by study), unemployment, or pollution determines what they are measuring and how comparable different studies are. In many cases, the "facts" remain the same. What changes is how those facts are labelled with an operational definition. What is called the poverty level or unemployment rate can vary simply by altering the operational definitions of these terms.

Reportive Definitions

A *reportive definition* provides the meaning of a term by reporting how it is used within a language community. Dictionary makers commonly construct definitions by finding a number of instances of the term and then constructing reportive definitions. This is one of the most common forms of definition.

Below is a dictionary entry for *argue*:

> **argue** v.—*tr.* 1. To put forth reasons for or against; debate. 2. To attempt to prove by reasoning; maintain or contend. 3. To give evidence of; indicate: *"Similarities cannot always be used to argue descent"* (Isaac Asimov). 4. To persuade or influence (another), as by presenting reasons.—*intr.* 1. To put forth reasons for or against something; *argued for dismissal of the case.* 2. To engage in a quarrel; dispute. [ME *arguen* < OFr. *arguer* < Lat. *argūtāre*, to babble, chatter, freq. of *arguere*, to make clear.][1]

This reportive definition provides several different meanings of the word, each of which is a different concept. For some of the definitions, it provides examples of the use of the term. It also indicates, through the etymology at the end, how the meaning of the term has changed over time, which is reflective of the constant evolution of language. For example, the term *gay* when introduced into the English language simply meant "merry." Over the course of centuries, it has also come to mean "homosexual." The term *bug*, meaning insect, was metaphorically extended to include errors in software logic when, in an early computer, a moth was found to have shorted out some of the circuits. *Nice* once meant foolish. The English word *lust* is derived from the German *lust*, meaning any kind of pleasure. This was the original meaning of the term in English; however, its meaning has since been narrowed to apply to a particular kind of sexual desire.

Language is fluid and contextual. Meanings of terms change as members of a language community extend and over time modify the uses of the terms. Since reportive definitions are simply accounts of how words are used in the language, there are many examples of terms that are used differently depending on the context or even who in the language community is using it.

---

[1] "Argue." Def. *ITP Nelson Canadian Dictionary of the English Language*, 1997.

Essential Definitions

In searching for the meaning of a concept, we must be clear as to whether we want a reportive or an essential definition. Whereas a reportive definition simply reports how a term is used in a given language community, an **essential definition** seeks to identify the necessary and sufficient conditions for the use of a concept.

One condition, a, is a **necessary condition** for another condition, c, if a must occur with c. a is also a necessary condition for c if a must occur for c to occur. That does not mean that if a occurs, c occurs. Rather, if c occurs, a must have occurred.

One condition, b, is a **sufficient condition** for another condition, c, if the presence of b is sufficient to define or bring about c. Whenever b is present, c is present. Having an atomic number of 79 is a sufficient condition for something being gold. If something is gold, then it has an atomic number of 79; and if something has an atomic number of 79, then it is gold. (See Module 4, Section 4.7 for more on necessary and sufficient conditions.)

An essential definition, therefore, seeks to identify the conditions that either must be met or would be adequate for something to be a referent of a concept. In regular dictionaries of the English language, some definitions are essential definitions but most are reportive definitions. Occasionally, dictionaries may provide both kinds of definitions — for example, in the case of a term such as *gold*.

Consider the term *gold* as applied to a metal commonly dug out of the ground and used for jewellery. One reportive definition states that "gold is a precious metal used for jewellery and certain industrial applications." This is reportive in that it tells how the term *gold* is used in a certain language community. There could well be a language community that does not value the metal we call gold and/or does not use it in the same ways. This reportive definition could change if we come to no longer treat gold as a precious metal or use it for jewellery or industrial applications.

The conditions identified in the reportive definition are not necessary or sufficient conditions for something being gold. Now consider the following essential definition for gold:

> Gold is a soft-yellow, corrosion-resistant element with an atomic number of 79, atomic weight of 196.967, melting point of 1,063 degrees Celsius, and a specific gravity of 19.32.

This definition seeks to provide the necessary and sufficient conditions for identifying the metal that we call *gold*. These conditions hold whether or not individuals realize that gold has these conditions. This definition would change only if we discovered that gold had additional essential properties or that these properties did not distinguish gold from other elements or metals. Most individuals who use the term *gold* and know the concept of it could not articulate these necessary and sufficient conditions; they are more likely to cite the reportive definition. Nonetheless, both definitions are true of the same referent.

Gold is an easy example. It is a specific thing whose essential properties we can discover. Sexual harassment is a more difficult concept. Not only may people disagree on its meaning but they may also disagree on what things constitute it. The disagreement is not just about the necessary and sufficient conditions for an agreed-upon set of objects but also about what objects will be included in the class of things the term refers to. As the set of objects (in this case, examples of sexual harassment) change, so, too, do the likely necessary and sufficient conditions for members of that class. As a result, with a concept like sexual harassment, we may be dealing with a variety of related concepts rather than one concept with a single essential definition.

Some terms may not have necessary and sufficient conditions or may have only one of these. For example, a game has no necessary and sufficient conditions, yet virtually all of us can use the term, identify things that are and are not games, and recognize problematic cases. At best, we can come up with reportive conditions, some possibly overlapping, for how the concept is used. We could say that games are characterized by conditions A through K, a family of conditions. However, few games will meet all of these conditions, yet we are willing to call things that meet a substantial number of these conditions *games.*

Some abstract terms —*justice, truth, freedom, democracy*— are particularly problematic. We sometimes treat them as having an essential set of properties that define them, which may well be the case — if we can agree on the class of things to which the terms refer. However, often such terms can refer to a variety of things, and different speakers will identify varying core sets of things that the terms refer to. In such cases, there may be not one concept but several described by the same term.

Stipulative Definitions

In a ***stipulative definition,*** an author specifies a specific meaning for a term, which may be a new term or one already in the language, in a given context:

> By *pornography,* I mean . . .

> By *metrosexual,* I will mean . . .

> In this essay, I will use the term *democracy* to mean . . .

Stipulative definitions can be a way of introducing a new concept into the language. Terms such as *informed consent* and *sexual harassment* did not exist until relatively recently. They were introduced to identify phenomena to which people wanted to draw attention. Stipulative definitions can also be very useful when there is not a clearly agreed-upon meaning for a concept or when the author wishes to restrict the discussion to a particular aspect of a number of available meanings associated with a term. Since *pythik* is an invented term, I would define it to show what I mean by it. *Pornography* and *democracy* are terms with multiple, contentious meanings. When using either, I would provide a stipulative definition (which may reflect a reportive definition) to clarify how I'd use the term in a given context. Not only is *metrosexual* new to the language; its meaning can and does vary considerably, so I would provide a stipulative definition to ensure that the reader knows what I am talking about.

Stipulative definitions can cause problems with terms already in use if the proposed definition is idiosyncratic or strays too far from common use. Providing a stipulative definition of *pornography* as portrayals of sexual violence against women (as some have done) may reflect the perception of one group of language users but does not connect with the more general understanding of *pornography* as any sexually explicit material, violent or not. A stipulative definition that can be confused with a corresponding reportive or essential definition may create ambiguity in the use of the term, a problem that can be compounded by different arguers introducing conflicting stipulative definitions.

One particular danger with using stipulative definitions is that of **circularity.** This occurs when the definition being stipulated includes claims the arguer seeks to establish, thereby making them true by definition.

> I define pornography as sexual material that portrays violence against and degradation of women. I will show in this paper that pornography degrades women.

In this stipulative definition of *pornography*, the author includes "degradation of women" as part of the definition, yet what he or she intends to show is that women are degraded by pornography. Since this is true by definition, there's nothing left to prove.

The term *sexual harassment* was invented to apply to a real phenomenon that did not yet have a name. Judging by the original definition, only women could be harassed and only when in positions of subordination. As other phenomena were identified and determined to be similar, the definition, and hence the concept, changed. The term came to include the notion that both men and women could be sexually harassed, and it recognized that coworkers could sexually harass one another without either one of them being in a position of authority. The definition broadened to the point where it now covers more referents. In the process, however, it may have become more like *game* than like *gold* in that it refers to a family of conditions rather than a set of essential properties. Part of the difficulty in working out a definition for a concept like sexual harassment is that the boundaries of the concept are still not clearly identified. Developing the criteria for the meaning of the concept is important to determining exactly which cases it applies to and which ones it does not.

Persuasive Definitions

A **persuasive definition** is one that uses evaluative language in an attempt to convince the reader to take the same point of view as the definition's author.

> Capitalism is the willful exploitation of the poor through the exploitation of their labour.

Persuasive definitions use emotionally laden language (such as *willful* and *exploitation* in the definition above) and contain a particular point of view (such as "capitalists exploit workers"), which is usually highly contentious. Many people would disagree with this definition of *capitalism*.

Consider two other examples:

> Abortion is the killing of unborn babies.

> Abortion is the removal of an unwanted piece of tissue.

Each of these uses emotionally laden language —*killing, babies, unwanted, tissue*. And each reflects a point of view that the definer wants the audience to accept. Contentious issues are brought into the definition. A more neutral definition of abortion is available:

> Abortion is the termination of a pregnancy and the expulsion of an embryo or fetus from the mother's body.

This definition does not take a stand on the issue of killing or the status of the embryo or fetus.

The stipulative definition of pornography, above, as the portrayal of sexual violence against and degradation of women is both a stipulative and a persuasive definition.

One of the dynamics of argumentation is that some people use persuasive definitions as a way of establishing their substantive claims. If arguers can get their audiences to accept a persuasive definition of a debatable term such as *pornography* or *abortion*, they are well on their way to establishing their position.

QUICK QUIZ 2.11   Identifying Kinds of Definitions

Identify the kind of definition used in each of the following statements.

1. For the purpose of the Income Tax Act, a student is someone who is enrolled in a full-time course of study at an approved educational institution.
2. An environmentalist is someone who wants to preserve the environment at the expense of humans.
3. In this paper, by *education*, I mean not only formal education but any informal learning individuals undertake to better themselves.
4. A bachelor is an unmarried male.
5. Suicide is the act of intentionally killing oneself.
6. Euthanasia is the unjust killing of another human being.
7. A student is one who studies.
8. For the purpose of this act, a motor vehicle is defined as any vehicle powered by a gasoline engine.

2.7 CRITERIA FOR GOOD DEFINITIONS

In addition to the criteria given for each type of definition above, the following criteria apply to virtually all definitions:

1. The definition should **not be too broad.** That is, the definition should cover only those cases to which it applies. If the definition includes referents that are not instances of the definition, then it is too broad.

   Defining *gold* as a yellow metal is too broad. The definition includes several other metals that are also yellow.

2. The definition should **not be too narrow.** That is, the definition should include all of the possible referents and not exclude significant ones. Defining *pornography* as the portrayal of sexual violence against women is too narrow. It excludes men and sexually explicit portrayals that are not violent.

   A definition can be both too broad and too narrow. "Sexual harassment involves the misuse of authority toward women" is both too broad and too narrow. Not all misuses of authority toward women constitute sexual harassment; the definition also excludes men as possible targets of sexual harassment.

3. The definition should be **phrased in neutral terms.** That is, emotionally laden terms and terms that skew the definition toward a particular point of view should not be used. The sample definitions of *capitalism* and *abortion* in our discussion of persuasive definitions above are not neutral.

4. The definition should use terms that are **clearer than the terms they define.** The point of a definition is to explain the concept. If the terms used are less familiar than the term being defined, the definition is not clear.

5. The definition should be **informative, not circular.** A circular definition is one that defines the concept in terms of itself. Defining *arguer* as someone who argues is circular and not informative.

6. The definition should **not beg the question.** A definition begs the question when it includes as part of the definition a contentious claim or set of criteria that need to be proven independently of the definition. Defining *intelligence* as an innate mental trait

measured by IQ tests assumes what still needs to be shown — that intelligence is an innate trait and that it is measured by an IQ test.

7. The definition should be **useful in the context.** Definitions are used in context. If I use a definition that is inappropriate or doesn't apply to the context, then it is not useful to the reader.

8. Where there are **alternate definitions,** and some of those are contentious, the person advancing the definition should identify the alternative possibilities and justify the definition being used.

QUICK QUIZ 2.12   Criteria for Good Definitions

For each of the definitions in Quick Quiz 2.11, given the kind of definition each is, explain whether the definition meets the criteria for a good definition.

MODULE SUMMARY

Before we can evaluate an argument, we need to know what the key concepts and claims in the argument mean. Language works by distinguishing words, concepts, referents, and meanings. Various uses and misuses of language, such as connotation, loaded language, vagueness, generality, ambiguity, euphemism, doublespeak, code words, hypostatization, and metaphor, can mislead us in our reasoning. We can clarify meaning by attending to context, identifying and relating the meaning to the referent, neutralizing loaded language, and providing definitions. There are several different kinds of definitions, each with strengths, limitations, and appropriate uses. A definition's value and usefulness can be assessed by using the identified criteria of good definitions.

KEY TERMS

ambiguity	euphemism	persuasive definition
analogy	hypostatization	prejudicial language,
beg the question	literal meaning	fallacy of
circularity	meaning/sense	reification
code words	metaphor	referent
concepts	missing qualifier	reportive definition
connotation	missing quantifier	statements
doublespeak	necessary condition	stipulative definition
elliptically	neutral claim	sufficient condition
emotive force	operational definition	vague
essential definition	ostensive definition	words

MODULE 3

ANALYZING ARGUMENTS

3.1 LEARNING OBJECTIVES

After completing this module, you should be able to
1. explain what an argument is;
2. explain what a claim is and distinguish it from nonclaims;
3. define and correctly use key terms in argument analysis;
4. identify and distinguish from other kinds of discourse text containing an argument;
5. identify and explain the function of cue words in identifying arguments; and
6. portray the structure of an argument, both in standard form and using arrow diagrams.

3.2 INTRODUCTION

The core of argumentation is the developing of, presenting of, analyzing of, critiquing of, and responding to arguments. Before engaging in argumentation, we must first be able to identify and analyze arguments.

An **argument** involves the giving of at least one reason for a conclusion. We offer an argument because the claim we seek to justify, the conclusion, is in doubt, is controversial, or is in need of validation in the context.

Claims are statements that can be affirmed or denied. In arguments, they may take the form of the **reason** (or **premise**) or the **conclusion,** as described above. How claims are used in a passage or dialogue determines their function, but not all claims must be part of an argument.

We need to verify that an argument is being given, distinguish the argument claims from ones extraneous to the argument, and then portray the argument's structure — that is, identify the reasons and conclusions and their relationship to one another. Cue words and the positioning and meaning of the claims help us determine whether an argument exists and, if so, the function of each of its claims. Once this is clear, we portray the argument structure, identifying the relationship between the reasons and the conclusion, either in a standard form or by using arrow diagrams.

3.3 IDENTIFYING CLAIMS

All arguments are based on claims. A claim consists of one complete thought — in English, usually in the form of a complete sentence. A claim can be either affirmed or denied, and evidence or support can be given to this end. The following are claims:

- My bike is red.
- The term bicycle includes any two-wheeled human-propelled vehicle; it does not include tricycles.
- Bicycles are more energy efficient than cars.
- Everyone should cycle to work.

Each can be affirmed or denied. The following are not claims:

- bicycle
- red bicycle
- more energy efficient than cars
- cycle to work

These are incomplete sentences, or fragments; they do not express a complete thought and they don't make a statement that can be affirmed or denied. Therefore, they are not claims.

To **affirm a claim** is to accept it or say that it is true; to **deny a claim** is to reject it or say that it is false. A **negative** claim is one that contains a negative, such as *not*; for example, "The term *bicycle* does not include tricycles." To affirm a negative claim, we repeat the claim: "The term *bicycle* does not include tricycles." To deny it, we claim it is not true: "The statement 'The term *bicycle* does not include tricycles' is not true." Or "The claim is false." Or "The term *bicycle* does include tricycles."

Not every grammatical structure is a claim. Questions ("Who is the prime minister of Canada?"), imperatives ("Do exercise six before next week's class"), and exclamations ("Oh!") are not claims and cannot be parts of arguments.

Nor are **performative utterances** claims. "I now pronounce you man and wife," said by a legal agent during a wedding ceremony performs the action of wedding a couple. When making a performative utterance, the speaker is performing an action, not making a claim about the world. The wedding ceremony complete, we might infer the claim that the bride and groom are now married. However, the performative statement itself is not a claim.

QUICK QUIZ 3.1   Identifying Claims

Identify which of the following are claims and which are not. Explain why each is or is not a claim.

1. Is marriage a sacred institution that deserves to be preserved by the state?
2. You're joking!
3. You smoke?!
4. Canadians tend to be more tolerant than their neighbours to the south.
5. Surely you don't support gay marriage, do you?

Answers for all Quick Quizzes in this text are provided in the Student Manual. After doing the Quick Quizzes, consult the Student Manual to check your understanding of the material.

3.4 WHAT IS AN ARGUMENT?

As explained in Module 1, an argument is a set of at least two claims that include a conclusion (the claim in need of defence) and one or more premises (a claim or claims advanced to support a conclusion).

Examine the following. Are they arguments?

Before continuing, review the conditions for an argument above. Then apply them to each example before reading the analysis.

1. **All Canadian residents are entitled to health care whether they can afford it or not.**

   Analysis: According to the criteria, this example is not an argument. It consists of one claim (the "whether" clause is a qualification of the claim, not a second claim). Although the claim may be controversial, no other claims are offered in support of it in this passage. This is simply an assertion. An ***assertion*** is an unsupported claim.

2. **All Canadian residents are entitled to a decent minimum of health care. Doctors and other health-care professionals work hard to ensure that this health care is provided.**

   Analysis: There are two claims here. The first claim is controversial. However, neither claim is a reason for the other — that is, neither of the claims serves as an answer to the question *why?* for the other. (For more on identifying reasons and conclusions, see Module 3, Section 3.4.) This passage is a ***description,*** a statement or set of statements that provides an account or report of the facts, details, or particulars of a situation, event, or topic.

3. **The Canada Health Act was inspired by the work of Tommy Douglas and the Cooperative Commonwealth Federation in Saskatchewan. Although there was strong resistance to universal health care from the medical profession and insurance companies when initially introduced, the people of the province embraced it. Seeing the popularity of Douglas's initiative, the federal government introduced a similar policy on the national level.**

   Analysis: Like the one above it, this passage is a description. It provides an account or report of the facts of the introduction of the Canada Health Act. No reasons are given for why it was introduced or why it was controversial, and there's no discussion of whether or not it should have been adopted. As well as being a description, this passage is a narrative. A ***narrative*** is a descriptive account that tells a story.

4. **Many countries have since initiated state-run health-care systems. Most European countries have such systems.**

   Analysis: Although this passage has two claims, one of which ("Most European countries . . .") might be confused with a reason, this is an illustration. The second claim illustrates (or provides an example of) the first. An ***illustration*** is a statement that provides an example of another claim. An example is not a reason.

5. **Tommy Douglas introduced universal health care in Saskatchewan because, as a boy, he had seen his father be refused medical treatment.**

   Analysis: This looks like an argument. It has two claims, and one of them is offered as a reason for the other (*because* indicates a reason). However, this is not an argument. It is an ***explanation*** — a statement or set of statements that identifies the causes, context, consequences, factors influencing, or motivations of an object, process, state of affairs, or behaviour. Explanations are used to clarify or make understandable such things by describing the relevant factors that produce them or the circumstances under which they occur. The passage above identifies Tommy Douglas's motivation for introducing universal health care in Saskatchewan.

   Explanations and arguments are often confused because they both appear to be giving "reasons" for something. There are, however, two critical differences between them. First, the conclusion of an explanation is usually not controversial. In the explanation above, it is assumed that it is a known fact that Tommy Douglas introduced universal health care in Saskatchewan. That is not contentious. What needs to be explained is the motivation for his actions. In an argument, on the other hand, the conclusion is contentious. The second critical difference is that in an argument, the arguer tries to justify the contentious conclusion by relating it to more widely accepted reasons, whereas in an explanation, the speaker identifies and connects other features — causes, context, motivations that help us make sense of what we already know.

This confusion is compounded by the fact that the term *reason* is ambiguous. It can be used to mean motivation or cause, or it can be used to mean the premise of an argument.

6. **All Canadian residents are entitled to health care. Therefore, we should ensure that everyone, including the homeless, receives a decent minimum standard of health care.**

Analysis: This is an argument. There are two claims. The first claim is offered as a reason for the second, the conclusion. And the conclusion is controversial: Some would argue that people should get health care only if they can afford it or if they qualify in some other way.

> Reason: **All Canadian residents are entitled to a decent minimum of health care.**
>
> Conclusion: **We should ensure that everyone, including the homeless, receives a decent minimum standard of health care.**

An argument's two fundamental components — the reason and the conclusion — are distinguished by their functions within a given argument. The claim that is being advanced that is controversial and in need of defence or justification is the conclusion. In the context of an issue analysis, it is also called a "position"; in the context of an essay, it is called the "thesis." Other terms may be used. The claim (or usually the set of claims) advanced to defend, justify, establish, or give support to the contentious claim is the reason, also referred to as the premise, the grounds, the support, the justification, and, sometimes, the evidence (although this term has other uses as well) for the conclusion.

To identify an argument, we need to determine the functions being performed by the claims. Any given claim may function as a conclusion in one argument and a reason in another.

QUICK QUIZ 3.2   Identifying Arguments

Which of the following are arguments? Why?

1. Although objectionable, racist materials should not be banned from schools.
2. The fundamental principles of justice demand that gay marriage be legalized.
3. Secondhand smoke causes harm to others. Therefore, it should be banned in any area that the public has access to.
4. Marriage is a sacred institution and deserves to be preserved by the state.
5. If pornography causes harm, then it should be banned.

QUICK QUIZ 3.3   Distinguishing Arguments from Other Prose

Identify whether or not the passages below contain arguments, explanations, illustrations, descriptions, narratives, or some other kind of discourse.

1. Céline took the job because she needed the money.
2. Céline had been looking for six months. She'd had numerous initial interviews but no follow-up interviews, and she was getting desperate.
3. Some of her friends had had better luck than she. Her friend Johan had gotten a job within three weeks of starting his job search.
4. Céline told her younger brother not to study philosophy in university because it wouldn't help him get a job when he graduated.

3.5 IDENTIFYING PREMISES AND CONCLUSIONS

Premises and conclusions can be identified and distinguished through meaning, the use of cue words (or "inference indicators"), or by their position within a passage. None of these methods is infallible, although cue words tend to be the most reliable.

Meaning: Why? Because . . .

Determining meaning requires understanding the relevance and intent of the passage. Is the passage trying to convince you of something? Is it trying to get you to accept a claim as true? Does it offer other claims in support of that claim? Asking yourself these questions can help you identify an argument. Once you've determined that an argument exists, probing further — "Why is this claim true?" or "Why should I accept this claim?" — can help you recognize the reasons. Of course, "a claim" in the above questions is the conclusion. Alternatively, you might want to ask, "What data is the author working from?" This exploration can lead you to uncover the basic reasons he or she gives in the argument. Then you can ask, "What inferences does the author draw from this data?" to identify the argument's conclusion.

If a passage has two claims that might be part of an argument, ask "Why?" of one of them and see if the other provides a "because"—a reason — for it. If so, an argument probably exists. If the answer to "Why?" is irrelevant or inappropriate, then it is likely that it is not an argument.

Cue (or Indicator) Words

English contains a number of words and phrases that indicate that one statement or a group of statements is functioning as a reason for another. These are called **inference indicators** or **cue words.** They indicate that there is a logical relationship between one claim or set of claims and another claim or set of claims. The words and phrases listed below generally, *but not always*, indicate that the statement that follows is a reason. (The following lists are not exhaustive.)

- because
- in view of the fact that
- seeing that
- since
- for the reason that
- for
- as indicated by
- on the correct supposition that
- follows from
- being that
- may be deduced from
- in the first place
- in the second place

The words listed below generally signal that what follows is a conclusion drawn from one or more other statements in the discourse:

- therefore
- thus

- consequently
- points to the conclusion that
- shows that
- accordingly
- proves that
- allows us to infer that
- hence
- leads me to believe that
- then (without a preceding *if*)
- demonstrates that
- it follows that
- so
- we may conclude that

A number of terms simply join thoughts. They should not be mistaken for inference indicators. Some of these include

- and
- also
- besides
- but
- yet
- nevertheless
- in addition
- furthermore
- as well as

There are exceptions to the inference indicator words. For example, *since* can be used to suggest time as well as being used to show logical connection.

> He has been acting strangely since taking his final exam.

Then often takes the role of indicator of sequence, instead of the role of logical indicator.

> She went to class. Then she went to the bookstore. Then she went home.

In the second and third sentences, *then* shows a sequence of events.

Thus, which can introduce a conclusion, can also be used to summarize what comes before it.

> She wrote out her rent cheque, and then her hydro, cable, and student loan
> cheques. Thus, she quickly went through her hard-earned paycheque.

Thus in this passage acts as an indicator of a summary statement meaning "in this way." We are not trying to prove that she went through her paycheque quickly, but rather we are outlining the steps that led to that result.

In analyzing a passage, circling any inference indicators that appear helps guide us in identifying an argument.

> You should get the Orange computer rather than the IBIS (because) it is
> more reliable and less vulnerable to viruses.

Cue words are often misused. The one probably most widely misused is *therefore*. Some writers begin every third sentence with a *therefore*, whether it is appropriate or not. When an inference indicator's use is questionable, it is wise to test its validity by using one of the other two methods of identifying the structure of an argument — meaning, discussed above, and position.

In presenting our own arguments, using indicator words to signal the premises and conclusions can help make our arguments clearer to the reader.

QUICK QUIZ 3.4   Identifying Inference Indicators

In the following passages, circle the inference indicator words that are being used as such. Make note of any inference indicators that are being misused. Identify the premises and conclusions by putting a *P* next to the premises and a *C* next to the conclusions.

1. Marriage is sacred; therefore, it should be preserved.
2. We should allow gay marriage because if we don't, we will be discriminating against people unjustly.
3. Marijuana should be outlawed. First, it is harmful; second, the claimed medical benefits are bogus; and finally, it undermines productivity and causes safety hazards in the work place.
4. The Tour de France has been happening since 1903; however, it didn't achieve its current international prominence until after 1980.
5. Abortion is wrong; therefore, the fetus is a person and therefore anything that kills a person is wrong.

Position

A third way of identifying premises and conclusions is through the position of the claims within a passage. Often the conclusion of a more complicated argument appears at the beginning or the end of a long passage or text. In a paragraph, it is often the first or last sentence. In an essay, it is often in the first or last paragraph.

The Order of Premises and Conclusions

Consider the following passage:

> The Canadian government has been debating the legalization of marijuana. Not only is it considering legalizing marijuana for medical reasons but it is also considering making possession of small amounts not a crime. Marijuana relieves symptoms of certain ailments such as glaucoma and reduces the nausea caused by chemotherapy. However, I am opposed to any legalization. Marijuana is a harmful substance and once we allow it, our kids will find ways to get their hands on it and we'll corrupt an entire generation.

Much of the early part of this passage simply sets up the argument by identifying the issue and the context. The argument comes in the final two sentences with the conclusion first and the reasons following.

The basic argument in this passage is:

Premise: Marijuana is a harmful substance.

Premise: Once we allow it, our kids will find ways to get their hands on it and we'll corrupt an entire generation.

Conclusion: We should not legalize marijuana.

The premises and conclusions in an argument can come in any order. When analyzing the passages of others, you will find that there is often a lot of material that is not significant to the core argument being made. Writers include illustrations, examples, descriptions, definitions of terms, and explanations of claims being made. Since these often contribute to making the material easier to understand, we cannot ignore them. However, they are not central to the analysis and evaluation of the argument.

Consider the following passage:

> Many high school students think it is cool to experiment with marijuana. After all, what is wrong with getting high? And marijuana is not harmful, especially when compared to heroin or tobacco. So what's the problem? Many of our parents used marijuana when they were young, and most of them turned out all right. Most people in Canada see nothing wrong with a little recreational use of marijuana. Consequently, I see no reason to ban it.

Much of this passage consists of **extraneous material,** material that is not part of the logical structure of the argument — anecdotes, illustrations, and examples — rather than the claims of an argument. Only toward the end does the writer present an argument. We can **paraphrase,** or reword, the argument in this passage as follows:

Premise: Marijuana does no harm.

Premise: It is widely accepted.

Premise: Many have used it and most turned out all right.

Conclusion: It should not be illegal.

QUICK QUIZ 3.5   Identifying Arguments and Providing Cue Words

In the following passages, identify the basic argument, and then provide the appropriate inference indicator words to help the reader follow the passage. You may reorder the sentences or paraphrase where necessary.

1. Abortion should be banned. It is morally wrong to kill an innocent human.
2. Capital punishment does not allow people to be rehabilitated, and it is immoral.
3. Kittens need to be trained. Instinct only goes so far with higher mammals. What is not governed by instinct needs to be taught. Kittens are higher mammals.
4. Most people believe that the woolly mammoths became extinct because of the Ice Age. This explanation is not satisfactory. Mammoths have been found entombed whole in glaciers in Siberia. Glaciers form and move too slowly to entomb woolly mammoths suddenly. The glaciers came later than the woolly mammoths. The mammoths were clearly the first alien abductions. Nothing else makes sense.
5. Everyone should wear a seat belt. This should be mandatory. Not wearing one increases the risk of death. When people are injured or killed in car accidents, their families are devastated. We all have an obligation to our family. And we all have an obligation to society. Not wearing a seat belt results in more injuries, which have to be paid for by the rest of society.

QUICK QUIZ 3.6   Ordering Claims in an Argument

Below are five claims that make up a single argument. Identify the basic structure of the argument and then, using only these, organize the claims so that the argument will be easy for the reader to follow. Add cue words to assist the reader. (Hint: Start with the most controversial claim and then look for the reason for that.)

1. Humans and apes have completely different genes.
2. Humans and apes inhabit the earth at the same time.
3. Humans could not be descended from apes.
4. The Bible claims that humans and apes were created distinctly and separately.
5. If two species have completely different genes, one could not have descended from the other.

3.6 PORTRAYING ARGUMENT STRUCTURE: STANDARD FORM

Portraying the structure of an argument involves identifying the different claims — reasons and conclusions — and their relationship to one another in that particular argument, and then displaying them in a visual way. There are two basic ways of showing an argument's structure: standard form and arrow diagram.

To portray an argument using ***standard form,*** we begin by writing out the premises, each on a separate line. We then separate the premises from the conclusion with a straight line and write the conclusion below it. Three dots forming an equilateral triangle are used as a conclusion indicator, which is placed in front of the conclusion statement. The three dots symbolize *therefore.* For easy reference, the claims can be numbered, as in the example below:

1.   Reason 1
2.   Reason 2 (if there is a second reason)

∴   3.   Conclusion

Consider the following argument:

> Simply by virtue of being human, all people are entitled to the basic necessities of life. Health care is a basic necessity of life. Therefore, everyone is entitled to health care.

When faced with such examples in this text, you should try to reason through them on your own before continuing. In this case, what are the premises (reasons) and what is the conclusion? Put the argument in standard form.

Portrayed in standard form, this argument would be displayed as follows:

1.   Simply by virtue of being human, all people are entitled to the basic necessities of life.
2.   Health care is a basic necessity of life.

∴   3.   Everyone is entitled to health care.

There are no strict rules for the order of the premises if there is more than one. However, it is useful to group them so that claims that are connected appear together. In this case, we have put the more general premise first.

Note that a claim that functions as a reason in one argument may function as a conclusion in another. Consider the following:

> Simply by virtue of being human, all people are entitled to the basic necessities of life. Health care is a basic necessity of life. Therefore, everyone is entitled to health care. And since the homeless are no less human than others, they are entitled to health care.

There are two arguments in this passage. The conclusion of one acts as the reason for the other, thereby linking them. We can portray this argument in standard form as follows:

1. Simply by virtue of being human, all people are entitled to the basic necessities of life.
2. Health care is a basic necessity of life.

∴ 3. Everyone is entitled to health care.

4. The homeless are no less human than others.

∴ 5. The homeless are also entitled to health care.

 QUICK QUIZ 3.7   Portraying Standard Form

Portray the following arguments in standard form.

1. All tortoiseshell cats are female. Felicity is a tortoiseshell cat. Felicity is female.
2. According to reports of the sightings of the Loch Ness monster, it would be an enormous size — at least six metres in length and a ton or more in weight. An aquatic creature of that size would have to eat literally tons of food each month. Yet, the loch has a far smaller food supply than that. The reported sightings must be wrong.
3. Although Lance Armstrong has won seven Tour de France races to Eddy Merckx's five, Merckx is the better cyclist. Armstrong has won only seventy-one classic races, including the Tour and the five stages he has won within the Tour. Merckx has won 471 classic races, including his stages within the Tour de France. Although they are both amazing and both legends, Merckx is the better all-round cyclist.
4. *Context: A couple had planned to go camping.* "I think we should stay home. It's going to rain all weekend."
5. I recommend that we fire Farah. She has been making decisions not within her job description and then contacting agencies and saying that her decisions are company policy. She has been warned twice that this is unacceptable behaviour and that it contravenes corporate policy, but she hasn't listened or learned. If she continues, she will cause serious problems not only externally to the company's relationships but internally as well. She's got to go.

3.7 PORTRAYING ARGUMENT STRUCTURE: ARROW DIAGRAMS

Portraying arguments using standard form works well for relatively simple arguments with a single line of reasoning. Once arguments become more complex, involving several lines of reasoning, the standard form can become quite cumbersome.

An alternate way of displaying the structure of an argument uses arrows and numbers to construct an **arrow diagram.**

1. Draw square brackets [ ] around each claim in the text.
2. Number each claim, starting from the first claim in the passage through to the last. Number all separate claims. Note that some sentences may contain multiple claims, and each claim, not each sentence, is assigned a separate number. (If some claims are not used in the argument, they can be dropped in the analysis of the structure.)
3. Circle inference indicators.
4. Use arrows to portray the structure of the argument. The blunt end of the arrow indicates the premise; the sharp end, the conclusion. Normally in the arrow diagram, the conclusion is at the bottom of the diagram.

Paraphrasing the argument first is sometimes helpful. Construct the paraphrase, and use the above strategy on the paraphrased argument. This works especially well with passages that have a lot of extraneous material or ones in which the basic claims in the argument need to be stated more clearly.

Consider the following argument:

You should major in psychology because you are good at dealing with people.

Numbering, bracketing, and circling inference indicators would produce the following:

1
[You should major in psychology] (because) [you are good at dealing with 2
people].

Diagramming using arrows produces an argument structure that looks like this:

2

1

All arguments with one premise and one conclusion are diagrammed this way.

If there is more than one premise in the argument, we can diagram the argument in one of two ways — as convergent or linked. In a **linked argument,** the two premises are related to one another and must be considered part of the same argument. In a **convergent argument,** the second premise stands entirely on its own — that is, it constitutes an independent reason for the conclusion, and each of the reasons offers independent support for the conclusion. In such arguments, each premise is represented by its own arrow, as follows:

1
[Legalizing marijuana will make a dangerous drug available to our kids.]

2

Furthermore, [there are no proven medical benefits to it.] (Therefore),

3

[we should not legalize marijuana.]

In this argument, claims 1 and 2 are unrelated reasons for the third claim, the conclusion. Each addresses a different feature of the debate over legalizing marijuana: a dangerous drug being made available to kids and the drug's alleged medical uses. When that is the case, we treat the premises as individual. This argument's diagram would be as follows:

By contrast, consider the following linked argument:

1   2

[We wouldn't knowingly expose our children to harm.] [Legalizing marijuana

3

would expose them to a harmful substance.] (Therefore), [we should not legalize marijuana.]

In this argument, premises 1 and 2 reinforce one another and, taken together, make the conclusion stronger. The premises would be treated as one unit in this argument's arrow diagram:

To show that the premises are linked, we not only join them with a plus sign but also draw a line underneath them, indicating that they are to be taken as one argument. When we diagram an argument with **linked premises,** we are claiming that the premises linked by the plus sign need to be considered together. This is called a *linked argument.*

Arrow diagrams are particularly useful when diagramming more complex arguments, including arguments with multiple premises and subpremises and several lines of reasoning leading to the same conclusion.

You can combine standard form and arrow diagrams by connecting the statements with arrows. This is a less common use of the conventions for portraying argument structure. The second argument above could be displayed as follows:

We wouldn't knowingly expose our children to harm.	+	Legalizing marijuana makes it easier for them to get their hands on a dangerously harmful drug.

∴   We should not legalize marijuana.

One primary purpose in drawing the structure of an argument is to be able to see at a glance what claims are being supported and what claims are offered in support. Since most arguments are written in prose, often their structures are not immediately apparent. Diagramming an argument helps us visually see and better understand the arguments we are analyzing. They also provide us with a convenient way of explaining the arguments to others.

QUICK QUIZ 3.8   Using Arrow Diagrams

Portray the arguments in Quick Quiz 3.7 using arrow diagrams.

3.8 DIAGRAMMING COMPLEX ARGUMENTS

The arguments presented thus far have been relatively simple. Many of the arguments we encounter are more complex than this.

> I can't write the exam because I am sick, and besides, my grandmother died and I have to go to the funeral.

numbering and bracketing, we get:

> 1
> [I can't write the exam] (because) [I am sick], and besides, [my
> 2
> 3   4
> grandmother died] and [I have to go to the funeral].

Although we have three premises and one conclusion in this argument, not all of the premises are inherently related. My being sick and my grandmother dying have no clear connection to one another. If two sets of premises are relatively independent of one another, and either could be treated as separate reasons for the same conclusion, then it is best to treat them as independent arguments (or independent lines of reasoning). We could portray the argument in standard form as follows:

Argument 1:

2.   I am sick.

_____

∴ 1.   I can't write the exam

Argument 2:

3.   My grandmother died.

4.   I have to go to the funeral.

_____

∴ 1.   I can't write the exam.

In this case, if the viewer doesn't read the conclusions, he or she will not know that there are two independent arguments for one conclusion. Portrayed in an arrow diagram, the structure is more obvious:

This is a convergent argument.

Consider the following passage:

> Smoking in public places should be banned because it causes harm to others. It is harmful to others because secondhand smoke can cause cancer, asthma, or lung disease.

This argument is also a complex argument, but it has a different structure.

1.   Secondhand smoke can cause cancer, asthma, or lung disease.

∴   2.   Smoking is harmful to others.

∴   3.   Smoking in public places should be banned.

Using an arrow diagram, this would be displayed as follows:

In this case, we have one premise (1) that acts as a reason for a conclusion (2), which, in turn, acts as a reason for yet another conclusion (3). One claim has two functions — it serves as a conclusion of one argument and a premise for another. *1* is a **basic reason** in that it is a starting reason for which no further justification is given. Basic reasons are the undefended starting points of an argument. *2* is an **intermediate conclusion** in that it is a conclusion from at least one reason and a reason for yet a further conclusion. *3* is the **final conclusion.** When the conclusion of one argument becomes the reason for another conclusion, the argument is called a **serial argument.**

> We should not legalize marijuana. Although some will experience minor health benefits with the legalization of marijuana, these benefits are outweighed by the increase in the number of people who will be attracted to

this dangerous drug by its legalization. In order to prevent more people from becoming addicted to this drug, it should not be made legally available for any purposes.

Some of the basic claims are repeated and some may be redundant, which often is the case when people make arguments. The following paraphrase (supplying cue words) captures the basic logic in the passage while eliminating the redundancies and extraneous claims.

We should not legalize marijuana. If we legalize it for any reason, more people will become addicted to it, and we don't want that to happen.

By numbering, bracketing, and identifying inference indicators, we get the following:

1   2
[We should not legalize marijuana.] [If we legalize it for any reason,
                                                                    3
more people will become addicted to it], and [we don't want that to happen].

Portraying this in standard form, we get the following:

2. If we legalize it for any reason, more people will become addicted to it.

3. We don't want that to happen.

_____

∴   1. We should not legalize marijuana.

Using an arrow diagram, this would be displayed as follows:

$$\frac{2 + 3}{}$$

When the premises are clearly linked to one another, are on the same topic, and, if taken together, help strengthen the argument, they are treated as a unit. In the above sample argument, the claims provide a stronger argument when linked. If we were to treat them as distinct arguments, we would have to provide additional reasons to link the premises to the conclusion, and the additional premises would duplicate the already stated claims.

When premises could be considered separately, and, if when considered separately, they would provide independent reasons for the conclusion, they should be treated as independent. Consider the following:

> We should not legalize marijuana for any reason. If we legalize it, it would only induce more people to try it and to become addicted to it. Furthermore, marijuana is a harmful drug. By legalizing it, we would be condoning the use of an unsafe substance. And we don't want to do that.

Using numbering and bracketing, we come up with the following:

1

[We should not legalize marijuana for any reason]. [If we legalize it, it

2

would only induce more people to try it and to become addicted to it.]

3   4

Furthermore, [marijuana is a harmful drug]. [By legalizing it, we would be

5

condoning the use of an unsafe substance]. And [we don't want to do that].

Argument 1:

2.   If we legalize it, it would only induce more people to try it and to become addicted to it.

∴ 1.   We should not legalize marijuana for any reason.

Argument 2:

3.   Marijuana is a harmful drug.

4.   By legalizing it, we would be condoning the use of an unsafe substance.

5.   We don't want to do that.

∴ 1.   We should not legalize marijuana for any reason.

Using arrows, we end up with the following:

2   3 + 4 + 5

1

The arrow diagram portrays more clearly the structure of the passage's argument. We have two independent arguments, one made up of three premises and both leading to a common conclusion. Each of the sets of premises can support the conclusion.

QUICK QUIZ 3.9   Interpreting Arrow Diagrams

Explain the meaning of each of the following arrow diagrams by identifying the premises and conclusions:

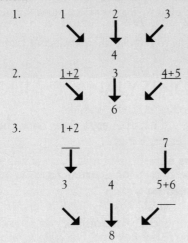

1.

1   2   3

4

2.

1+2   3   4+5

6

3.

1+2

3   4   5+6

8

QUICK QUIZ 3.10   Diagramming Complex Arguments

Portray the structure of the following arguments.

1. Marriage is a private matter between the partners in a marriage. The state has no right to interfere in the private affairs of its citizens. Therefore, the state has no right to prohibit gay marriage.
2. The state does have a right to regulate marriage, including gay marriage. The state is entitled to enforce morals and values, and sexual relations between individuals of the same sex are immoral and an abomination to God. Moreover, marriage is fundamentally about conceiving and raising children, and gay couples can't do this. So the state has a right to prohibit gay marriage.
3. The recent dramatic increase in gas prices is a good thing because it will result in less drain on oil reserves. We are running low on oil reserves and need to conserve them.
4. Capital punishment is not effective as a deterrent. It is a form of cruel and unusual punishment. And we risk killing innocent people by enforcing capital punishment because some innocent individuals have been convicted of what would be capital crimes. Therefore, capital punishment should not be allowed.
5. The Atlantis portrayed by Plato and on which all later stories of the lost continent are based could not have existed. Plato says that Atlantis was in the Atlantic Ocean, that it was destroyed by tidal waves and earthquakes and sank to the bottom of the sea virtually overnight, and that it was an extremely advanced culture that existed 10,000 years before his day. Extensive mapping of the Atlantic Ocean floor reveals neither the kind of rock of which continents are made nor a land mass even approximating the presumed size of Atlantis. From geology, we know that tidal waves and earthquakes cannot cause a land mass of Atlantis's alleged size to sink to the ocean bottom, much less overnight. Nor is there any evidence for any kind of advanced civilization existing 10,000 years before Plato. Plato's story is a myth.

3.9 ANALYZING PASSAGES WITH MIXED PROSE

As discussed earlier, many passages that contain arguments also contain extraneous material, which may include background information, examples and illustrations, definitions, descriptions, elaboration, repetitions of the basic claims, explanations, and simply irrelevant information.

In analyzing a passage for the argument, we want to remove the extraneous material and focus on the argument structure.

1. Read the passage.
2. Circle inference indicators and underline key concepts in the passage.
3. Examine each sentence for its role in the passage. What does each claim do in the overall context of the passage? Among other things, a sentence may

   - contain a claim that acts as a premise or conclusion in an argument;
   - set the stage with relevant background information;
   - provide information to help the reader understand an issue;
   - define an issue;
   - provide examples or illustrations;
   - define key terms;
   - restate claims in a slightly different way; or
   - make an aside or digression from the main point.

Many or all of these functions are useful in presenting an argument in prose. However, in analyzing an argument, we are looking for only what is essential to the logic of the argument.

1. Identify the main point (conclusion) of the passage. You may find a stated claim that captures the main point exactly. In some cases, you may need to formulate the main point in your own words.
2. Check the conclusion against the passage. How do the other claims fit with this claim?
3. Identify the structure of the argument.
4. If there are any unclear, ambiguous, or vague terms that are central to the argument, clarify them.

Consider the following passage:

> The debate over gay marriage has become particularly heated over the past two years. By gay marriage, I mean the right of same-sex couples to enter into a legal union that gives the partners the rights normally shared by heterosexual couples who marry. Gay men and women have demanded that they be given the legal right to marry. Many conservatives have rejected the idea on the grounds that this will undermine the sanctity of marriage. I contend that we should allow gay marriage because if we don't, we will be denying one significant segment of the population the basic rights shared by the rest of the population.

By numbering and bracketing the basic claims, we get the following:

1
[The debate over gay marriage has become particularly heated over the
2
past two years.] [By gay marriage, I mean the right of same-sex couples to
enter into a legal union that gives the partners the rights normally shared by
3
heterosexual couples who marry.] [Gay men and women have demanded that
4
they be given the legal right to marry.] [Many conservatives have rejected
the idea on the grounds that this will undermine the sanctity of marriage.]
5
(I contend that)[we should allow gay marriage] (because) [if we don't, we will
6
be denying one significant segment of the population the basic rights shared
by the rest of the population].

The key to extracting the argument from such a passage is to examine each sentence to determine its role:

Statement 1 provides information about the escalation of the controversy.

Statement 2 defines gay marriage.

Statement 3 presents the position of one side in the debate.

Statement 4 presents the position of another side in the debate. ("On the grounds that" could be interpreted as a reason indicator.)

Statement 5, preceded by a conclusion indicator, identifies a controversial claim.

Statement 6, preceded by a reason indicator, gives a reason for the controversial claim.

Claims 1 through 4 provide background information but are not part of the argument. Although there is an argument within 4, it is not the main argument of the passage. That is given in claims 5 and 6:

> If we don't allow gay marriage, we will be denying gay people basic rights shared by the rest of the population.

> ∴ We should allow gay marriage.

An analysis involves not just analyzing the arguments in the passage but interpreting the passage and trying to clarify the meaning. Sometimes when we do this, we end up with something other than what the author intended. Some passages are simply muddled, so in interpreting them we may have to say, "If the author means *x* by this," where *x* is our reconstruction, "then here is what is right or wrong with this argument."

QUICK QUIZ 3.11   Identifying Arguments in Passages with Extraneous Material

In the following passages, identify whether or not there is an argument. If there is no argument, explain why. If there is an argument, identify the basic argument. Be especially attentive to extraneous material and do not include it in your analysis. If there is extraneous material, explain why the material is irrelevant to the argument.

1. 1 Transgender people are individuals who believe that their proper genders are different from the sex of the bodies they inhabit. 2 Some transgender people seek to change their bodies to conform to what they feel is their proper gender identity. 3 Some psychiatrists have argued that these individuals have a serious personality disorder and that such attempts at transformation are signs of this. 4 I disagree. 5 They don't have a personality disorder at all, and 6 psychiatrists have failed to provide any evidence to the contrary. 7 Moreover, if it were a personality disorder, transgender people would have the various characteristics of a personality disorder. 8 And generally speaking, they don't. 9 This is just another example of psychiatrists trying to impose their narrow values on anyone they see as different.

2. 1 Marijuana, like heroin and cocaine, is an addictive drug. 2 It has become widely available in Canada. 3 Much of the marijuana available in Canada is grown domestically. 4 Once grown only in fields, it is increasingly being grown in grow-houses, houses taken over by drug dealers and used to grow marijuana. 5 Because it is addictive, 6 marijuana should not be legalized for either medical or recreational uses. 7 There are far more effective drugs that could be used medically. 8 And because it is addictive, 9 it should not be used recreationally.

3. 1 Hate speech should not be prohibited. 2 It is simply speech. 3 Some people find what is called "hate speech" upsetting. 4 However, many people find many things upsetting. 5 For example, some people find particular ads upsetting. 6 Others find violence in movies upsetting. 7 Some people find couples being the same sex upsetting. 8 Some find even the mention of such things upsetting. 9 That is not sufficient grounds for the prohibition of anything. 10 If we did that, we would prohibit all kinds of unpopular ideas and beliefs. 11 Hate speech is simply speech. 12 And all speech, even unpopular and unpleasant speech, should be tolerated. 13 It is far better to counter such verbal communication with good arguments than to suppress it. 14 No, hate speech should not be suppressed.

3.10 DIAGRAMMING CHALLENGES AND RESPONSES

The conventions for diagramming and displaying arguments do not yet provide us with an easy means for dealing with challenges and responses. A ***challenge*** involves a denial of a claim. A ***response*** to a challenge is a challenge to the challenge, or the denial of the challenge. In effect, with a response, we are saying that claim *x* should not be accepted for reason *y*. So as not to get confused by using the same notation as for a reason and a conclusion, we will use a wavy arrow to indicate the relationship between a challenge and a claim or between a response and a challenge.

This is read as *C* is not true (is false) because *R*. In this case, *R* is a reason for rejecting *C*.

A response to a challenge is read the same way.

We read this diagram as C is false because R; and R is rejected (false) because A.
Consider the following argument:

Original:
            1   2
[Abortion is immoral] (because) [the fetus is a person.]

                    not 2   3

Challenge:
[The fetus is not a person] (because) [a person is a moral

                                        4
agent], and [moral agents are capable of making decisions].

               5   6
[Fetuses can't make decisions,] (so) [they can't be treated as
moral agents.]

               7   8

Response:
[Infants are not capable of making decisions], yet [we treat
them as persons.]

This can be diagrammed as follows:

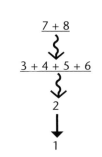

This notation reads as follows: *2* supports *1*; *2* is false because of *3* and *4*; and *5* and *6* deny *3* and *4*. In this context *3* and *4* are a challenge to *2*, and *5* and *6* are a response to that challenge.

QUICK QUIZ 3.12   Diagramming Challenges and Responses

Diagram the following arguments using the notation for challenges and responses.

1. A: *The Adventures of Huckleberry Finn* is racist because it uses the N-word over 200 times, and that is offensive to many people.
   B: The dictionary uses the N-word, and it is not racist.
   C: The dictionary is defining the term; *The Adventures of Huckleberry Finn* uses the term to refer to a group of people.

(continued)

2. A: Euthanasia is immoral because it denies an individual autonomy.
   B: It does not deny an individual autonomy; rather, it allows the individual to choose how and when he or she will die, and that is upholding an individual's autonomy.
3. A: Pornography is degrading to women because it shows women in sexual positions.
   B: It shows men in sexual positions. Is it not degrading to men as well?
   C: No. Men have positions of power in society and cannot be degraded, whereas women are degraded by being shown in sexual positions.

MODULE SUMMARY

The central unit of argumentation is the argument. Arguments are composed of claims, which are statements that can be affirmed or denied. An argument consists of at least two claims, one of which, the premise or reason, is given as the justification for the other, the conclusion. We use cue words (inference indicators), position, and meaning to help identify arguments and distinguish between the premises and the conclusion. In order to identify the structure of the argument — the relationship between the premises and the conclusion — we diagram the argument, using either standard form or an arrow diagram. Often we need to eliminate extraneous material to find the core logical structure of a passage. Paraphrasing a passage can help clarify the claims and identify the basic argument structure.

KEY TERMS

Note: The list of key terms may include terms introduced in the Student Manual.

affirm a claim
argument
arrow diagram
assertion
basic reason
challenge
claims
convergent argument
conclusion
cue words (inference indicators)
deny a claim

description (versus argument)
explanation
extraneous material
final (or main) conclusion
illustrate/illustration
inference indicators (cue words)
intermediate conclusion
linked premises
linked argument
narrative

negative
paraphrase
performative utterances
portraying the structure of an argument
premise
reason
response
serial argument
standard form
structure of an argument

MODULE 4

ASSESSING DEDUCTIVE ARGUMENTS

4.1 LEARNING OBJECTIVES

After completing this module, you should be able to

1. explain the difference and distinguish between inductive and deductive arguments;
2. explain and apply the criteria for assessing arguments;
3. define and correctly use key terms in assessing argument structure;
4. explain the difference between a valid argument and an invalid argument;
5. determine and explain why a given deductive argument is valid or invalid using the topics model and the patterns model;
6. supply missing premises for a deductive argument; and
7. identify and challenge invalid arguments using the argument counterexample method.

4.2 INTRODUCTION

We give an argument because we have some doubts about the acceptability (truth) of the conclusion or because we want to identify the reasoning, assumptions, and claims that support a given conclusion. We are trying to show that the conclusion rests on claims that are more readily acceptable than the conclusion and provide a strong or compelling reason to accept the conclusion. This means that not only must the reasons be true but they must also adequately support the conclusion. If an argument meets all of these conditions, it is said to be *sound.*

For the reasons to support the conclusion, they must be relevant to the conclusion as well as sufficient to support the conclusion. Both deductive and inductive arguments provide reasons that support the conclusion. They differ in the strength of that support. Deductive arguments guarantee the conclusion, whereas inductive arguments can only provide, at best, very strong reasons for the conclusion. This module examines the logical conditions for good deductive arguments — validity and invalidity. It introduces two methods for determining validity — logical patterns and the topics model — and one method for demonstrating invalidity — the counterexample method. Patterns and the topics model provide means for supplying the assumed premises needed to make an argument valid. Module 5 addresses inductive arguments.

4.3 DEDUCTIVE AND INDUCTIVE ARGUMENTS

Consider the following argument:

Beethoven was the greatest composer of the nineteenth century.

∴ The moon is made of green cheese.

If someone were to offer this as an argument, we would probably have reason to doubt both their seriousness and sanity. Even if the premise were true, there appears to be no connection or relationship between the premise and what it is supposed to justify. There simply is no relevance between composing music and the composition of the moon.

Consider another example:

> Beethoven was the greatest composer of the nineteenth century.
>
> _____
>
> ∴   Every university student should study Beethoven.

In this argument, the premise does constitute a possible reason for the conclusion. That is, it is the kind of claim that would be **relevant** to establishing the conclusion. However, it is not sufficient for establishing the conclusion. That Beethoven was the greatest composer of the nineteenth century might be a reason for some people to study him but not necessarily for all university students to study him. To guarantee this conclusion, we would need an additional claim or claims that would connect Beethoven's being the greatest composer of his time to it being made compulsory for all university students to study him. The premise in this argument is, as stated, relevant but not sufficient for establishing the conclusion.

> Beethoven was the greatest composer of the nineteenth century.
>
> Every university student should study the great composers.
>
> _____
>
> ∴   Every university student should study Beethoven.

In this argument, the premises are not only relevant reasons for the conclusion but, if accepted, they would be **sufficient** to establish the conclusion. That is, in this argument, you could not accept the premises and deny the conclusion. If you did, you would contradict yourself. Arguments with this kind of structure, in which accepting the premises logically forces us to accept the conclusion, are called **deductive arguments.**

Not all arguments, however, are of this type.

> I bought this coffee in the college dining hall.
>
> It is overpriced.
>
> _____
>
> ∴   All coffee sold on campus is overpriced.

Although the sample is relevant to establishing that all coffee on campus is overpriced, it is not sufficient. The premises provide weak grounds for the conclusion, so even if we accept them, we are not logically forced to accept the conclusion. To infer that all coffee on campus is overpriced, we would need to know how many coffee outlets there are on campus, whether they are controlled by one body that sets a common price or whether they all set their own price structures, and what each charges.

This is an inductive argument. An ***inductive argument*** is one in which the premises provide plausible or probable reasons for the conclusion, but do not absolutely guarantee the conclusion. In the following inductive argument, the reasons provide probable grounds for accepting the conclusion. However, accepting the premises does not guarantee that the conclusion is true.

Ninety-seven percent of the part-time faculty voted to go on strike.

Nayla is a member of the part-time faculty.

∴   Nayla must have voted to go on strike.

Nayla might be one of the three percent who voted not to go on strike. In this case, the premises provide strong but not conclusive support for the conclusion.

Inductive arguments are judged in terms of the strength of the support that they provide for accepting the conclusion. That strength can range from very weak, as in the price of coffee example above, to very strong, as in the example involving Nayla.

Both inductive and deductive arguments require that the premises be relevant to the conclusion. Where they differ is in whether or not the sufficiency condition is met. In a deductive argument, the premises fully support or guarantee the conclusion. In an inductive argument, the premises only partially support the conclusion, providing a degree of probability but nothing conclusive. The rest of this module discusses the criteria for assessing deductive arguments.

QUICK QUIZ 4.1   Identifying Deductive and Inductive Arguments

For each of the following,

- portray the structure of the argument;
- identify whether the argument is inductive or deductive; and
- assess whether the premises are relevant and sufficient to establish the conclusion.

If the argument is inductive, assess whether the premises strongly or weakly support the conclusion.

1. Daphne is a cat. All cats are playful. Therefore, Daphne is playful.
2. Nigel is a dog. Some dogs are playful. So Nigel is playful.
3. The defendant knew the victim. She had the motive to want him dead. She was in possession of a weapon that could have been the murder weapon. She was in the vicinity where the victim was killed. She was seen by three eyewitnesses talking to the victim just before he was killed. Therefore, she must have killed him.
4. If something is immoral, it should be illegal. Adultery is immoral. So it should be illegal.
5. I didn't receive any mail last week, yet there were no holidays. My mailman must be falling down on the job.

Answers for all Quick Quizzes in this text are provided in the Student Manual. After doing the Quick Quizzes, consult the Student Manual to check your understanding of the material.

4.4 ASSESSING DEDUCTIVE ARGUMENTS: VALIDITY

Deductive arguments are assessed in terms of validity and invalidity. A deductive argument is **valid** if accepting the premises logically requires that one accept the conclusion. Accepting the premises and denying the conclusion would result in a contradiction. Validity is a function of the relationship between the premises and the conclusion. A deductive argument is **invalid** if we can affirm the premises and deny the conclusion.

The following is a valid argument:

>   All mammals nurse their young.
>
>   Whales are mammals.
>
> _____
>
> ∴   Whales nurse their young.

The premises in this argument happen to be true. If we have an argument that is valid (i.e., in which the premises support the conclusion), and if the premises are true, then the truth of the conclusion is guaranteed. This is the ideal whenever we present an argument. An argument like this is called **cogent.** To be cogent, an argument must meet two criteria: the argument must be valid and the premises must be true. Unlike a cogent argument, a valid deductive argument does not by definition have true premises.

Consider the following argument:

>   All mammals nurse their young.
>
>   Alligators are mammals.
>
> _____
>
> ∴   Alligators nurse their young.

Again, _if_ we accept the premises in this argument, we must also accept the conclusion or consequently contradict ourselves. However, in this argument, one of the premises happens to be false. So, although the argument is valid, it is not cogent.

We can also have valid arguments in which the premises are false and the conclusion is true.

>   Mammals lay eggs.
>
>   Alligators are mammals.
>
> _____
>
> ∴   Alligators lay eggs.

This argument is valid. If we accept the premises, we must accept the conclusion; there are no circumstances under which we could accept the premises yet not accept the conclusion. However, in this case, the premises are, in fact, false, and the conclusion happens to be true.

Knowing that an argument is valid does not assure us that the conclusion is true. Validity is concerned simply with the relationship between the premises and the conclusion — relevance and sufficiency.

To summarize, a valid argument may have

- true premises and a true conclusion;
- false premises and a true conclusion; or
- false premises and a false conclusion.

A valid argument may not have

- true premises and a false conclusion.

An invalid argument, on the other hand, may have any combination of true and false premises and conclusions. That is, with an invalid argument, the truth of the premises does not guarantee the truth of the conclusion. Because the relationship between the premises and conclusion is not properly established, knowing the truth of the premises tells us nothing about the truth of the conclusion.

QUICK QUIZ 4.2   Validity Comprehension

Which of the following claims are true and which are false? If the claim is false, explain why.

1. A valid argument can have true premises and a false conclusion.
2. A cogent argument must be valid.
3. A cogent argument can have false premises.
4. A valid argument must have a true conclusion.
5. Validity is an indication of the truth of the claims in the argument.
6. Cogency is an indication of the truth of the claims in an argument.
7. Validity is concerned with the relationship of the claims to one another.

4.5 VALID ARGUMENT FORMS

Validity is a function of how terms or statements are related to one another. An argument is considered valid not by the truth of its content but by the relationship of its claims. We call this relationship the **logical structure** or the **logical form** of an argument. Since we are not concerned with an argument's substance when determining validity, we need only look at the structure (the logical form) and not the content (meaning of the statements) of the argument. An argument form can be identified by replacing the claims of an argument with **variables** (e.g., *a*, *b*, *c*) and leaving only the logical terms and variables. **Logical terms** include, among others,

If . . . then . . .

All . . . are . . .

Some . . . are . . .

None . . . are . . .

Not (and its variations)

Either . . . or . . .

. . . and . . .

The statement "If there is life on Venus, there must be water on Venus" implicitly contains the logical term "If . . . then . . ." and the content terms "there is life on Venus" and "there is water on Venus." The logical form of this statement is "If a, then b."

The statement "There is life on Venus" contains no logical terms and is simply translated as a. The statement "There is no water on Venus" contains the logical term *not* and would be stated as "not b."

When we translate a claim such as "If there is life on Venus, there must be water on Venus" into "If a, then b," we are turning a claim with content into a claim with variables and thereby identifying the logical form of the claim.

The following are not logical terms:

but

however

although

even though

Consider the following argument:

If there is water on Venus, then there may be life on Venus.

There is water on Venus.

_____

∴   There may be life on Venus.

We can determine this argument's logical form by identifying the logical terms and the content terms and replacing the content terms with variables. Each repetition of a content claim gets the same variable. Replacing the content terms with variables in each of the above arguments would give us the following logical form for the argument:

If a, then b

a

_____

∴   b

This is a valid argument form. (See Section 4.6 on conditional arguments, below, for an explanation of why.) Any argument with this form or pattern is valid. One cannot accept its premises and deny its conclusion. Knowing this logical form enables us to identify and determine the validity for any argument having this form.

Because arguments are *valid* or *invalid* solely in terms of their logical form, we can determine the validity of an argument solely by examining its logical form. Some logical forms are valid, and some are invalid. A valid form will never produce an invalid argument, and an invalid form will never produce a valid argument.

Logicians have developed a number of different ways of establishing validity: truth tables, Venn diagrams, and logical derivations. Using each of these requires mastering a somewhat technical set of skills. Less formal methods of determining validity and invalidity include identifying the most basic common argument patterns, the topics model, and the method of argument counterexample. Since our purpose with this text is not to become logicians but to develop the skills for critiquing and developing good arguments, we will focus on the less formal methods.

Conditional and disjunctive arguments are two of the most common types of arguments. Fortunately, the valid and invalid argument patterns for each of these are relatively few, so we can simply learn the patterns. Many arguments don't, however, fit into those patterns. The topics model method allows us to determine validity for most of the remaining patterns without having to learn a large number of argument forms or more complicated methods for determining validity.

QUICK QUIZ 4.3   Identifying Logical Terms and Content

Identify the logical terms and content terms in each of the following, and then turn the content terms into variables.

1. Either I study for the exam or go partying with my friends.
2. Some stars are relatively cool compared to our sun.
3. No stars are as cool as a planet.
4. If I am late for the interview, I won't get the job.
5. All cats chase mice.

4.6 CONDITIONAL ARGUMENT PATTERNS

One of the most common argument patterns is the conditional argument. A **conditional argument** is an argument that contains at least one conditional statement. A **conditional statement** asserts that one state of affairs is conditional upon another. It does not state that either is true, but only that if one is true, then the other will be true (if the conditional statement as a whole is true).

The following is a conditional statement:

If he is a logician, then he is mad.

It claims that a person is mad under certain conditions. This statement contains the logical term "If . . . then . . ." and the content terms "he is a logician" and "he is mad."

We substitute a different variable for each of the content terms in the statement. Substituting a for "he is a logician" and b for "he is mad," we thereby get the following statement:

If a, then b.

"If . . . then . . ." is the most common form of a **conditional claim.** A conditional statement (or claim) is a single claim, and it always consists of two conditions, one of which is dependent in some way on the other. A conditional statement cannot be broken into its component parts unless we have further information. From the statement "If he is a logician, then he is mad," we do not know that anyone is a logician, much less that he is mad. All we know is the condition — that *if* someone meets the condition of being a logician, then he is mad.

As long as we are consistent about substituting the same letter for the same content term throughout an argument, we can portray the logical structure or form of the argument.

In the argument below, by following through with the substitution, we can discover the logical form.

> If he is a logician, then he is mad.
>
> He is a logician.
>
> _____
>
> ∴   He is mad.

This becomes

> If a, then b
>
> a
>
> _____
>
> ∴   b

In this argument, the conditional statement is "If *a*, then *b*." In this statement, *a* is called the **antecedent** (because it comes before the "then"); *b* is called the **consequent** (because it comes after). "If . . . then . . ." is the basis for identifying the antecedent and the consequent. Other variants of the conditional are identified below under "Translating Claims into the Conditional Form." No matter how a conditional is worded, it can always be translated into the base form, "If *a*, then *b*."

QUICK QUIZ 4.4   Identifying Antecedents and Consequents

In the following, identify the antecedents and the consequents.

1. If the sun is powered by nuclear fusion, then its life span is far longer than anyone expected.
2. We will go to the party if I can borrow the car.
3. If the province raises tuition fees, fewer students will be able to go to university.

In order to understand validity, we need to understand what we can do with a claim. With any given claim, we can either affirm it or deny it. To **affirm a claim** means that we say that the claim is true. By affirming the claim "Saindon is a logician," I am saying that this claim is true. To **deny a claim** is to say that the claim is false. By denying the claim "Saindon is a logician," I am saying "It is false (not the case) that Saindon is a logician" or, more simply, "Saindon is not a logician." We can deny either affirmative or negative claims. Denying an affirmative claim would produce a negative claim:

> Saindon is a logician.

would become

> Saindon is not a logician.

Denying this negative claim would, in turn, produce a positive claim:

> Saindon is a logician.

Given these basic functions of affirming and denying, we have six choices with the conditional claim "If a, then b":

1. We can **affirm the antecedent.**
2. We can **deny the antecedent.**
3. We can **affirm the consequent.**
4. We can **deny the consequent.**
5. We can **affirm the conditional.**
6. We can **deny the conditional.**

The first four provide us with our basic conditional argument patterns:

Affirming the antecedent	If a, then b	
	a	
	_____	VALID
	∴ b	

Denying the antecedent	If a, then b	
	not a	
	_____	INVALID
	∴ not b	

Affirming the consequent	If a, then b	
	b	
	_____	INVALID
	∴ a	

Denying the consequent	If a, then b	
	not b	
	_____	VALID
	∴ not a	

Stating the conditional before portraying the argument is simply a matter of convention. It makes the argument easier to follow. If we portray our argument in standard form with the conditional as the first premise, then the name of the kind of argument is derived from what the second premise does in the argument — affirms the antecedent, denies the consequent, and so forth. To illustrate, we'll use the following claims as substitutions for *a* and *b*:

a = I drop the chalk.
b = The chalk will break.

Making these substitutions, we get

If I drop the chalk, the chalk will break.	If a, then b
I dropped the chalk.	a
∴ The chalk broke.	∴ b

Affirming the antecedent—VALID

There are no conditions under which, if the premises were true, the conclusion could be false. If I drop the chalk and it doesn't break, we are shown that the first premise is false, not that the argument is invalid. To show the argument to be invalid, we would have to find a condition in which both premises could be true and the conclusion could be false. And we can't find that.

If I drop the chalk, the chalk will break.	If a, then b
I didn't drop the chalk.	not a
∴ The chalk must not be broken.	∴ not b

Denying the antecedent—INVALID

This argument is invalid because both premises could be true and the conclusion could be false. Just because I didn't drop the chalk doesn't mean it is not broken. It could have rolled off the table when I set it down; I could have snapped it with my fingers or sat on it. So both premises could be true, yet the conclusion could be false — the chalk *is* broken.

This is the nature of the conditional statement. A conditional statement holds that if (or whenever) *a* occurs, then *b* will follow. If I drop the chalk, then it will break. However, the chalk could break for a number of other reasons. My not dropping the chalk does not tell me anything about the current state of the chalk — whether it is broken or unbroken.

If I drop the chalk, the chalk will break.	If a, then b
The chalk is broken.	b
∴ I dropped the chalk.	∴ a

Affirming the consequent—INVALID

Again, this is invalid. The premises could be true but the conclusion false. I might have sat on the chalk and broke it, or it might have rolled off the table. Dropping the chalk is just one way of guaranteeing (according to *a*) that the chalk will break. However, it can be broken in a number of other ways. Knowing that if I drop it, it will break, and that it is broken does not allow me to infer that I must have dropped it.

If I drop the chalk, the chalk will break.	If a, then b
The chalk isn't broken.	not b
—	—
∴ I didn't drop the chalk.	∴ not a

Denying the consequent—VALID

If we know the conditional is true and the consequent is false, then we must know that the antecedent is also false.

Now that you know these four basic conditional argument patterns, you can handle the vast majority of conditional arguments that you encounter. Simply identify their pattern and you can determine whether they are valid or invalid.

Translating Claims into the Conditional Form

Some conditional claims are not stated in the "If *a*, then *b*" form, but they can be translated into it. For example "a, unless b" can be restated as "If *b*, then not *a*."

Other types of statements that appear not to be conditionals at all can often be rewritten as such. Universal claims such as "All cats are mammals" can be understood as a conditional: "If something is a cat, then it is a mammal." Similarly, "No cats are reptiles" can be understood as either of the following conditionals: "If something is a cat, then it is not a reptile" or "If something is a reptile, then it is not a cat."

The following claims can be turned into conditionals:

All *a*'s are *b*'s	= If something is an *a*, it is a *b* (e.g., All cats are mammals. = If something is a cat, it is a mammal.)
a only if *b*	= If *b*, then *a* (note that "only if" is not the same as "If . . . then . . ."; e.g., You may take this course only if you are a fourth-year student. = If you are a fourth-year student, then you may take this course.)
a on the condition that *b*	= If *b*, then *a* (e.g., It is a mammal on the condition that it is a cat. = If it is a cat, then it is a mammal.)
No *a*'s are *b*'s	= If something is an *a*, then it is not a *b*, and If something is a *b*, then it is not an *a* (e.g., No cats are reptiles. = If it is a cat, then it is not a reptile, and If it is a reptile, then it is not a cat.)
Only *a*'s are *b*'s	= If *b*, then *a* (e.g., Only fourth-year students may take this course. = If you take this course, you are a fourth-year student.)

| *a* unless *b* | = If *b,* then not *a,* and if *a,* then not *b* (e.g., John goes home on weekends unless he has a test on Monday. = If he has a test on Monday, John does not go home on the weekend, and If John goes home on the weekend, then he does not have a test on Monday.) |

QUICK QUIZ 4.5   Translating Claims into Conditionals

Translate the following claims into conditional claims.

1. No students like tuition increases.
2. Only the ignorant take action without considering the consequences.
3. He will graduate unless he fails critical thinking.
4. He will graduate only if he passes critical thinking.

QUICK QUIZ 4.6   Determining Validity: Conditionals

In each of the following, portray the structure of the argument and then determine whether or not the argument is valid or invalid. Show validity or invalidity by labelling the claims with variables and identifying the argument pattern.

1.   If Watson's fingerprints are found on the money, then he committed the robbery.
       His fingerprints are not on the money.

∴   He didn't commit the robbery.

2.   If the moon has an atmosphere, then there would be few signs of impacts with meteors.
       There are signs of a large number of meteor impacts on the moon.

∴   The moon does not have an atmosphere.

3.   If Mars is inhabitable, we would find water on Mars.
       We found water on Mars.

∴   Mars is inhabitable.

4.   If I park here overnight, I will get a ticket.
       I have to park here overnight.

∴   I will get a ticket.

4.7 NECESSARY AND SUFFICIENT CONDITIONS

The conditional patterns defined above are true because of the nature of the conditional claim itself. In a conditional claim, the antecedent is a sufficient condition for the consequent. However, the consequent is only a necessary, not sufficient, condition for the antecedent. A *sufficient condition* is one that, if it occurs, is sufficient to produce the condition that depends on it. For example, a sufficient condition for the presence of oxygen is for there to be a fire. If there is a fire, then there must be oxygen present. The antecedent in a true conditional claim is always a sufficient condition for the consequent. In a course in which one exam makes up 100% of the mark, passing the exam is a sufficient condition for passing the course. If the final were worth only 40%, passing it, by itself, would not be sufficient to pass the course.

A *necessary condition* is a condition that must be present for the resultant condition to occur; however, the necessary condition cannot, by itself, produce the result. Oxygen is a necessary condition for fire. However, oxygen is not sufficient to produce fire. There are a number of conditions that must be met if fire is to occur: There must be oxygen, some burnable material, and a kindling (ignition) temperature raised to the flash point. A necessary condition for passing some courses is that the student pass the final exam. However, passing the final may not be sufficient. The student may have a failing grade in the course-work yet pass the final exam by one point and fail the course.

A necessary condition does not need to be a sufficient condition, although in some situations it can be; and a condition may be a sufficient condition without being a necessary condition. My dropping the chalk is sufficient to break it. However, my dropping the chalk is not necessary for breaking it, nor does the fact that the chalk is broken mean that I dropped it. A sufficient condition may be one of several ways of producing the result, so the presence of the result need not indicate that a particular sufficient condition occurred.

We do not have to use conditionals to identify necessary and sufficient conditions. "Fire needs air." "To get a B on this essay, you will have to do a critical review of five papers."

We sometimes talk of sets of necessary conditions, sets of sufficient conditions, or sets of necessary and sufficient conditions. A set of conditions is two or more of the relevant conditions that, together, would be either necessary or sufficient.

QUICK QUIZ 4.7   Identifying Necessary and Sufficient Conditions

In the following, identify the necessary and sufficient conditions.
1. If something is a whale, it is a mammal.
2. All critical-thinking instructors have Ph.D.s.
3. No reptiles live in arctic climates.
4. Some logicians are mad.

4.8 THE DISJUNCTIVE PATTERN *EITHER/OR*

Another common type of pattern is the either/or pattern. The either/or pattern is based on an either/or claim, called a **disjunction.**

> Either I study for the exam or I will fail it.

The components of the disjunction — in this case, "I study for the exam" and "I will fail it" — are called **the disjuncts.** Logically, it does not matter which disjunct comes first and which second. A disjunction normally has two disjuncts. However, it may have three or more (although grammatically *either* takes only two disjuncts, logically, it may take two or more):

> I will take either psychology, fine arts, or economics next semester.

The disjunctive claim becomes the basis for a disjunctive argument in the same way that the conditional does. As with the conditional form, we can either affirm or deny a disjunct to construct an argument. There is one valid and one invalid disjunctive argument form. Since disjuncts are logically symmetrical, it doesn't matter which disjunct appears after the "either" and which after the "or" (although it may make a difference in terms of language flow). Consequently, it doesn't matter which of the disjuncts we deny or affirm.

Formulating an argument for the above claim, we might get the following:

Either I study for the exam or I will fail it.	Either a or b
I didn't study.	not a
∴ I will fail the exam.	∴ b

Denying a disjunct—VALID

For the claim "Either *a* or *b*" to be true, at least one of the two disjuncts must be true, although it is possible that under certain conditions both could be true (I may study for the exam and still fail it). Therefore, the minimal condition for a disjunction being true is that one of the claims is true. Hence, I can draw a valid inference that if I know that the disjunction is true and that one of the claims that make it up is false, then the remaining claim in the disjunction must be true.

Either I study for the exam or I will fail it.	Either a or b
I failed the test.	a
∴ I didn't study for the test.	∴ not b

Affirming a disjunct—INVALID

Since it is possible that both claims in a disjunction can be true, knowing that one is true tells me nothing about the other. I might have studied for the exam and still failed. The premises would be true, but the conclusion could be false. And that makes the argument invalid.

The disjunctive forms are based on the fact that in most disjunctive statements, the statement can be true if either disjunct is true or if both are. Thus, knowing one is true does not guarantee that the other is false. However, knowing one is false guarantees that the other is true. And that is the only way to be guaranteed a true conclusion from a disjunctive claim. As mentioned above, in the claim "Either I study for the exam or I will fail it," it is possible that I both study and fail the exam. When the either/or includes the possibility that both are true — either *a* or *b*, or both — it is called an **inclusive disjunction** claim.

One kind of disjunctive claim, however, is more restrictive: "Either I study or I don't study." In this kind of disjunctive claim, knowing the truth of one *does* guarantee the falsity of the other. This is called an **exclusive disjunction** claim and occurs with disjuncts whose truth conditions are linked so that asserting one automatically denies the other. They have the form "Either *a* or not *a*."

The disjunctive patterns built on the inclusive disjunction form apply to both forms.

QUICK QUIZ 4.8 Assessing Disjunctive Arguments

In the following, portray the structure of the argument and identify whether the argument is valid or invalid.

1. Either Harris did it or his wife is lying. His wife is not lying. So he must have done it.
2. Either the fuse is faulty or the TV's picture tube has gone. The fuse is faulty. So the picture tube is OK.
3. Either we improve our response time in getting to fires or more people are going to die needlessly. I guess more people are going to die needlessly because we can't improve our response time.

4.9 COMPLEX ARGUMENT PATTERNS

The various structures we have identified thus far can be combined to form more complex argument patterns. For example, we can have an argument that combines a conditional and a disjunction:

If a, then b or c

a

_____

∴ b or c

In this simple argument, the antecedent is affirmed, the consequent is a disjunction, and the argument is valid. It says that if a given antecedent is true, then one of two outcomes is possible. We don't know which.

If a or b, then c

a

_____

∴ c

This structure says that if one of two possible antecedent conditions (*a* or *b*) is true, then a given consequent (*c*) is true. In this case, the antecedent is a disjunction. We know that a disjunction is true if one of the disjuncts is true. Since we know that *a* is true and that a disjunctive claim is true as long as one of the disjuncts is true, then we know that the claim "*a* or *b*" is true and we can infer *c*. Try substituting "Fluffy is a cat" for *a*, "Fluffy is a dog" for *b*, and "Fluffy is a mammal" for *c*.

Contrast this with the following:

> If a and b, then c
>
> a
>
> ————————
>
> ∴ c

This is not a valid argument. The claim "*a* and *c*" is a **conjunction,** and the components *a* and *c* are called **conjuncts.** For a conjunction to be true, both conjuncts must be true. In the argument as stated, we have affirmed only *a*. Until we know that *b* is true, we cannot conclude that *c* is true.

We can sometimes construct complex arguments using the various simple forms.

> If a, then b or c
>
> a   Affirms the antecedent—VALID
>
> ————————
>
> ∴ b or c
>
> not b   Denies the disjunct—VALID
>
> ————————
>
> ∴ c

The first argument here is a conditional argument; the second is a disjunctive one. In this particular example, both arguments are valid. It is possible, however, for one of the inferences to be valid and the other invalid:

> If a, then b or c
>
> a   Affirms the antecedent—VALID
>
> ————————
>
> ∴ b or c
>
> b   Affirms the disjunct—INVALID
>
> ————————
>
> ∴ not c

One relatively common conditional pattern is the conditional chain argument:

If a, then b

If b, then c

_____

∴   If a, then c   Valid conditional chain

This form of the conditional chain argument is valid. We know that if the two premises are true, then the conditional in the conclusion is also true. The following is an invalid conditional argument pattern:

QUICK QUIZ 4.9   Complex Argument Patterns

Consider the following patterns. Are they valid or invalid? Explain.

1.   If *a* then *b* or *c*
        not *b*

   _____

   ∴   not *a*

2.   Either *a* or *b*
        not *b*

   _____

   ∴   *a*
        If *a*, then *c* or *d*

   _____

   ∴   *c*

3.   If *a* or *b* or *c*, then *d* or *e*
        a
        not *d*

   _____

   ∴   *e*

4.   If *a* and *b*, then *c* or *d*
        a
        b
        not *c*

   _____

   ∴   *d*

5.   If *a*, then *c* and *d*
        a
        not *d*

   _____

   ∴   *c*

If a, then b

If a, then c

∴   If b, then c   Invalid conditional chain

There are situations in which accepting the premises would result in a false conclusion. Substituting "Something is a cat" for a, "Something is a mammal" for b, and "Something that purrs" for c presents true premises and the false conclusion "If something is a mammal, it purrs." There are several other invalid argument chain patterns. The strategy for showing invalidity of the pattern is outlined in Section 4.11.

So far, we've identified only some valid and invalid argument forms. Arguments without a clear logical form or with a different logical form need to be assessed using the method of counterexample or the topics model, below.

4.10 THE TOPICS MODEL

An alternate model that works for determining validity as well as helping in constructing arguments, analyzing issues, and writing essays is the **topics model.** The topics model works by identifying the key terms (topics) in the conclusion and comparing those with the topics in the premises.

A claim connects two or more topics. A **topic** is a subject for discussion — a subject about which we can say something. In this context, a topic is usually the grammatical subject, verb phrase, or object of a sentence. Occasionally, it may be a qualifier — an adjective or adverb. (We will deal here with claims that have only two topics.)

Critical Thinking should be a required course.

"Critical Thinking" is one topic; "should be a required course" is another topic. We can say something about "Critical Thinking," and we can say something about "things that should be required courses." The verb "should be," in this case, is not a topic by itself. It is not something we can say something about; rather, it simply connects two topics.

We can identify the topics in a claim by drawing a single line under the first and a double line under the second (we can also number them "1" and "2"), as follows:

1   2
Critical Thinking <u>should be a required course</u>.

Relevance and sufficiency are established by connecting the topics in the premises with the topics in the conclusion. If none of the topics in the conclusion appear in the premises, then the premises are irrelevant to the conclusion. That is the case with the Beethoven and the moon-is-made-of-green-cheese argument in Section 4.3.

If only some of the topics in the conclusion are mentioned in the premises, then the premises, though likely relevant, are insufficient to establish the conclusion. Validity of an argument is established by properly linking the various topics in the premises with the topics in the conclusion. If the topics mentioned in the premises are not connected appropriately to those in the conclusion, validity cannot be established.

To use the topics model to determine validity, start by underlining and numbering the topics in the conclusion. Focus on the subject of the sentence as one possible topic, and the verbs and objects as others. Remember that important qualifiers may be additional topics. Next, identify the topics that recur in the premises and give them the same underline pattern and number. New topics are assigned a different number and underline. This has been done in the following argument:

<blockquote>
3   2
<u>Murder</u> is <u>immoral</u>.

---

1   2
∴ <u>Abortion</u> is <u>immoral</u>.
</blockquote>

In this argument, there are three topics:

- murder (occurs only in premise)
- abortion (occurs only in conclusion)
- immoral (occurs in both premise and conclusion)

The conclusion has two topics: "abortion" and "is immoral." "Murder" is a new topic introduced in the premise. It gets a different underline and a new number.

However, the topic "abortion" is not mentioned in the premise. Unless we mention "abortion" and connect it to the rest of the topics in the premise(s), we cannot be sure that the conclusion follows from the premise(s). For the conclusion to be established, we need premises that say something about all of the topics that are present in the conclusion. This provides us with a basic rule for validity: **For an argument to be valid, all of the topics mentioned in the conclusion must be mentioned in the premises.** The above argument, as stated, fails that condition.

Consider the argument with an additional premise:

<blockquote>
1   4
<u>Abortion</u> is the <u>taking of a human life</u>.
</blockquote>

Adding this premise would satisfy the condition. However, the argument would still not be valid. Neither "abortion" nor the fourth topic, "the taking of a human life," has been connected to the other two topics —"murder" or "is immoral."

This demonstrates a second rule for determining validity: **For an argument to be valid, all of the topics mentioned in the conclusion must be connected to the topics in the premises, and those must be connected to one another.** Since "abortion" is already connected with "is immoral" in the conclusion, the only other term it can be connected with in the original argument is "murder". Instead of adding the premise above and introducing a new topic, we can add the following premise to the existing argument to make it valid:

<blockquote>
1   3
<u>Abortion</u> is <u>murder</u>.
</blockquote>

"Abortion" is connected to "murder"; "murder" is connected to "is immoral." "Abortion" can now logically be connected to "is immoral."

Another way of using the topics model to make an argument valid is to recognize that we can ask two linked questions of any claim, each dealing with one of the topics in the conclusion. The verb–object topic in a conclusion claim will usually indicate a general set of conditions that must be met for the claim to be true; the subject topic will indicate something that fits those conditions, meaning it is narrower than the verb — object topic. Likewise, the premise involving the verb–object topic will usually be more general than the premise involving the subject topic. Applying this, we get the following two questions (where *x* is the verb — object topic and *y* is the subject topic):

1. Under what conditions does/is something *x?*

2. Does *y* meet those conditions?

In turn, applying this to the abortion argument, we get

1. Under what conditions is something immoral?

This question is general. It says nothing specific about abortion or any other moral action. However, once answered, it will give us a condition or set of conditions under which any action is immoral.

The second question is asked with the first one in mind. What we want to do is connect the topic in the second question with the answers generated by the first question. The following question does this:

2. How does abortion meet the conditions for something being immoral?

The two questions are linked. An answer to one provides information about answering the second. Applying these to the argument in question, we get the following:

1. Under what conditions is something immoral?
   Something is immoral if it involves murder. = Murder is immoral.

2. Does abortion meet those conditions?
   Abortion does meet those conditions: It is a form of murder. = Abortion is murder.

The argument must answer both questions in order to establish relevance and sufficiency. If it answers only one of the questions, the argument is incomplete — the premises, as stated, are relevant but not sufficient.

QUICK QUIZ 4.10   Identifying Topics

Identify the topics in the following claims and arguments.

1. Adultery is immoral.
2. Anything that is immoral should be illegal. Adultery is immoral. So it should be illegal.
3. Whatever is gained easily is not valued. University degrees are becoming too easy to achieve. As a result, they will not be valued.
4. You ought to study economics. Of all the options, it is the only one with real-world application.
5. Personal testimony based on experience, though vivid, is often not reliable. Our perceptions and memory are often flawed and limited in perspective.

For the exercises that consist simply of a claim in Quick Quiz 4.10, identify the two questions that would have to be addressed if that claim were the conclusion of an argument. For the exercises that contain arguments, identify the two questions that need to be asked of the conclusion.

4.11 THE COUNTEREXAMPLE METHOD FOR SHOWING INVALIDITY

The method of **counterexample** is a means of showing that an argument pattern is invalid; however, it will not show us that an argument pattern *is* valid. If you encounter an argument that you believe is invalid, you can use this method to confirm its invalidity.

Since a valid argument is one in which the premises, if true, must lead to a true conclusion, if we can show that the pattern of an argument can have true premises and a false conclusion, we have shown that the argument pattern cannot be a valid pattern.

Consider the following argument:

> All logicians have Ph.D.s.
>
> All college teachers have Ph.D.s.
>
> ───────────────────────
>
> ∴   All logicians are college teachers.

In identifying the argument pattern, we look for the logical connectives, listed in Section 4.5. We then substitute a letter, or variable, for each same statement consistently throughout. Finally, we try to find a substitution for the letters that will give us true premises and a false conclusion. If we can find such a substitution, we know that the argument form is invalid. Not being able to find a substitution does not prove that the argument is valid, however. It may simply be a testament to our limited imagination in finding a substitution.

In the above argument, we can make the following substitutions:

> *a* for "logicians"
>
> *b* for "have Ph.D.s"
>
> *c* for "college teachers"

This gives us the following argument structure:

> All a's are b's
>
> All c's are b's
>
> ───────────────
>
> ∴   All a's are c's

If I can now find substitutions for *a*, *b*, and *c* that will make the premises true and the conclusion false, I will have found a counterexample for this argument form. In other words, I will have shown that with this argument form, it is possible to have true premises and a false conclusion, which would, in turn, confirm that this form is not valid. Remember that for a pattern to be valid, it must *always* lead from true premises to true conclusions.

One substitution for the above would be

a = cats

b = mammals

c = dogs

Simple biological categories like these tend to work well since the connections become quite obvious, and it becomes clear when the premises are true and the conclusion false. The above substitutions give us the following invalid argument:

All cats (a's) are mammals (b's). True

All dogs (c's) are mammals (b's). True

———————————————————

∴ All cats (a's) are dogs (c's). False

It's now clear that this is an invalid argument form. Any argument having this form will be invalid even if the premises and conclusion happen to be true.

QUICK QUIZ 4.12   Using Argument Counterexamples to Show Invalidity

For each of the following arguments, provide a counterexample.

1. All logicians are mad. Saindon is not a logician. Saindon is not mad.
2. Some logicians are mad. Saindon is a logician. So Saindon must be mad.
3. Anyone who works hard will pass the course. I haven't worked very hard. It looks as though I won't pass.
4. If you don't have perfect attendance, then you won't be entitled to a bonus at the end of the year. I had perfect attendance. So I will get the bonus.
5. Treating animals kindly is a sign that individuals will treat other people kindly. Michael doesn't treat his dog very well. He must not treat his wife very well.

4.12 ASSUMED (OR MISSING) PREMISES

In many deductive arguments, the arguer does not present all of the premises needed to prove validity. Such arguments have an assumed, or missing, premise. An **assumed premise** or **missing premise** is a claim that is required by the argument to establish relevance or sufficiency or both (validity) between the premises and the conclusion.

The purpose of supplying a missing premise is to identify all of the assumptions necessary to make an argument valid. It can help us analyze and critique the argument by showing what the argument is committed to.

When supplying a missing premise, we try to meet two conditions: (1) Where possible, we supply a missing premise that makes an argument valid rather than invalid, and (2) Given a choice between supplying a true or a false missing premise, we supply a true premise. These are necessary to satisfy the truth-seeking principle. Meeting both conditions may not always be possible. The arguer may have simply given an invalid argument, or his argument may assume a false claim. In such cases, we should indicate that the argument cannot be reconstructed cogently and explain why.

To identify and supply missing premises, we can use either argument patterns or the topics model.

Using Argument Patterns to Supply Missing Premises

Using valid argument patterns to supply missing premises is relatively straightforward. Identify the existing pattern of the argument: Start with the conclusion; then examine the premises. If there is a conditional, compare the existing parts of the argument with the valid argument forms. Supply what is necessary to make the argument valid. If there is no conditional, then supply the conditional necessary to make the argument valid.

Ali told Ellen he inflated his expense report.

_____

∴   Ali is dishonest.

This argument has two claims. The pattern is

a

_____

∴   b

Comparing this structure to the valid argument forms, we could either affirm the antecedent or deny the consequent to make this valid. If we try to affirm the antecedent, we need to supply "If *a*, then *b*" (If Ali told Ellen he falsified his expense report, then he is dishonest). If we try to deny the antecedent, we need to supply "If not *a*, then not *b* (If Ali did not tell Ellen he inflated his expense report, then he is not dishonest). We have to insert the negatives into the statement because the claim in the argument is a positive. To act as a denying claim, it would have to be denying a negative claim.

In this situation, the simplest of these two methods is affirming the antecedent:

If a, then b

a

_____

∴   b

Or, in English,

A

[If Ali inflated his expense report, then he is dishonest.]

Ali told Ellen he inflated his expense report. (Treat as equivalent to "Ali inflated his expense report.")

—————————————————————————

∴   Ali is dishonest.

To identify supplied missing premises in an argument diagram, we put square brackets around them and label them with capital letters instead of numbers.

Depending on the context of the argument, we may sometimes want to make the conditional a general claim rather than a specific one: "If someone inflates his expense report, then he is dishonest." It is not just Ali's inflating his expense report that is dishonest. Anyone who inflates his or her expense report is dishonest. Making the claim broad gives us the general conditions, not just conditions as they apply to Ali.

Which valid pattern to use — affirming the antecedent, denying the consequent, or the valid disjunctive form — will depend on what makes the most sense and is most enlightening in a given situation. Any is acceptable. If an argument is invalid, however, no matter which you use, it may not be possible to make it valid.

If the breeding grounds had been contaminated by lead, the birds would have stopped nesting.

—————————————————————————

∴   The breeding grounds must have been contaminated by lead.

The only possible missing premise here —"The birds have stopped nesting"— would give us an invalid argument, as it affirms the consequent.

QUICK QUIZ 4.13   Using Valid Patterns to Supply Missing Premises

Identify the structure of the argument. Using the valid argument forms, supply the missing premises for the following arguments. If you cannot make the argument valid, explain why.

1. We want to reduce speeding, so we should use red-light cameras.
2. If he is a good lawyer, he reads the fine print in contracts. So he is not a good lawyer.
3. If something is intellectually challenging, it is not designed for a mass audience. So university is not designed for a mass audience.
4. If he is a good lawyer, he reads the fine print in contracts. So he doesn't read the fine print in contracts.

Using the Topics Model to Supply Missing Premises

The topics model can also be used to supply missing premises. Identify, number, and underline the topics in the conclusion and then the stated ones in the premises. Supply a claim that will connect the unconnected topics. Using the questions we used to assess validity can help.

Using the argument below, we will walk through these steps.

1. Identify, number, and underline the topics in the conclusion.

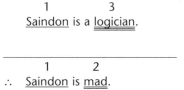

Saindon is a logician.

_____
        1   2
∴   <u>Saindon</u> is <u>mad</u>.

2. Identify, underline, and number the stated topics in the premises.

     1   3
<u>Saindon</u> is a <u>logician</u>.

_____
        1   2
∴   <u>Saindon</u> is <u>mad</u>.

3. List the topics in the argument.

- Saindon

- mad

- logician

"Saindon" is used twice; the other two terms, once. "Saindon" is connected to each of the other two terms. The other two terms, however, are not connected to one another. These need to be connected.

4. Using the topics model, work from the conclusion and identify the questions that need to be answered for the argument to be valid.

1. Under what conditions is someone mad?

2. Does Saindon fit those conditions?

5. Which, if any, question is answered by the stated premise? If neither is answered by the stated premise, then the premises are likely irrelevant to the conclusion. In our example, the stated premise identifies a condition that Saindon meets — he is a logician (Question 2). We can infer that being a logician is a condition for being mad, which will give us the answer to Question 1: Anyone who is a logician is mad.

Another way of using this is to notice that "Saindon" appears in both the premise and the conclusion. "Is mad" and "is a logician" each occur only once in the argument, so these are the two terms that need to be connected in the premises for the argument to be valid. The missing premise is

[All logicians are mad.]

In supplying a missing premise, we are trying to supply only what is minimally necessary, given the materials in the existing argument to make the argument valid. For example, although we could supply any of the following as possible missing premises, none of them will enable us to connect the terms in the argument.

[Saindon has been diagnosed with a mental disorder.]

[Logicians are odd people.]

[Logicians spend their lives interacting with arguments rather than people.]

None of these would make the argument valid. Each introduces a new term that would then have to be connected to the terms in the conclusion.

QUICK QUIZ 4.14   Using the Topics Model to Supply Missing Premises

Portray the structure of the following arguments and use the topics model to supply the missing premises for each argument. Identify the two questions for each conclusion and show how the stated premise and missing premise answer those questions.

1. Fred shouldn't be allowed to drive. He drives dangerously.
2. Creationism should not be taught in biology classrooms because it is not science.
3. Stem cell research can help in the search for a cure for Alzheimer's. Therefore, we should support stem cell research.

4.13 ASSESSING COGENCY

A cogent argument is a valid argument that has true premises. Assessing an argument for cogency involves first assessing it for validity and then determining whether the premises are acceptable. We start with validity because we want to make sure that the premises actually support the conclusion. It also enables us to determine what the argument is committed to. We can use any of the techniques in this module to determine if the argument is valid or invalid. If an argument is invalid, then we can stop the assessment: The author has not established the conclusion.

To assess the truth of the claims, examine each claim in the premises. Is each sufficiently clear and precise in context that you know what would count as evidence for and against it? Is it a claim that is either widely known or acceptable to everyone who would likely read the argument, or, if it is contentious, has it been supported by independent lines of argument? If a claim is false, doubtful, or contentious, develop your reasons to show why it is and how that affects the argument.

Don't simply accept the premises because you agree with the conclusion. Test the truth of the premises. Under what conditions could they be false? One of the most common errors in reasoning is **confirmation bias.** This occurs when we look for evidence to support our claims rather than for the possible evidence that might disconfirm or challenge our claims. In most cases, we can find some evidence that will support our position, especially if we have to interpret the evidence. Since we can usually find some evidence that could be interpreted to support our prior positions, finding evidence that confirms those positions does not necessarily prove them to be true. Rather, what we need to do is subject our positions to a more rigorous test by looking for the evidence that might disconfirm our basic position.

Consider the following:

> Withholding information is the same as lying. So withholding information is wrong.

The argument can be analyzed as follows:

1. Withholding information is the same as lying.
A. [Lying is wrong.]

_____

∴ 2. Withholding information is wrong.

The argument is valid. We can show this using the topics model.

Under what conditions is something wrong?

Something is wrong if it involves lying. = Lying is wrong.

Does withholding information fit those conditions?

Withholding information is the same as lying. (Stated)

Alternatively, we could translate the missing premise into a conditional: If something involves lying, it is wrong. The argument then becomes a standard affirming the antecedent.

The argument is not cogent. Although I can think of some exceptional circumstances in which the stated premise could be interpreted as true, the stated premise is false. Withholding information is not always the same as lying. I withhold information about my personal life from my students. I do not lie to them. That is simply something they have no right to know. If I withheld information from my students about, for example, the specific contents of the final exam, I would also not be lying. Lying might be intentionally telling students a false date for the exam. Therefore, lying and withholding information are not the same. Here we have used a claim counterexample to show that the premise as formulated is false. The argument is not cogent.

It is not sufficient to assert that a claim is false. We also need to provide reasons why it is false. To do this, we need to construct an argument.

Consider the following passage:

> We are justified in torturing and even killing terrorists without trial or due process. Terrorists have no concern for the rights of the innocent citizens they slaughter. Therefore, we should not grant them any rights once we have caught them.

We can analyze this argument as follows:

           If   a   then b

A.   [If (people have no concern for the rights of others), then (they should not be given any rights themselves).]

1.   Terrorists have no concern for the rights of the innocent citizens they slaughter.   a

---

∴ 2.   We should not grant them any rights once we have caught them. *(I treat this as the same as "we are justified in torturing and even killing terrorists without trial or due process," because this simply explains "not grant them any rights.")*   b

A is a missing premise, supplied to make the argument valid. With this claim, the argument is valid: It affirms the antecedent.

The argument, however, is not cogent. Premise 1 may be false, but I have no evidence to indicate that it is. However, the missing premise, A, is false. If we were to accept its claim, then we are saying that we would be justified in denying rights to anyone accused of a crime. One could argue that anyone who commits a crime has shown that he or she has no concern for the rights of those whose rights were violated by the crime itself. Further, if this is applied to everyone accused of a crime, then those who are accused would lose their rights simply on the grounds of having been accused, not on the grounds of having been convicted. Since the arguer is referring to due process and a trial as part of the rights being denied, this would mean that we could simply imprison or execute people on the grounds of their having been accused of a crime, not on the grounds of their having been convicted. This would result in many innocent people being falsely imprisoned and/or convicted. And this would not be just. The missing premise is unacceptable.

If a passage contains several independent lines of argument supporting the conclusion, then we need to examine each line of argument. As long as there is one cogent argument, the arguer has made a case for his or her conclusion.

QUICK QUIZ 4.15   Assessing Cogency

Assess the following arguments for cogency using the skills developed thus far. Give reasons for your assessments of validity and of cogency.

1. Teachers should not be allowed to strike because their going on strike disrupts students' learning.
2. We should censor anything that is crude and offensive. And much of rock music is certainly crude and offensive. So we should censor it.
3. The novel *The Adventures of Huckleberry Finn* uses language that many consider racist. Therefore, the novel is racist and promotes racism.

MODULE SUMMARY

This module identifies the criteria for assessing the support that premises give to conclusions and for determining the overall acceptability (cogency) of an argument. There are two basic types of arguments, inductive and deductive, classified according to the degree of support the premises give the conclusion. Support is based on the relevance of premises to the conclusion and the sufficiency of the premises in establishing the conclusion. Deductive arguments seek to provide indisputable support, whereas inductive arguments provide probable support for the conclusion. We can assess the support (relevance and sufficiency) separate from the acceptability of the premises. The support in deductive arguments is assessed in terms of validity or invalidity. We can determine validity and invalidity through identifying argument forms or patterns and through the topics model. We can show invalidity through the method of argument counterexample. Once we have assessed a deductive argument for validity, we can assess it for cogency by determining whether the premises are in fact true. A cogent argument is valid and has true premises.

KEY TERMS

affirm the antecedent
affirm a claim
affirm the consequent
affirm the disjunct
antecedent
assumed premise
cogent
conditional argument
conditional claim
conditional statement
confirmation bias
conjuncts
conjunction
consequent

counterexample
deductive arguments
deny the antecedent
deny a claims
deny the consequent
deny the disjunct
disjuncts
disjunction
exclusive disjunction
inclusive disjunction
inductive argument
invalid
logical form
logical structure

logical terms
missing premise
necessary condition
relevant
sound
sufficient condition
topic
topics model
valid
validity
variables

ASSESSING INDUCTIVE ARGUMENTS

5.1 LEARNING OBJECTIVES

After completing this module, you should be able to

1. identify the various kinds of inductive arguments;
2. identify the key criteria for assessing inductive arguments; and
3. use those criteria to assess inductive arguments.

5.2 INTRODUCTION

Inductive arguments were introduced and explained in Section 4.3. Unlike with deductive arguments, in which the connection between the premises and the conclusions can be assessed solely in terms of logical form, assessing inductive arguments requires examining the content of the argument in order to assess its strength. Inductive arguments do not have a set of logical terms and logical forms by which relevance and sufficiency can be assessed. And since there are different kinds of inductive arguments, each has its own criteria for assessing relevance and sufficiency.

In inductive arguments, the premises give support to the conclusion but do not guarantee the conclusion. Instead of validity and invalidity, we say that the premises of an inductive argument weakly, strongly, or very strongly support the conclusion, depending on how well the sufficiency condition is met. If the premises of an inductive argument strongly support the conclusion and are true, we say that the argument is *sound.*

Some of the most common types of inductive arguments include inference to the best explanation, inductive generalization, causal argument, appeal to authority, and statistical argument. All but statistical arguments, which require more in-depth study and explanation than we can provide in this text, will be dealt with in this module.

5.3 INFERENCE TO THE BEST EXPLANATION

In an *inference to the best explanation,* the conclusion is offered as an explanation for the facts cited in the premises. Consider the following:

1. Fred was desperate to get his bookie off his back.

2. Fred bought a gun the day before the bank robbery.

3. He was seen getting into a white 1998 Blazer two miles away from the robbery fifteen minutes before the robbery.

4. A 1998 white Blazer was the getaway car.

5. Although the robbers were masked, Fred's height and weight fit the description of one of the bank robbers.

6. Fred can't account for where he was at the time of the robbery.

7. Fred paid off his bookie debt the day after the robbery.

∴ 8. Fred robbed the bank.

The conclusion is not a deductive certainty. However, the probability that Fred is one of the bank robbers is extremely high. If we just had the first two and last two claims, we would have reasonable doubt about Fred's guilt. As additional pieces of evidence tie Fred to the time and location of the robbery, the probability that Fred was involved increases. Nonetheless, we could imagine a situation in which all of the premises are true and the conclusion false — Fred did not rob the bank. On the other hand, casting doubt on the truth of the claims or providing **alternate explanations** for the facts in the premises decreases the probability of the conclusion.

Key criteria we use for assessing such arguments include:

- the truth of the claims;
- the plausibility of the explanation;
- the simplicity of the explanation;
- the completeness of the explanation; and
- whether the explanation better explains or rules out likely alternatives.

One way of examining an inference to the best explanation is by considering one or more alternate possible explanations and applying these criteria to them. Where an alternate is not given, we need to come up with one. To illustrate, we'll consider the following example:

A friend reports that she saw a UFO. I ask why she believes that it was a UFO. Her response is that it was an unusual light in the sky, and she doesn't know what it was. Her argument could be stated as follows:

Shantal saw an unusual light in the sky.

She couldn't explain it.

∴ It was a UFO.

Alternate explanations for the conclusion include that Shantal saw a satellite, Venus, a meteor, or a plane. Each of these is plausible. The hypothesis that she saw a UFO is less plausible. A claim is **plausible** if, given a background set of information, the claim could be true, is supported by independent evidence, and is likely or worth considering. The UFO hypothesis above is minimally plausible in the sense that there have been numerous reports of UFOs. However, there is little or no solid evidence for their existence and good evidence against them. At best, the existence of UFOs is highly controversial. By contrast, each of the other alternatives has independent evidence and each has been mistaken many times for a UFO. Those alternates are more plausible than the UFO hypothesis. An implausible alternative might be that my friend was witnessing angels crossing the multidimension barrier from the seventh dimension. Nothing in our background knowledge supports such a claim.

The seventh-dimension claim also fails the criterion that the conclusion adequately explain the facts. It is not clear how angels would produce what was observed.

The alternate explanations are simpler in the sense that they involve postulating fewer new entities, and the explanation involves fewer unsupported assumptions. This is called **Occam's Razor,** a principle of simplicity that says that when faced with alternative explanations, we should prefer the simplest — the one that has the fewest principles or postulates the fewest entities or unsupported assumptions as long as there are no differences in the observed consequences. In other words, if there are two explanations for the same phenomenon and the repercussions of accepting either are the same, we should choose the simplest unless the more complex one explains more. In the UFO example, satellites, landing jets, Venus, and meteorite sightings are all simpler explanations than the UFO alternative. The UFO alternative posits an unknown entity for which there is no independent evidence, whereas there is independent evidence for each of the others.

An explanation is most **complete** if it links together all or more of the relevant considerations than the alternatives. An alternate explanation for Fred that did not address premises 3, 6, or 7 would be less complete and, hence, a less satisfactory explanation.

In assessing an inference-to-the-best-explanation argument, consider what additional information would strengthen or weaken the argument. When possible, check that information out. For example, if you are considering the Venus alternative to the UFO hypothesis, you might investigate where Venus was at the time of the sighting. Discovering that Venus was not visible at that time would rule out that alternative. Finding out that when Fred entered the Chevy Blazer, he was wearing the same clothes that the bank robber was reportedly wearing would strengthen the case against him. Part of assessing an inference to the best explanation is identifying what additional evidence would count for or against the proposed explanation.

QUICK QUIZ 5.1   Assessing Inference-to-the-Best-Explanation Arguments

Formulate the following arguments. Assess each argument in terms of strength — very strong, strong, weak — and explain why you assess it that way. Use the criteria for assessing inference-to-the-best-explanation arguments.

1. Raj and Janet are friends. They have studied together all year. They sat next to each other in the exam. Not only did they both get the same letter grade on the exam but both got the same questions right and most of the same questions wrong. They must have cheated on the exam.
2. The Loch Ness monster has to exist. Hundreds of people have seen the creature over the centuries. Furthermore, there are photographs and even videotapes of the monster.
3. Gasoline prices go up at the beginning of a long weekend and down just after. And this happens all over the country. This shows that the major oil companies are controlling gas prices.
4. The developer withdrew $25,000 from his business account. He then immediately called a local city alderman and met him fifteen minutes later in an underground parking garage. Over the next week, $23,000 was deposited to the alderman's account in five deposits. All deposits were in $100 bills. The alderman claims that the money was a gift from his father-in-law. However, there is no evidence of withdrawals from the father-in-law's account and no independent evidence for the source of the money. The alderman spoke strongly for a proposal favouring the developer over the next few months and convinced many of his colleagues to support the developer's proposal. I contend that the alderman took a bribe from the developer.

Answers for all Quick Quizzes in this text are provided in the Student Manual. After doing the Quick Quizzes, consult the Student Manual to check your understanding of the material.

5.4 GENERAL CLAIMS AND GENERALIZATIONS

We can distinguish between a summary, a generalization, and a general claim. A **summary** is simply the bringing together of a set of observations in a general claim. "I observed ten instances of people driving badly. Eight of these people were driving SUVs. Summary: Eighty percent of those observed driving badly were driving SUVs." Rather than enumerating each of the cases, they are summarized in a simple statement or set of statements. We can show a summary is false by showing that the observations on which it is based are false or that the summary is inaccurate.

A **generalization** is the result of a process of reasoning from a limited number of cases. "I observe that three people driving badly were driving SUVs. I conclude that all SUV drivers are bad drivers." The conclusion generalizes from a smaller set of instances. We cannot directly observe a generalization, although we can observe the instances on which it is based and assess the inference from those instances to the generalization. We can show a generalization is false by showing that the observations on which it is based are false or the inference is erroneous.

A **general claim** is simply that — a claim about a group or class with no indication of the process of reasoning behind it: "All SUV drivers are bad drivers." No observations on which the general claim is based are identified. General claims can be addressed either by asking for the evidence on which they are based, in which case we can treat them as generalizations, or by counterexamples — "My cousin drives an SUV and is a good driver." A counterexample for a general claim involves giving a specific example that shows the generalization to be false.

Assessing Generalizations

Generalizations are the result of a process of inference from a limited number of cases. The person making the inference makes a limited number of observations and draws a conclusion about the whole set of things to which the observations are assumed to apply. I note that the chalkboards in five classrooms on campus are green. I draw the general conclusion that all chalkboards on campus are green.

To determine if this is a good generalization, I need to know not just about the accuracy of the observations but also about the population, the sample, the representativeness of the sample, the variability and frequency of the items in the sample, and any possible bias.

The group of things that we are drawing the conclusion about is called the **population.** The population I am interested in is that of all chalkboards on campus.

The set of things I actually observe to draw the generalization is called the **sample.** My sample is the chalkboards in the five classrooms I have visited.

For an inference to a generalization to be a good inference, not only must the original observations be accurate, but the sample must be **representative** of the population. To ensure that the sample is representative, we need to assess whether the sample we have selected adequately represents the variability in the population and the frequency of that variability. **Variability** refers to the range of difference or variation within the population in respect to relevant characteristics. **Frequency** refers to how often those characteristics occur within a population. If I am trying to judge the proportion of coloured balls in a jar, variability would depend on whether there are two colours or ten. Frequency would refer to the relative proportion of the colours to one another: one red to one white (1:1), two red to one white (2:1), or ten red to one white (10:1), in the case of two colours; one red to two black to two blue to five green to ten white (1:2:2:5:10), in the case of five colours. Chalkboards can be black or green — that is their variability. The proportion of green to black on this campus would be the frequency. At the start of my study, I may know neither of these.

In examining the sample, I need to determine if there is anything about the sample that might be biased. A **biased** sample is one that skews its representativeness in some way so that not all of the variability and frequency among the items have an equal chance of being in the sample. If all of my observations of chalkboards were made in classrooms in one building, that might indicate a limitation (bias) to my sample. I might more reliably generalize about the chalkboards in that building than about all chalkboards on campus. Based on other information, I may or may not be able to extend my generalization. For example, if I knew that all of the classrooms on campus were built at the same time by the same contractor, I might be able to more reliably generalize about all classrooms on campus. The variability in the population would be decreased. However, if I realize that the various buildings on campus were built over a thirty- or fifty- or one-hundred-year time span by various contractors, I might have less confidence in my generalization of all chalkboards on campus. If I know that prior to 1960, only black chalkboards were made and that between 1960 and 1980, green chalkboards gradually replaced them, I might be able to refine my estimates of frequency and my conclusions.

If we are sure that every item in a population is identical (that is, there is no variation), then a sample of one would be sufficient to establish the basis for a generalization. If I am trying to judge the colour of identical balls within a jar, then a sample of one is sufficient. Once there is variability within a population, we need to know what the relevant differences are and how frequently they occur to know if a sample is representative. If there is a great deal of variability in the population (five colours of balls), then a substantially larger sample would be required to ensure that we have captured not only the range of variability in the population but also the frequency of that variation. If I don't know the range of variation (how many colours of balls there are), then it is more difficult to establish a representative sample.

This is the realm of probability and statistics. Although we do not have the space in this text to go into all of the conditions that make for good generalizations, we can identify some of the major features. A **reliable generalization** is one

1. that is based on evidence — that is, on the observation of a number of cases;
2. in which the observations are systematic;
3. in which the evidence is identified;
4. in which the population is identified or easily inferred;
5. in which the sample is identified;
6. in which the sample is representative of the population;
7. in which the range of variation in the population is identified or easily inferred; and
8. in which the generalization does not overgeneralize in relation to the population.

To defend a generalization as reliable, we should establish each of these conditions. Challenging a generalization as unreliable involves challenging it on one or more of these conditions. Although these eight conditions are rarely met explicitly except in some scientific and social-scientific literature, often enough, information is given or is implicit in the context to allow us to judge the reliability. We can use the criteria for a reliable generalization, given above, to help us develop our intuitions about assessing generalizations.

Both generalizations and general claims are easier to defend if they are limited in scope. **Limitation of scope** refers to limiting the population about which we are generalizing. Instead of generalizing about all chalkboards, I can restrict my generalizations to one specific building or those buildings constructed after 1980. Generally, questions of scope have to do with quali-fiers such as *all, some, most, a few, 51 percent, more than half, two-thirds,* etc. The more precise we can be with these and the more limited in scope the conclusion is, the more likely we can defend the claim. On the other hand, the more wide-ranging and less qualified the general claim is, the easier it is to challenge.

For more on generalization, see the fallacy of hasty generalization in Module 7.

QUICK QUIZ 5.2   Assessing Generalizations

In the following, identify the population and the sample, and assess whether the sample is likely representative of the population. Using the criteria specified in the text, how reliable would you judge the conclusions reported? Justify your reasoning.

1. Most people think that the government should lower the taxes on gas.
2. A radio journalist interviews five people at a parking lot in the city about their views on what the government should do about rising gasoline prices. Four of the five think that the government should intervene to lower the gas tax. The journalist reports that eighty percent of the population think the government should lower the gas tax.
3. A student surveys a class of sixty students on whether they approve of a proposal to introduce a student health levy. Forty-five of the sixty students interviewed agree with the proposal. The student concludes that seventy-five percent of the 10,000 students at the university support the proposal.
4. A student surveys a cross-section of 200 students, balanced for year of study, gender, ethnicity, and major, on whether they approve of a proposal to introduce a student health levy. One hundred and fifty students agree with the proposal. The student concludes that the majority of the 10,000 students at the university are likely to support the proposal.

QUICK QUIZ 5.3   Defending General Claims and Generalizations

Qualify each of the bolded claims below by limiting the scope to make it a more defendable claim in the context of the passage. (You are not being asked to supply reasons or justifications.)

1. The Sponsorship Scandal shows that **politicians are corrupt.** [The Sponsorship Scandal involved a number of politicians and civil servants allied with the Liberal Party providing government advertising contracts for little or no work and, in return, receiving kickbacks to the Liberal Party in Quebec.]
2. I was in Montreal for a month and saw really bad driving. Drivers ignore the rules of the road. They speed, run red lights, and go through crosswalks as children are crossing. **Society is becoming more lawless.**
3. I read in the *New York Times* (online version, November 16, 2005) that **many young urban professionals are self-medicating.** In interviews with a number of people under thirty-five, the *Times* found that these people are trading prescription medications both with friends and via the Internet. Some of them fake symptoms to get the prescription medications they want.

5.5 CAUSAL ARGUMENTS

A *causal inference* involves drawing a connection between two states of affairs and inferring that one causes the other. Although some causal inferences involve generalizations, they do not have to. The claim that a specific automobile accident was caused by alcohol and speeding involves a causal inference but does not involve a generalization. However, saying that alcohol and speed cause most automobile accidents is both a general claim and a causal inference. In order to establish a causal connection, we need to establish

- *temporal priority* — the cause must come before the effect or be nearly simultaneous with it.
- *spatial connection* between the two events — the cause and the effect must be connected in some way. A cause may produce an effect at a distance, but we then need to understand the intervening mechanism.
- *covariance* — the two things must vary together. As one increases, the other increases, or as one decreases, the other decreases. This is usually established through correlation.
- a *reasonable mechanism* that establishes the connections between the two items and shows which causes which and why — this is what helps us establish the cause.

The purpose of a causal argument is to establish that one event is the result of another, or that one event caused another. To establish a cause–effect relationship, we must establish two things: (1) that the cause preceded and was spatially connected with the effect, and (2) that the effect would not have occurred without the cause. Ideally, in order to establish the second condition, we normally have to establish the mechanism by which the cause produces the effect. Without that, we simply have a correlation.

A *correlation* is a claim that two things vary together. For example, the more a person smokes, the more likely he or she is to get lung cancer. A *direct correlation* holds that the two factors vary together. The preceding claim is a direct correlation. As people smoke more, their chances of getting lung cancer increase, and as they smoke less, the likelihood decreases. An *inverse correlation* holds that two factors vary inversely — the more of one, the less of the other. The more leafy green vegetables and fruits a person eats, the less the likelihood of that person getting colon cancer. Eating leafy greens and fruits and contracting colon cancer are inversely correlated.

Establishing a correlation does not establish a causal connection between the two events. "I am always exhausted when I arrive home from teaching class. My cats always meet me at the door when I get home." Although there may be a perfect correlation, I cannot conclude that my cats cause me to get tired. My being tired is caused by a long day. My cats greet me in the hope of getting fed. The two factors, though correlated, are independent of one another.

In order to establish cause, we need to establish a mechanism. In the example of smoking, extensive research has been done to establish some of the causal mechanisms linking smoking and lung cancer. This includes identifying the ingredients in tobacco smoke, the effects of those on lung tissue, genetic predispositions, and so on. Some of these mechanisms have been well enough established that we can say that smoking causes lung cancer.

That we usually have imperfect rather than perfect correlations complicates establishing cause. A *perfect correlation* is one in which *in every instance* whenever one of the correlated items varies, the other also varies. We know that smoking causes lung cancer. However, not everyone who smokes gets lung cancer. And some of those who do not smoke and are not exposed to smoke do get lung cancer. This is an *imperfect correlation.* In this case, not every change in one produces a change in the other. What we do know is that a much higher percentage of those who smoke get lung cancer than those who don't.

The problem with establishing a perfect connection between smoking and lung cancer is that what we identify as the cause is only one of several conditions that produce the effect. Often we need conditions *a*, *b*, and *c* to produce effect *p*. Other conditions, *d*, *e*, and *f*, may act as **countervailing causes** — factors that minimize the influence. And other factors, *g*, *h*, and *j*, may independently cause *p*. Yet we don't know all of the conditions, *a* through *j*. Moreover, when we are dealing with something like smoking and lung cancer, there are numerous variables that lead to the effect. Smoking may produce it, but so, too, may air pollution. Knowing the mechanisms help us make the connection between the cause and the effect, even when we don't appear to have a perfect correlation.

Scientific and academic methods of research have developed quite detailed methods for establishing causal connections. Our focus here is not on those more detailed methods but on how we attribute cause in everyday life. Often we attribute cause when only one of these conditions for causality has been met, usually temporal priority or covariance. When this occurs, we have committed the fallacy of false cause (see Module 7).

Consider the following claim:

> There is a high incidence of exposure to pornography in New York City, and there is a high incidence of rape in New York City. Therefore, pornography causes rape.

This is a common type of argument. We will grant the claims that there are both a high incidence of exposure to pornography and a high incidence of sexual assault in New York City. Is that sufficient to establish the causal connection?

1. The argument does not establish temporal priority — that exposure to pornography comes before the sexual assault. There was likely a high incidence of sexual assault before pornography became widely available in New York in the 1970s. This suggests other factors lead to sexual assault. Did the rates of sexual assault increase after pornography became widespread? Adding this information might strengthen the correlation.
2. While there appears to be a spatial connection — both exposure to pornography and the high incidence of sexual assault occur in New York City — nothing establishes that the individuals exposed to pornography are the ones who commit sexual assault. We also don't know what happens in the absence of pornography. Are there areas that do not have exposure to pornography in which the incidence of sexual assault is low? Without a comparison group, we don't know whether it is the exposure to pornography or something else that produces the effect.
3. The argument establishes a minimal correlation — that both happen often in New York City. It does not establish that there is covariance — that as one increases, the other increases, and as one decreases, the other decreases. At best, there could be an imperfect correlation. It is possible that some people exposed to pornography do not commit rape and some people not exposed to it do.
4. The argument identifies no mechanism.
5. The conclusion, that pornography causes rape, goes far beyond the scope of the evidence. It overgeneralizes as well as fails to establish a causal connection.

In summary, to defend a causal claim, we need to establish

- temporal and spatial connection;
- covariation; and
- a proposed or possible mechanism.

To challenge a causal claim, we can challenge

- the temporal or spatial connection by showing that the two events are not connected;
- the correlation/covariance by showing that some other factor could produce the appearance of correlation/covariance; or
- the lack of a mechanism, or we can propose an alternate mechanism that suggests that the two events are not connected.

QUICK QUIZ 5.4   Assessing Causal Connections

In the following, identify whether or not a causal connection is being claimed. If one is being claimed, identify the claimed cause and effect and then assess whether a satisfactory causal connection has been established.

1. Taking large doses of vitamin C prevents colds. My whole family took twice the recommended daily dose of vitamin C everyday, and none of us had a single cold all winter.
2. Surveys show that teens are reporting using drugs and having sex at a younger age than was reported five years ago. Sociologists suggest this is because of the increased pressures on them to succeed and the fewer opportunities they have.
3. In November 2005, some of the poorer immigrant areas of France erupted into violent riots. Most of the rioters were young males between 16 and 25, unemployed, and subjected to discriminatory behaviours from authorities. Experts suggested that the riots were a natural outcome of the conditions, pointing to the social law that when young males are marginalized, deprived of opportunities, and feeling little hope, given an opportunity, they often resort to antisocial, antiestablishment, and illegal behaviour — drug use, crime, and, sometimes, revolutionary activity. As one expert pointed out, we do not see these reactions in middle-class areas where individuals are not marginalized and do have hope.

5.6 APPEAL TO AUTHORITY OR EXPERTS

When we know little about a particular subject and don't have the time or expertise to become an expert in that subject, we appeal to those who are authorities or experts. Such appeals can be legitimate or illegitimate. The conditions for a legitimate **appeal to authority** are as follows:

1. The area is a defined area or field of empirical knowledge.
2. There is consensus within the field.
3. Someone is an expert in the field.
4. The expert is identified.
5. The expert could back his or her expertise with a survey of the evidence if required.
6. The expert is not in a conflict of interest.

There must be a **field** or **body of empirical knowledge** about which the expert can testify. **Empirical** means based on observation of the world. We appeal to an expert to cite the knowledge gathered within a given discipline. A **field** or **body of knowledge** is an area of inquiry in which there is widespread consensus on the basic claims, evidence, and theories based on evidence available to anyone; this consensus is recognized by others as authoritative. If there is no field or body of knowledge about a subject, there can be no expert knowledge of that area and hence no experts. The sciences and many other academic fields have bodies of knowledge about which there is widespread agreement.

Some areas are not fields about which we can have empirical knowledge; for example, ethics, religion, and esthetics. We can have reasoned opinion. An expert in the area of ethics could testify about the theories and practical implications of various ethical theorists but not about what the "best moral course of action" for me is. The former is part of an academic study about which agreement is possible; the latter is not. Any disinterested inquirer could investigate and discover what theories of morality have been proposed and developed. However, when it comes to giving a judgment invoking normative criteria, there is no agreement on which normative criteria take precedence. Hence, there is no **expert opinion** in the case of what one *ought* to do. Similarly, a theological scholar could testify about the doctrines of a particular church — what they are, when they were passed, how they have been interpreted, any disputes about them — but not about which religion is "the true religion." Ultimately, on such issues, people have to make their own decisions, based on their own reasoning.

A Catholic theologian, knowledgeable about the Catholic Church's view on abortion can give an authoritative answer as to what that view is. There is a body of knowledge about what the Catholic stand on abortion is. It is a matter of public record, and, as a doctrine of the Church, there is consensus among Catholic theologians on it. However, I cannot ask for the Christian view on abortion, for there are a variety of conflicting Christian views on the subject. If I want the answer to "Is abortion morally justified?" there is no expert or authority who can answer the question.

Not only must there be a body of knowledge, there must be **consensus within the field.** In some fields where we can have knowledge — for example, some areas of inquiry in science — we may not have consensus. In such situations, the expert testimony can tell us only that there is a lack of consensus. Experts cannot be used, in their capacity as experts, to testify that one side is truer than the other in such a situation, for the evidence does not establish that. If there is no consensus, then we have to justify why we prefer one expert's support of the position to another's opposition of it. And to do that, we need to supply independent evidence for their positions. And if we do that, we don't need to provide expert testimony.

The requirement for consensus on the subject within a field does not mean that absolutely every expert must agree. Within virtually any field, a few mavericks can be found who challenge the general opinion. So by *consensus*, we mean the agreement of the vast majority of people working within the field. The fact that a few doubt the claim does not destroy the consensus.

This explains one of the common strategies used in legal trials that confuses many lay people. Lawyers call opposing experts to give their opinions. Sometimes, however, the experts are not equal. One lawyer may use a well-recognized authority and the other, someone on the fringes of the discipline. If both are well-recognized experts and one's view differs from the consensus within the field, the maverick (the one whose view differs) is testifying not necessarily as an expert but on his or her educated opinion. This strategy is often used by lawyers in an effort to suggest that there is no consensus on the subject.

That those within a field agree (i.e., have reached consensus) on certain facts and ideas within their field does not mean that those facts and ideas are, in some ultimate sense, true. Instead, what this means is that, according to the criteria and standards of evidence used within the field, at this point in time, the "facts" are the best we have; virtually all scholars working in this area agree on this. New evidence, the development of more sophisticated measuring devices, or new criteria may lead them to reject these facts and ideas later on.

Many people with few or no qualifications pose as experts. As lay people, when assessing whether someone is an expert, we need to consider such things as the person's involvement with the field: Is our expert a scholar recognized by peers as knowledgeable and worthy of citing, or a quack on the fringes of the field? Is he or she doing research in the field? Is he or she cited by others? Does our expert belong to professional societies? Does he or she have proper credentials and qualifications? None of these guarantees that the person is an expert. However, if we are going to quote someone as an expert and expect that person's testimony to further our argument, we should, at minimum, investigate his or her credentials, qualifications, and standing within the field.

The expert *must be identified*. Claims that "experts agree" do not allow arguers to check the credentials of the experts in question. "Unidentified sources" in news reports provide us no way of knowing if the sources are reliable, credible, or knowledgeable.

The expert's *claim to expert status should be supported*. In other words, identify the parts of the expert's background that are relevant for establishing such a status.

There should be *no conflict of interest or obvious bias*. The expert should not have a stake in what he or she is testifying about. If a scientist owns shares in a particular company, that scientist's testimony about the technological process that company is introducing becomes suspect. Instead, a neutral or disinterested party should testify on its effectiveness. Having a member of a nuclear generating company testify about the environmental benefits of nuclear power is also somewhat suspect. This does not mean that the person's claims are false but that they are potentially tainted by the member's association with the company. It does not even mean that the person is consciously distorting his or her assessment of the evidence. However, because an employee could be subconsciously influenced, it is better to have a neutral expert who could make the same claims.

These criteria are arranged in order of importance from the most important to the least important. If the first fails, then it doesn't matter who the expert is or that there is no conflict of interest — the claim to an expert opinion fails. Failure to identify the expert's credentials is less serious than there being no consensus in the field.

QUICK QUIZ 5.5   Assessing Appeals to Experts

Treat each of the following claims as an appeal to authority. Identify what body of knowledge is being appealed to and who is being appealed to as an expert. For each of the following claims, determine, using the criteria for a proper appeal to authority, whether the person being appealed to would qualify as an appropriate authority for the claims being made.

1. News broadcaster gives his opinion on a current political event.
2. The author of a popular book on negotiating strategies makes claims about the most effective way to negotiate. He bases his claims on twenty-four years' experience of negotiating in various contexts.
3. Pollution Probe (an environmental organization opposed to nuclear energy) testifies at a public hearing on the reopening of Ontario's nuclear generating facilities that such a move would be costly and environmentally unsound.
4. Wayne Gretzky, a hockey superstar, claims in an advertisement that Motrin is a good medication for arthritis.
5. A management consultant who teaches negotiation is called as an expert witness to testify at a trial about whether a contract was negotiated in good faith.

QUICK QUIZ 5.6   Assessing Experts

What expertise would be required to establish someone as an expert on the following topics? Be as specific as you can be. To the best of your knowledge, are these fields of knowledge about which expert testimony is possible?

1. The claims of astrology
2. The truth of astrology
3. The origins of humankind
4. International banking policy
5. The effects of the Roe–Wade decision (a United States Supreme Court decision on the legal acceptability of abortion)

Expert Opinion vs. Informed Opinion

It is all too easy to say that someone is not an expert and, therefore, we should dismiss his or her opinion. However, some people can have an informed opinion without meeting all of the criteria for being experts on the issue. A sportscaster who is knowledgeable about hockey could have an informed opinion on the likelihood of a particular team winning the Stanley Cup. Despite there not being consensus on an issue like this (nor a field of knowledge), some individuals' opinions are more informed than others.

We need to distinguish between expert opinion, informed opinion, and uninformed opinion. Expert opinion relies upon there being a body of knowledge, consensus about that knowledge, and a person having expertise in that body of knowledge. The expert testifies to the state of knowledge about which there is consensus in the field.

Yet in many cases we rely on *informed opinion* — opinions of individuals who are knowledgeable about a particular subject, even though there may not be consensus on that subject. Each year, at the beginning of the hockey season, various informed observers are asked their opinions about the likely rankings at the end of the season. The opinions are based both on the person's knowledge of the teams' strengths and weaknesses and their knowledge of hockey in general.

Much of what passes in modern political, social, athletic, and entertainment discourse is opinion. Whether it is informed depends on our assessment of who is making the comments, their knowledge, and their reasoned consideration of the issues. Someone who has extensive experience and has thought about an issue is more likely to give an informed opinion than someone who has not. At best, informed opinion becomes information we ought to consider, not expertise we ought to accept in the absence of contrary evidence. And if it is backed by reasoning and evidence, then we have grounds for making our own judgment.

QUICK QUIZ 5.7   Experts, Informed Opinion, and Opinion

In each of the following, identify whether the appeal is made to expert opinion, informed opinion, or just opinion. Explain.

1. My brother, who has worked as a motorcycle mechanic for thirty years, says that Harley-Davidson motorcycles are more reliable than Suzukis.
2. Based on an extensive survey of motorcycles, Consumers Union reports that Harley-Davidson motorcycles are more reliable than Suzukis.
3. Dr. Hamm in the physics department says that Harley-Davidson motorcycles are more reliable than Suzukis.

MODULE SUMMARY

The premises in inductive arguments can provide only some degree of probable support for the conclusion. Accepting the premises in a strong inductive argument does not guarantee the absolute certainty of the truth of the conclusion. Some inductive arguments are stronger than others. None absolutely guarantees the conclusion. Different kinds of inductive arguments — inference to the best explanation, generalizations, causal arguments, appeals to authority — rely on different criteria. Each needs to be assessed in terms of the criteria relevant to it. An inductive argument is one in which the premises strongly support the conclusion and are true is sound.

KEY TERMS

alternate explanations
appeal to authority
biased
causal inference
complete
conflict of interest
consensus within a field
correlation
countervailing causes
covariance
direct correlation
empirical
expert within a field
expert opinion
field or body of knowledge
frequency
general claim
generalization

imperfect correlation
inference to the best explanation
informed opinion
inverse correlation
limitation of scope
Occam's Razor
perfect correlation
plausible
population
reasonable mechanism
reliable generalization
representative
sample
sound
spatial connection
summary
temporal priority
variability

MODULE 6

ASSESSING CLAIMS

6.1 LEARNING OBJECTIVES

After completing this module, you should be able to

1. identify the different kinds of claims — empirical, normative, and conceptual;
2. identify the kinds of support relevant to establishing each kind of claim;
3. assess various kinds of claims for acceptability;
4. generate and respond to counterexamples; and
5. identify and assess presuppositions and corollaries.

6.2 INTRODUCTION

Good arguments require both good structure and good content. This module focuses on the content of an argument — the different kinds of claims that can be used in an argument and the conditions under which they are acceptable or unacceptable. (Module 3 discusses identifying claims and distinguishing them from other kinds of utterance.)

Not all claims are the same. Different kinds of claims — empirical, conceptual, normative — require different kinds of evidence or support. Empirical claims rely on observations about the world to establish their truth or falsity. The acceptability of conceptual claims relies on our knowledge of the language. Normative claims, including ethical ones, rely on judgment and criteria.

We use the term *acceptability* rather than *true* when discussing normative and conceptual claims. *True* applies, most strictly, to empirical claims. The grounds for an empirical claim's truth are different, however, from those for the acceptability of normative and conceptual claims.

In addition to assessing claims based on their content, we can use the additional tools of counterexample, presupposition, and corollary to probe the acceptability of claims.

 QUICK QUIZ 6.1   Preliminary Quiz: Kinds of Claims

Before continuing, examine this list. For each claim, consider how you would establish that it is true (acceptable) or that it is false (unacceptable). Identify the specific evidence that would be required to prove or disprove each of the following claims. Be as specific and detailed as you can be. You do not need to gather evidence. Rather, you are being asked *what would count as evidence* for or against the claim. If you are unsure about what evidence would be relevant, explain your uncertainty. If there are several possible interpretations of the claim's meaning that would affect how you assess the acceptability of the claim, explain. Having identified the specific evidence that would count for or against each of the claims, examine your list and analyze it to see what different *kinds* of evidence are used.

1. The chalkboard in my critical thinking classroom is green.
2. Every chalkboard on this campus is green.

(continued)

3. Every chalkboard ever made has been green.
4. It is in the nature of chalkboards to be green.
5. Caesar crossed the Rubicon in 49 B.C.E.
6. The earth is 4.5 billion years old.
7. Water freezes at 32 degrees Fahrenheit (0 degrees Celsius).
8. The atomic number of gold is 79.
9. Scientists believe that AIDS is not one single virus but several kinds of viruses.
10. AIDS is caused by HIV.
11. Getting unauthorized information about an exam prior to that exam is cheating.
12. This classroom is overcrowded.
13. Pornography is any depiction of sex or nudity that degrades women or children.
14. Pornography degrades women and children.
15. Prostitution is immoral.
16. Humans are, by nature, selfish.

Answers for all Quick Quizzes in this text are provided in the Student Manual. After doing the Quick Quizzes, consult the Student Manual to check your understanding of the material.

6.3 KINDS OF CLAIMS

Different kinds of claims require different kinds of evidence. Empirical claims are based on observational evidence; conceptual claims are based on meaning; normative claims are based on criteria of evaluation; mixed claims are based on a combination of the preceding.

Before examining these in more detail, it is worth noting that we can take four approaches to dealing with the acceptability of a claim:

1. We can accept the claim as true or acceptable.
2. We can suspend judgment if there is insufficient evidence to establish the claim. A variant of this is to show that the claim is **problematic,** which is to say that we have some reason for doubting it, although neither the claim nor the evidence for it has conclusively been shown to be faulty.
3. We can set off the claim with brackets for further examination on the grounds that we don't know exactly what it means or what kind of evidence would count for or against it.
4. We can reject the claim as unacceptable.

See Exercise 6.1 in the Student Manual for additional exercises on identifying kinds of claims.

6.4 EMPIRICAL CLAIMS

Empirical claims are claims whose truth is ultimately established by observation of the world around us and the inferences we make based on those observations. The inferences — generalizations, causal claims, and appeal to expert testimony — are discussed in Module 5.

How do you know that the chalkboard in the next classroom is green? *I observed it.* How do you know that Lance Armstrong won the Tour de France seven times? *I watched the sixth and seventh races and have read many reports by people who were there for the other five.* How do you know that an electron is a bundle of energy and not a particle? *I rely on the testimony of experts who have studied electrons and made observations about them.* How do you know that gay couples are entitled to spousal benefits at your place of employment? *I consulted the company's written policies.* All of these claims are confirmed by some kind of observational evidence: observing directly, referring to some kind of authoritative document, or getting information from an authority. Ultimately, their truth or falsity rests on someone's observations about the world.

Empirical claims include

- personal sensory observations (e.g., The text I am reading is printed on white paper.);
- general knowledge based on the observations of others (e.g., Caesar crossed the Rubicon in 49 B.C.E.);
- generalizations based upon a few or many observations (e.g., All swans are white.);
- theoretical knowledge of empirical science (e.g., A falling body descends at the rate of 32 feet per second); and
- the factual testimony of experts (e.g., Scientists believe that AIDS is not one single virus but several kinds of viruses.)

> "Somewhere in the universe is a planet other than Earth inhabited by intelligent beings capable of space travel."

Above is an empirical claim. We don't know if it is true or false because we haven't yet been able to make the appropriate observations. In time we may be able to. While we don't know the actual truth or falsity of the claim, it is still an empirical claim since its truth or falsity *could be* established by observation through one of the five senses. A claim's status as empirical relies not on whether we have actually made the observations that would establish it as true or false but whether observations are the kind of evidence needed to establish whether it is true or false.

Claims that through observation have been shown to be false are nevertheless empirical claims. "The chalkboard in the next room is black" is an empirical claim even if the board is green; it is a false empirical claim. To say that a claim is empirical is to identify the kind of evidence that is relevant to establishing its truth or falsity. It says nothing, however, about its actual truth or falsity.

The various kinds of empirical claims have different considerations relevant to establishing their acceptability. Consider the following kinds of observational claims in terms of their reliability:

1. Direct and immediate observation: "The chalkboard in front of me is green."
2. Report of a past direct observation: "The last time I was in University College, I noted that the chalkboard in room 224 was green."
3. Report of a direct observation made by another person: "Mary reports that the chalkboard in room 230 is green."
4. Report of a report of a direct observation made by a third party: "Mary says that one of her classmates reported that the chalkboards in Vanier College's room 102 are also green."
5. A summary of observations: If I have observed ten classrooms with chalkboards on campus and Mary has observed another ten in different buildings, then I could summarize by saying, "All the chalkboards we have seen on campus are green."
6. An inference drawn from an observation: "Green chalkboards must be easier to read since they are installed in more recent buildings, whereas black chalkboards are more common in earlier buildings."
7. A generalization inferred from one or more direct observations: "In the ten classrooms I visited, all of the chalkboards were green. All the chalkboards in this university are green." (A generalization differs from a summary in that it goes beyond what was actually observed and draws an inference to a wider group than was actually observed.)
8. Causal inferences from observations: "The university administration prefers green chalkboards."

9. Expert testimony by someone in a position to know: "The person in charge of building maintenance for the university says that all the chalkboards on the campus are green."

Although these are all empirical claims, there are some important differences. The first five claims are direct observation reports. The remaining go beyond direct observation to inferences and judgments.

Direct Observation Reports

Direct observation reports are based on the direct observations made by an observer or observers. Their acceptability differs depending on how proximate the report is to the observer. Memory reports become less reliable over time as memories fade or are reconstructed. Reports of second or third parties depend on the accuracy of their observations and other factors.

We judge these observation reports on the basis of

- how reliable the observer is;
- how attentive the observer was when making the observation;
- whether the report is confirmed by other, preferably independent, observers;
- how recent the observation was;
- how detailed the report is;
- whether the report is confirmed or can be confirmed by independent observable evidence;
- the categories the person uses to make the report ("I saw a bright light in the night sky" vs. "I saw a UFO." The latter is an inference based on an observation not directly reported); and
- how distant the report is from the actual observer (second-, third-, fourthhand).

A report that fails in some of these criteria is not necessarily false or even erroneous. It may not, however, be reliable enough for us to base an inference on.

The last three categories of observation reports in Section 6.4 above are somewhat different. Generalizations (which include scientific laws) go beyond what we immediately observe to incorporate claims about a whole group or class of things. Causal connections involve inferences to which situation caused another situation. Expert testimony is usually about the general knowledge within a field and is a mixture of observation and inference as well as opinions within that field. Although all of these are empirical claims because their truth or falsity is ultimately based on observations, they go beyond the directly observable.

The remaining four items on the list above (6 through 9) involve inferences based on observations — inferences to the best explanation, assessing generalizations, causal claims, and appeals to authority — and are discussed in Module 5.

QUICK QUIZ 6.2   Assessing Empirical Claims

In each of the following, identify the empirical claim, the evidence offered for it, and how reliable each claim is based on the evidence.

1. Last year when I was in Scotland, I visited Loch Ness and saw a number of photographs of the Loch Ness monster. It is a forty-foot-long dinosaur-like creature that lives in the loch.
2. Although there are no photos of the Loch Ness monster before 1900, we have over a dozen drawings. All of these show a seagoing dinosaur-like creature.
3. Ancient dinosaur-like creatures must exist because they have been seen. The Loch Ness monster is a good example of one.

6.5 CONCEPTUAL CLAIMS

Conceptual claims are claims about the meanings of terms and expressions: for example, "A bachelor is an unmarried male." The truth of such claims is determined not by examining the physical world but by examining language and its use. What we *mean* by *bachelor* is an unmarried male. Conceptual claims have to do with the meanings of concepts and terms. Their acceptability is determined by investigating the denotations and connotations of the concepts, how the concepts are used, and how various concepts are related to one another.

Dictionaries can be a useful starting point for clarifying the meaning of a term. If you don't know the definition of *euthanasia* and you are presented with a claim on the subject, your first resource should be a dictionary. However, a dictionary's entry is not sufficient for all conceptual problems. It would not, for instance, help us come up with claims to answer the following: "Was Canada a *democracy* before the introduction of voting rights for women?"; "Do animals feel *pain?*"; "Is a *fetus* a person?" Instead, we need to explore how the concepts of "democracy," "pain," and "fetus" are used in the language and, in some cases, make decisions about their proper use. Conceptual analysis is explored more fully in Module 9. For more about meaning, see Module 2.

The criterion for assessing the acceptability or unacceptability of a conceptual claim is the use of that claim in the language or within a particular conceptual system. In reviewing definitions, we normally don't discuss their truth or falsity; rather, we talk of their usefulness, acceptability, or accuracy. Similarly, we judge a conceptual claim by its ability to help us understand the concept, its consistency with the use of the term within the language, and its usefulness in interpreting the world. If I use "a yellow metal" as the meaning of the concept *gold*, it may be sufficient if I am trying to distinguish it from aluminium or tin, but it would not be sufficient if I were trying to distinguish it from iron pyrite (fool's gold).

> **QUICK QUIZ 6.3**   Assessing Conceptual Claims
>
> Identify which of the following are conceptual claims and explain why.
>
> 1. Objectifying women is wrong.
> 2. Objectifying women means treating them as less than human.
> 3. Objectifying women results in their being treated as less than human.

6.6 NORMATIVE CLAIMS

Normative claims are claims whose acceptability or unacceptability is based on some criterion of value or standard of evaluation. They are claims about what should or should not be done, or about what states of affairs are good or bad, desirable or undesirable: for example, "Stealing is wrong"; "This paper deserves a B."

There are two basic kinds of grounds for normative claims:

1. Claims based on a personal expression of preference, such as "I like broccoli," are **preference claims.**
2. Claims based on some kind of general criterion or criteria for judging or evaluating, such as "This paper deserves a B" are **criterial claims.**

In a preference claim, the only ground given for the claim is the individual's personal preference or evaluation. I do or don't like it, prefer it, want it. The only real challenge to a preference claim is to the person's sincerity in making the claim. "You say you hate broccoli, but yesterday you told Andre that you eat it at least three times a week. Are you sure you hate broccoli?"

A criterial claim, in contrast, provides at least one criterion for evaluating that extends beyond the individual's preference. The criteria for awarding a paper a B can be articulated, defended, and challenged. More than mere personal preference, these claims can be argued about, defended, and determined to be appropriate or not in a given circumstance.

The two types of normative claims can be easily confused. "That was a good movie" might simply be the speaker's way of saying "I liked it" (just as he or she would say "I like broccoli"), or it might be based on some critical standards of evaluation: "That was a good movie. It was acted well, had a good plot, was brilliantly photographed, and was well scripted." Which it is depends on context and whether reasons are or can be given for the claim. In the latter case, the movie evaluator is providing criteria for determining whether a movie is good or bad. Advanced as grounds on which any person could make a similar evaluation, the criteria are rationally defensible (and challengeable), unlike with a preference claim.

To assess the acceptability of a criterial normative claim, we must identify the criteria for evaluation; determine whether what is being evaluated meets the criteria; and decide whether these are the best possible criteria for assessing that specific thing in these specific circumstances. Applying this to the movie example, we would ask, (1) "What criteria are being used to evaluate the movie?" (2) "Does the movie meet these criteria?" and (3) "Are these the best possible criteria for evaluating this movie for these purposes?"

Often we simply get the normative judgment without any justification for it. "This paper deserves a B" does not state any criteria for evaluation. We have to probe for that: "What criteria are being used that justify this paper being given a B?"

Normative criterial claims are evaluations; they assert judgments about what states of affairs are good or bad, desirable or undesirable, should or should not be pursued. These claims depend upon the application of some evaluative criteria. Assessing normative claims, then, depends upon two separate activities:

1. The identification of a state of affairs — that is, the relevant conditions of whatever it is we are evaluating.
2. The application of a criterion or standard of evaluation to those characteristics.

If I were to defend my evaluation that a paper deserves a B, I would need to do two things:

- **Specify my criteria for evaluating papers.** Papers with the following characteristics receive a B:
  1. They are reasonably well structured; have no or few grammatical, spelling, or typographical illiteracies; and address the assignment at a better-than-average level of competence.
  2. They develop an argument that supports the conclusion.
  3. They show some level of originality in the development of the argument.

- **Show that the paper has those characteristics.** This paper meets criterion 1 because it has the following characteristics: x, y, z. It meets criterion 2 because . . . And so on.

The criteria I use are *evaluative*. That is, they depend upon the assigning of relative merits. In this case, papers without grammatical illiteracies and spelling errors are more valued than papers with; papers that are on topic are more valued than those that are unfocused; and well-argued papers are more valued than poorly argued ones. If I were teaching English composition, I might use other criteria, placing more importance on style, grammar, and creativity than on logical criteria. Which criteria I choose to use will depend on my objectives in evaluation.

We can elaborate, giving a more detailed set of criteria for evaluating criterial claims:

1. The purpose of the evaluation (e.g., evaluating an English essay or philosophy essay; evaluating public conduct or private conduct; evaluating the esthetic or economic merits of a painting).
2. The criteria we are using for evaluation, which are based on our purposes for evaluating (e.g., for an essay, research, style, cogency of argument, or facility with English).
3. The weighting of the criteria — where there are multiple criteria, one criterion might have more weight than another. (e.g., For an English essay, I might weight style more heavily than research; for a science paper, I might weight research more heavily than style).
4. The condition of whatever it is we are evaluating (e.g., the specific features of the item to which the criteria are being applied).
5. Whether the conditions in 4 satisfy the criteria in 2; the application of the criteria to the conditions (e.g., whether the paper actually meets the criteria specified).
6. Whether the criteria in 2 are the best for accomplishing the purposes in 1; it might be argued that other criteria would be better suited to accomplishing the aims in 1. (e.g., If I am trying to teach students philosophy, a colleague might argue that I cannot expect students to develop an original, coherent argument until they have examined and analyzed the works of others and that I should make my first assignment a précis and critique of the work of a major philosopher, rather than an original essay.)
7. The underlying value(s) behind the criteria; sometimes the values that motivate the criteria are not clear and identifying them can help us see alternate potential values and raise these as possible challenges. (e.g., What are my underlying values in emphasizing style?)
8. Alternate values that may supersede or challenge those in 7. This points to different underlying values and how to apply them. (e.g., The challenger suggests that critiquing the arguments of others is a better way to learn how to develop an original argument than simply trying to develop an argument. I would have to address this with an argument.)

QUICK QUIZ 6.4   Distinguishing Normative Claims

Determine whether each of the following is a factual claim, preference normative claim, or criterial normative claim, and explain why. If you are undecided, explain your indecision.

1. Ken Dryden was a better goalie than Patrick Roy.
2. Despite their respective records, the Toronto Maple Leafs is a better team than the Montreal Canadiens.
3. I like the Leafs better than the Canadiens.
4. The Canadiens have scored more goals this year than the Leafs.

Assessing Normative Claims

Normative claims can be defended by identifying the criteria being used, supporting the criteria as the best possible for the situation, and showing clearly that the criteria apply to the situation.

Normative claims can be challenged by showing that criteria have not been plainly identified, asking for a clear statement of the criteria, challenging the criteria as not the best for the situation, and then showing that the criteria have not been thoroughly applied in the situation or that applying them leads to a different evaluation.

QUICK QUIZ 6.5   Assessing Normative Claims

For each of the normative claims below, identify (1) the kind of normative claim; (2) the purpose of the evaluation, if it can be determined; (3) the criteria used; and (4) other possible criteria that might challenge these criteria.

1. This book is poorly written. It is very difficult to understand, and the author's language is highly technical.
2. *Said in a discussion between a couple deciding where to vacation this year:* "I think we should go camping and cycling in Quebec this summer rather than visit my sister in Calgary. We both like camping and cycling, and it would be cheaper. Besides, we saw her last year, so it's her turn to visit us — and cycling and camping would be more relaxing than staying with family."
3. *Said in an election campaign:* "You should elect the Conservatives because they will form a better government. They will interfere less in the lives of citizens."

Esthetic, Practical, and Ethical Claims

Various types of subject matter give us a second way of categorizing normative claims — we divide them into esthetic, practical, and ethical claims. **Esthetic claims** are concerned with art and beauty. Criteria for esthetic claims depend on the kind of material being assessed — novels, sculpture, architecture, paintings, photographs — and may include such things as proportion, contrast, harmony, realism, nonrealism, craftsmanship, plot, and character portrayal. **Practical claims** are concerned with decisions about appropriate courses of action. Evaluation of student essays, the comparative merits of different university majors, the choice of best mp3 player, and the comparative merits of different political policies can be assessed practically — in terms of costs, infrastructure required, feasibility considerations, et cetera. These are practical normative judgments. **Ethical claims** are concerned with issues of right and wrong behaviour, fairness, equity, duty, obligation, and justice. When a person says that certain actions are right or wrong, moral or immoral, just or unjust, he or she is claiming that the actions satisfy some criteria of evaluation based on "ethical" considerations. These criteria or ethical principles are based upon our understanding of what is and is not desirable behaviour for us as humans.

Anything — a movie, for example — can be evaluated on any of these terms. When I judge a movie as "good" because the plot is well developed, the acting well done, and the script well written, I am using criteria of craftsmanship, which is esthetic. Were I to judge the movie as "good" because it made lots of money, I would be using practical standards of evaluation. Were I to judge it in terms of its possible corruption of youth, I would be making an ethical judgment.

Although the terms **morals** and **ethics** are often used interchangeably, we can use them to distinguish between two kinds of discourse. *Morals* and *morality* can be used to refer to the specific principles, rules, and behaviour of individuals and groups. *Ethics* can be used to refer to the systematic examination "on ethical grounds" of those rules and principles as well as the developing of a system of conduct based on rational grounds. We can say the morals (i.e., the specific moral code and practices) of a given society, *x,* justify slavery. In that sense, we are describing the moral principles that the society follows. We can go on to talk about the ethics of that practice, asking, "Is this the way we should treat people?" An ethical judgment appeals to a value or set of values independent of the specific code of that particular society, so we might answer, "The moral code of *x* is unethical in its treatment of those individuals it enslaves."

Several **ethical principles** have been proposed: Individuals ought to act so as to create the greatest good or the greatest happiness for the greatest number of people. Or individuals ought to act so as to ensure that each person is treated fairly. Or individuals ought to act so as to ensure human well-being, where well-being is characterized as ensuring access to those goods, and the development of those traits, that are essential for humane treatment of others — health, personal security, food, shelter, autonomy, freedom of thought and action, and so on.

An ethical principle identifies a core value and enshrines it in a general claim. The value identified in the first example of an ethical principle above is human happiness. How that is to be accomplished is not specified. The third principle refers to ensuring human well-being and lists a number of subordinate values that contribute to that. Again, there is no indication as to how they are to be applied in a specific situation nor are there specific ethical rules that follow from them.

An **ethical rule** is a rule of behaviour or judgment that identifies a specific kind of action as right or wrong: "Stealing is wrong" or "You shouldn't lie." Ethical rules are concerned with a relatively specific kind of action. If we probe deeper to find out why stealing is or should be wrong, we may come up with a variety of reasons. For example, someone might say that stealing is wrong because it violates a basic agreement we have with others in our society to treat them fairly. In this case, there is a basic principle — *we have an agreement with others in our society to treat them fairly.* Taking another's property without permission is treating that person unfairly. The basic value enshrined in this principle is the fair treatment of all members of one's own society. Different ethical systems can be based on different fundamental values: Obedience to the will of a deity, satisfying the needs and wants of human beings as living creatures, respect for the autonomy of individuals and human choice are a few that have served as the foundations of ethical systems.

Ethical rules and ethical principles operate in ethical arguments in the same way that normative criteria work in normative arguments; that is, they identify a criterion or set of criteria to be applied to a situation or judgment. Where we agree on an ethical rule, we can use it as a basic principle in an argument. Where we disagree on an ethical rule, we have to back up the rule with more general and accepted ethical principles.

In defending a moral judgment, we use the same kind of criteria we found with criterial normative claims:

1. What ethical criteria are being used in this situation?
2. Do the criteria apply to the case in point?
3. Are these the best possible criteria to be used, given the purposes of the evaluation?

The difference is that we use specifically ethical criteria — ethical principles or ethical rules and the underlying moral values on which they are based.

Consider the following situation:

> Michel stole some money from Aine's purse. Stealing is wrong. Therefore, what Michel did was morally wrong.

An ethical rule—"Stealing is wrong"—is used to show that Michel's actions were immoral. We could challenge this by showing that the criteria do not apply in this situation. If Michel borrowed the money with Aine's approval, he did not steal it. This does not invalidate the ethical rule. It simply says that it does not apply here.

We could also challenge it by arguing that this criterion can be overridden by a more important value in this situation; that is, the criterion being used is not the best possible or most appropriate under the circumstances. Michel did steal the money, but he stole it to buy medicine for his sick wife, without which she would have died. In this case, we are claiming that there is another ethical rule: Stealing (or other unethical behaviour) can be excused when it is done for a higher purpose.

The second challenge rests on identifying an alternate ethical value and arguing that the alternate value overrides the stated one in this situation. The no-stealing rule defends the value of private property. The stealing-is-justified-to-save-a-life rule defends the value of preserving life. The claim is that saving a life overrides the value of private property in certain circumstances.

This helps explain why some people assert that normative claims are subjective or "just a matter of opinion." Different individuals in different situations may invoke different normative criteria as relevant and appropriate. While this shows variability in assessments and criteria, it does not mean that we cannot argue and reason about the criteria and their application.

We can defend ethical claims by clearly identifying the criteria being used, defending the criteria as the best possible for the situation, and showing clearly that the criteria apply to the situation.

We can challenge ethical claims by showing that criteria have not been plainly identified and asking for a clear statement of the criteria; showing that the criteria are self-contradictory or confused; challenging the criteria as not appropriate or not the best ones to use in the situation; or showing that the criteria have not been clearly applied in the situation or that applying them leads to a different evaluation.

QUICK QUIZ 6.6   Identifying Ethical Claims

For each of the ethical claims below identify (1) the ethical claim being argued for; (2) the criteria being invoked; and (3) other possible criteria that might challenge these criteria.

1. The United States should be condemned for systematically using torture in its conducting of the war on terror and the war in Iraq. Torture violates the basic human rights of its victims.
2. Paying women less than men for doing the same job is immoral. Therefore, we shouldn't do it.
3. A student charged with a breach of the rules of the university should have the right to a fair hearing before a disinterested party and the right to counsel at such a hearing. This is only a matter of natural justice.

6.7 MIXED CLAIMS

Mixed claims are claims whose criteria for acceptability depend upon some combination of empirical, conceptual, and normative criteria. This typically occurs when a claim requires conceptual clarification before one of the other sets of criteria can be invoked.

> Computers are not capable of human thought.

This claim is both empirical and conceptual. Its acceptability depends on examining computers and determining if they have certain characteristics. But first, we have to clarify what is meant by "capable of human thought."

Consider another example:

> Anything that causes harm to another is immoral.

This is a mixed ethical and conceptual claim. Before we can assess it on ethical grounds, we need to know what is meant by "causing harm to another."

Mixed claims are usually conceptual–empirical or conceptual–normative claims. In either case, we usually have to clarify the conceptual part of the claim before dealing with the remainder of the claim.

QUICK QUIZ 6.7   Identifying Mixed Claims

Identify any mixed claims below. Determine which are conceptual–empirical and which are conceptual–normative. Explain what would be required to determine the claim's acceptability.

1. The Conservatives have the best policy on child care.
2. Feminism is making a comeback among female university students.
3. Low-income earners have greater health problems and lower life expectancies than middle- and high-income earners.

6.8 ADDITIONAL TOOLS FOR CHALLENGING CLAIMS

Thus far in the module, we have considered the kinds of evidence that would be relevant to assessing different kinds of claims and the kinds of evidence that would make a claim acceptable or unacceptable. One common type of claim we encounter is a **general claim** (defined in Module 5). A basic technique for challenging general claims is the counterexample.

Counterexamples

A **counterexample,** as we have seen, is a specific instance that is designed to counter (show the limitations or falsity of) a general claim. It is a key tool in argumentation as most arguments contain general claims of some sort. Providing a counterexample allows us to test the adequacy of those general claims.

Different kinds of general claims require different kinds of counterexamples.

> All cats are black.

This claim has the form "All *a*'s are *b*." If I can find one *a* that is not *b*, then I have shown that the claim is false. So I need to find a specific instance of a nonblack cat in order for the counterexample to work. If I just say, "Some cats are not black," I am simply asserting the contrary of the other person's statement, without providing any support for believing that my counterclaim is true. If, on the other hand, I give a specific example or instance, then I have provided evidence through the specific case: "Pandora is a cat, and she is white." I have thereby shown that the other person's original claim is false in that there is at least one cat to which it does not apply.

> If I drop this piece of chalk, it will break.

This claim has the form of a conditional statement: "If *a*, then *b*." I can counterexample this by showing or identifying conditions under which *a*, the antecedent (the term following the "if," described in Module 4), could occur and *b*, the consequent (the term following the "then," also described in Module 4), would not occur. The claim "If I drop this chalk, it will break" is probably true under most "normal" conditions — if I drop it from a sufficient height, if the piece of chalk is sufficiently large enough, if it is dropped onto a hard surface, if it has not been specially treated to avoid breakage, and so on. If some or all of these conditions are not met, the chalk will not break. These are the normal **reservations,** the **"unless" conditions** that apply to most universal claims. Normally, pointing these out might be considered "picky"; however, under certain conditions, it might be necessary to introduce them.

When we make a general claim, we are saying that all instances of a particular kind should be treated alike. We call this the **Principle of Similar Cases:** All things that are alike should be treated alike. The corollary of this is that whenever we encounter any two things that appear to be alike and that we propose to treat differently, we must provide some justification for the difference in treatment.

When faced with a counterexample to our own claim, we can have the following choices:

1. **Accept the counterexample as relevant and withdraw or modify our claim.** For example, in response to the claim that all swans are white, an arguer counterexamples with "Black swans are found in Australia." In response to the counterexample, we can modify the original claim to "All swans outside Australia are white," qualifying the scope of our claim. Alternatively, we could simply withdraw the claim, admitting we were wrong about the colour of swans.
2. **Reject the counterexample as not relevant.** For example, if we offer as a counterexample to the claim "All swans are white" that newborn swans are brown, our argument partner might respond that he or she is referring to adults, not newborns.

Whether or not an argument partner changes views when we generate a counterexample, we learn something about his or her position.

When making a general claim, we are asserting that all instances of that general claim are true. The counterexample is designed to establish a limitation of that general claim. It can show that the universal claim is false (i.e., that there is at least one instance in which it is not true) or that it is limited (i.e., that the claim is true under certain conditions).

Two additional techniques — presuppositions and corollaries — provide further tools for assessing claims.

QUICK QUIZ 6.8   Counterexamples

For each of the following claims, identify at least one possible counterexample.

1. All SUV drivers are a menace on the roads.
2. If a person is a financial success, then he or she is a good person.

3. In making all of their decisions, chief executive officers have in mind the best interests of the stockholders.
4. Everyone who uses a public roadway should have a motor vehicle licence or be banned from using it.

Presuppositions

A *presupposition* is a claim that logically precedes one under consideration. The presupposition must be true in order for the claim under consideration to make sense or be true. Alternatively, if a given claim, *a*, is to be considered true, then a prior claim, *p*, must be true. If *p* is false, then the truth of *a* is in doubt. The prior claim, *p*, is the presupposition. All claims have presuppositions.

Suppose you are presented with the following argument:

> A student tells her instructor that she could not write the exam because her father died and she had to attend the funeral.

This seems to be reasonable grounds for the person not having written the exam. However, the instructor discovers that the person's father had died several years before. The problem is not that the argument has false claims in the obvious ways. Rather, the claim "my father died" presupposes that her father had been alive near the time of the exam and that his funeral was going to be held at or near the time of the exam. The student hasn't made an explicit claim that this is the case. Rather, the claims she makes presuppose a prior claim — a presupposition. And the presupposition is false. If the presupposition of one or more of the premises of an argument is false, then the argument is defective and should not be accepted.

Consider the following:

> We need to make our meetings more democratic by ensuring that every member has a significant say.

The above claim presupposes the following claims:

- I belong to a group that holds meetings.
- The group has already held some meetings.
- Meetings can be made more democratic.
- Meetings should be more democratic.
- The meetings the group has held have not been democratic or not as democratic as they could be.
- Something in the meetings has prevented at least one and possibly more members from having a significant say in the proceedings.
- Democracy is assured by ensuring that every member has a say.

We might challenge a number of these claims, including the claim that meetings should be democratic and the claim that the past meetings have not been democratic. In critically assessing a passage, we want to focus on those presuppositions that are significant.

There are various kinds of presuppositions:

- **Existence:** A claim may presuppose the existence of something. The claim about making meetings more democratic presupposes that we are holding meetings.
- **Properties:** Properties of the thing talked about are assumed. Meetings can be democratic.
- **Relations:** A claim may presuppose that one thing is related to another in a certain way. I belong to a group.

- **Context:** A claim may presuppose features of the context. In a specific organization, the context presupposes that meetings should be democratic.

This list of types of presuppositions is not exhaustive.

Consider the following:

Context: A Christian minister is telling the story of the exodus of the Israelites from Egypt. He makes the following claim:

> Moses led the Israelites out of Egypt and to the Promised Land.

Before continuing, examine this claim using the various kinds of presuppositions listed above:

Existence:	Moses, Israelites, Egypt, and the Promised Land are all presupposed to exist.
Properties:	Moses was the kind of person who could be a leader.
Relations:	Moses was the leader of the Israelites.
	The Israelites were capable of being led. Or the Israelites were willing to follow a leader.
	Egypt was not the Promised Land.
	One can get from Egypt to the Promised Land.
	This happened in the past (*led* is past tense). [Note that we include possible temporal relations in the category of "relations."]
Context:	The Bible's story of the exodus of the Israelites is a real story.
	The Israelites were enslaved in Egypt.

The contextual presuppositions require knowledge of the Biblical context and all that goes with this particular story, just as the contextual presuppositions in the earlier example require knowledge of the university's examination policies.

Contrast this with the situation in which one is telling what is clearly an imaginary story — the referents (Moses, etc.) would be presupposed to exist only in the context of the story, whereas, in the context of the minister's telling, the story is presumed to be true and to refer to real people. The context includes how and why a story is being told or a set of claims is being made.

In some cases, context is set within the passage; in some cases, the passage presumes a common cultural knowledge. For example, a claim made about a legal or political system may presuppose common knowledge about that legal or political system. A claim made about the legal system in Quebec may presuppose different things from a claim made about the legal system in the rest of Canada. Quebec operates under the Napoleonic code; the rest of Canada operates under the English system of common law.

Some claims related to a given claim may not be presuppositions. The claim "Moses was an Israelite" is not a presupposition. Given the original claim, it might be possible that Moses was someone who, although he led the Israelites from Egypt, was not himself an Israelite. For that we need independent knowledge. After all, someone who leads a group is not necessarily a member of that group.

QUICK QUIZ 6.9   Presuppositions

Identify the presuppositions in the following claims. Using the list of kinds of presuppositions might be helpful here. Identify at least one claim related to the claims in the passage that is not a presupposition of the claim given.

1. You need to replace your engine. It has over 350,000 km on it.
2. Kidnapping, torture, and extortion are legitimate strategies in waging war.
3. Marijuana should be legalized for medical reasons.

Corollaries: Implications and Consequences

A *corollary* is a claim that follows from an explicit statement.

> The Canucks have a much improved team this year.

The above claim has the corollary that the Canucks should win more games this year than last year. Any statement, whether or not it is part of an argument, can have a corollary.

One way of challenging a statement is to show that its corollary (the claim that follows from it) is false, unacceptable, or otherwise problematic. If the statement is the conclusion of an argument and the corollary is not true, either something is wrong with the argument used to support the conclusion or the argument has been framed in too narrow a way — that is, a key issue in the situation has not been addressed by the argument. An example of the latter would be the proposal of a project, presented with good reasons for undertaking it, but the costs being prohibitive.

Consider the following claim:

> A study has shown that astrologers have been far more accurate than stock analysts in predicting market variations.

If we accept the claim as true, then one corollary is that if I want to make money in the stock market, I am more likely to do so by following the advice of astrologers. Yet if I have reason to doubt that — astrologers have been inaccurate in predicting my future — then I might reject the claim.

Consider the following claim:

> Israel should accept the PLO's offer to return to the peace table.

If we accept this claim as true, there may be a number of corollaries. One might be that Israel's actions will be seen as conferring legitimacy on the PLO's offer. That may be objectionable to Israeli leaders and therefore something they will not want to do.

When identifying a corollary, we are in effect determining what follows from the claims in question if we accept them as true. By showing that there are unacceptable corollaries, we generate reasons for rejecting the original claim.

There are two significant types of corollaries: consequences and implications. **Consequences** relate to causal effects; **implications** relate to meaning. A consequence of building a domed stadium in the centre of a city is that there will be an increase of traffic in the downtown core. An implication of building a domed stadium in the centre of a city is that that location is considered more important or valuable than others in the region. The first has to do with the causal effects of the stadium's location; the second has to do with the meaning or significance of the stadium's location.

Presuppositions differ from corollaries in that presuppositions are claims that must be true if another claim is true, whereas implications and consequences are more just possibilities, other things being equal. In identifying corollaries, it's important to know something about the social, political, and personal contexts, among others, surrounding the things in the statement.

For example, consider the claim:

> Paul Bernardo was convicted of first-degree murder.

In the Canadian context, the consequence of this is that Paul Bernardo will spend a minimum of 25 years in a federal penitentiary. In the context of the Canadian Criminal Code, that is the minimum sentence before parole can even be considered. The consequence may be different in other jurisdictions. One of the significant attributes of implications and consequences is that they are identified only with some knowledge of the subject of the claim.

QUICK QUIZ 6.10   Corollaries

Identify the implications and consequences for the following claims/situations.

1. Situation: Marijuana is going to be legalized for medical reasons.
2. Situation: A student is trying to get an exemption from the rule that he can't take a particular course without first taking its prerequisite. In talking with an advisor, he is caught lying about his grade in a previous course and why he got the low grade.
3. Claim: Tuition for general undergraduate education will increase next year by ten percent.

MODULE SUMMARY

The assessing of claims is central to assessing the soundness of arguments. Different kinds of claims — empirical, normative, conceptual — require different kinds of evidence to establish them. Empirical claims are ultimately based on observations. Generalizations and causal claims involve reasoning connected with such observations. We often use an appeal to experts or, sometimes, informed opinion as a basis for supporting empirical claims. Challenging the claims means challenging the reliability of the observations, the inferences from the observations to the generalizations or causes, or the expertise of the authorities. Conceptual claims are claims about the meanings of concepts and are ultimately checked by how the terms are used in the language. Normative claims are claims of value and are based on identifying and defending standards or criteria of evaluation. Criterial normative claims, as opposed to preference normative claims, can be argued and reasoned about.

In addition to knowing the kinds of evidence relevant to different claims, two additional ways of challenging claims are through their presuppositions and corollaries. General claims can be challenged with counterexamples.

KEY TERMS

conceptual claims
consequences
corollary
counterexample
criterial claims
direct observation reports
empirical claims
esthetic claims
ethical claims
ethical principles
ethical rule
ethics
evaluative

general claim
implications
mixed claims
morals
normative claims
practical claims
preference claims
presupposition
Principle of Similar Cases
problematic
reservations
"unless" conditions

FALLACIES

7.1 LEARNING OBJECTIVES

After completing this module, you should be able to

1. explain what a fallacy is;
2. identify different kinds of fallacies;
3. identify and explain a fallacy within a passage;
4. neutralize a fallacy;
5. avoid committing fallacies in your own writing;
6. distinguish between look-alike fallacies; and
7. determine when an argument that appears to be a fallacy is not a fallacy.

7.2 INTRODUCTION

Consider the following passages:

1. Since my opponent has not clearly indicated his opposition to the new federal gun-control bill, he must obviously be in favour of it.
2. Incest must be wrong because virtually every society, both past and present, has forbidden it in one form or another.
3. *Daughter:* "If two people really love each other and have committed themselves to each other, I don't see any reason why they shouldn't live together. Azan and I really do love each other, Mother. Someday we may get married, but right now we simply want to be close to each other."
   Mother: "The way I see it is that you're just looking for an excuse to go to bed together. Your whole attitude about this thing makes sex something cheap!"
4. No, I don't want my boys to join the Boy Scouts. Did you know that the Boy Scouts was organized as a paramilitary organization? They even trained the young boys in accordance with a military scouting manual. The "scouts" in "Boy Scouts" literally refers to *military* scouts. None of my children are going to join such an organization with my blessing.

Each of the above could be formulated and assessed as an argument. Through assessment, we would *eventually* find what is wrong with them. Knowing some of the patterns of bad reasoning, however, can help us identify and gauge such arguments more efficiently. Each of these is a **fallacy,** a pattern of faulty reasoning.

A fallacy meets at least two conditions:

1. **It is a pattern of reasoning.**
2. **There is something fundamentally flawed about that pattern of reasoning.**

In everyday language, we sometimes refer to a false claim as a fallacy. What we mean is that it is false or somehow incorrect. In this text and in the study of logic as a whole, the term *fallacy* refers to a pattern of reasoning or an argument that is fundamentally erroneous. Claims are false. Only arguments can be fallacious.

What does it mean to say that a fallacy is "a pattern of faulty reasoning?" Consider the following argument:

> We shouldn't accept what Sophie has to say about abortion because Sophie is a lesbian and lesbians are all radicals trying to destroy the family unit.

Something is wrong with this argument. It is not just that some of the claims are false — that all lesbians are radicals, that all lesbians are trying to destroy the family unit, or that the presupposition that one's stand on abortion is an attempt to destroy the family unit. There is something wrong not just with this particular argument or the specific claims in it but with the kind of reasoning that this argument exemplifies.

The argument structure is

> x is a y.
>
> y is discredited.
>
> _____
>
> ∴   We shouldn't accept what x has to say.

Let us examine a similar argument.

> In the Ontario legislature, Dalton McGuinty, leader of the opposition, has challenged Premier Ernie Eves about a possible conflict of interest involving Eves's government. Eves's response suggests members of the legislature should disregard McGuinty's charges because McGuinty is "sleazy." (*Toronto Star*, June 10, 2003)

This has the following structure:

> Dalton McGuinty has advanced a charge that the government is involved in a conflict of interest.

The (former) premier's response, formulated as an argument, is the following:

> Dalton McGuinty is sleazy.
>
> _____
>
> ∴   We should disregard his charges. (= His charges are false.)

Although the content of this argument and that of the preceding one are quite different, both have a common pattern:

> We should reject what someone says because of who he or she is.

In both cases, the arguments are being dismissed, not because they have been shown to be wrong but because of the person asserting them — Sophie is a lesbian; Dalton McGuinty is a sleazy politician.

This pattern of reasoning is fundamentally flawed for two reasons. First, the premises do not provide good reasons for accepting the conclusions. Even if the premises were true, they are irrelevant to showing that the arguments are not sound. The only way of showing that the arguments are faulty is to assess them, and the premises do not do that. Second, this pattern of reasoning violates several of the constitutive rules of argumentation (see Module 1) — the truth-seeking principle, the respect principle, and the argument principle. Argumentation is about assessing the claims and arguments for a position, not assessing the person making the claims. This argument pattern fails that.

Fallacies are patterns of reasoning that undermine the basic aim of argumentation — the pursuit of truth about an issue. Fallacies prevent us not only from discovering possible points of agreement and disagreement; they also thwart the possibility of reaching any resolution on an issue.

The idea that fallacies are a pattern of erroneous reasoning is similar to the idea of validity in that the error is a structural or patterned error (see Module 4). Affirming the consequent is a pattern of reasoning that is always erroneous, regardless of the specific content. Any argument with a fallacious pattern of reasoning is always a fallacious argument. The kind of structure or pattern differs between validity and fallacies. With validity, the structure is a formal pattern related to the conveying of truth. With fallacies, the structure relates to the aim of argumentation.

The more common fallacies have names based on how the error occurs. The particular pattern of argument illustrated on page 116 involves attacking the person rather than the person's position. It's called *ad hominem,* which translates to "to the man": we take the argument to the person rather than to the reasoning. You will see in this module that fallacies' names relate clearly to the various patterns of bad reasoning.

Each of the fallacies in this module has been developed using these steps:

1. Identify examples of a type of faulty reasoning.
2. Abstract from the examples their particular patterns of reasoning, which are the criteria for the fallacy.
3. Identify why this pattern of reasoning, as a pattern of reasoning, is faulty. This can be done in one of two ways: (1) by showing how the pattern violates one or more of the constitutive rules of argumentation, or (2) by showing that such a pattern of reasoning does not guarantee the truth of the conclusion.
4. Provide a descriptive name for the pattern of reasoning.

Rather than going through this entire process with each fallacy, we will use a simpler form that gives the name of the fallacy (#4 above), the criteria for the fallacy (#2), a brief explanation of why it is an error in reasoning (#3), and one or several paradigm examples (#1) of the fallacy.

The examples provided in the text are designed to be paradigms or models of the fallacies. A *paradigm case* is a clear and unambiguous example of what we are trying to identify — here, a fallacy.

By identifying the fallacy, showing what is wrong with its reasoning, and explaining how the error in reasoning manifests itself in a particular argument, we neutralize the fallacy. This is developed further in Section 7.4.

QUICK QUIZ 7.1   Understanding Fallacies

For each of the following, state whether the claim is true or false.

1. A fallacy as used in this text is a false claim.
2. All bad arguments are fallacies.

(continued)

3. In challenging a fallacy, one should attack the person for making the mistake in reasoning.
4. A fallacy is a violation of one of the constitutive rules of argumentation.
5. In challenging a fallacy, it is sufficient to be able to name the fallacy committed.
6. Any error in reasoning is a fallacy.
7. All fallacies are bad arguments.

Answers for all Quick Quizzes in this text are provided in the Student Manual. After doing the Quick Quizzes, consult the Student Manual to check your understanding of the material.

When we encounter arguments with fallacies in the real world, the fallacies will not always be evident and may not precisely fit the criteria. Passages may commit multiple fallacies, and it may be challenging to disentangle them. Also, some fallacies resemble one another, and we may have difficulty trying to decide between several types. In such cases, the existing criteria might not be precise enough for the purpose, and we may have to adopt further criteria to help us distinguish the *look-alikes* (different fallacies that have similarities; for more on look-alikes, see Section 7.5). Finally, some things that appear to be fallacies may not be fallacies. Name-calling is not necessarily a fallacy. (See Section 7.6.)

The context and the function of the utterance within that context are critical in determining whether or not a fallacy has been committed. Saying Dalton McGuinty is sleazy is a fallacy if it is used as part of an argument to dismiss what he has to say. If it is simply a comment on a particular political maneuver he has engaged in, it is not.

The context is often not specified in examples given to illustrate and learn fallacies. In the absence of background, consider various possible contexts and how they might affect whether or not a fallacy is being committed. In more complex examples, context will be specified.

QUICK QUIZ 7.2   Context

For each of the following, identify a possible context in which the claim or argument would be an *ad hominem* fallacy and a possible context in which it would not be. Explain the difference.

1. You have lied in the past. How can I trust what you are saying now?
2. Of course she would say that. She is a feminist.
3. A stockbroker has been charged with insider trading. After hearing the stockbroker's lawyer's explanation, the investigator says, "Of course you'd have an explanation. You're a lawyer."

7.3 THE FALLACIES

There are many ways of classifying fallacies. Sometimes different fallacies can be identified by the same name, and sometimes the same fallacy can be identified by different names — for example, *ad hominem* can also be called "attacking the person." What is most important about fallacies is not knowing their names but being able to recognize, first, that there is an error with the reasoning and, second, what exactly the error in reasoning is. These — the criteria for the fallacy — are more significant than the name.

An argument can commit more than one fallacy at a time. Identifying just one, however, is sufficient to show that the argument is not sound.

The fact that an argument or appeal is fallacious does not mean that its conclusion is false. What it means is that the reasons given for that conclusion are irrelevant, insufficient, or false. The conclusion of a fallacious argument could be true, just as the conclusion of an invalid argument could be true.

1. Appeal to Force or Threat

An arguer commits the fallacy of **appeal to force** or **the threat of force** when, instead of offering rational grounds, he or she uses or threatens to use coercion to get another to do something or to accept an idea. Such an appeal violates the truth-seeking principle, the respect principle, the argument principle, and the resolution principle.

Consider the following:

Example 1   I don't think it would be wise to run a story on my son's driving escapades. After all, my firm does thousands of dollars of advertising business with your paper.

Example 2   Refugees who come to this country from other cultures have no right to try to preserve their own customs and beliefs. If it weren't for us taking them in, they would be dead. If they keep on insisting on their cultural integrity, we should ship them back home.

These could be formulated as the following arguments:

1.   My firm does thousands of dollars of advertising business with your newspaper.

2.   If you run a story on my son's driving escapades, I will withdraw that advertising business.

3.   You don't want to lose my advertising dollars.

∴   4.   You shouldn't run the story on my son's escapades.

1.   If refugees from other cultures insist on cultural integrity and retaining their own customs and beliefs, they should be shipped back to their homelands.

2.   If they are shipped back home (= If we don't take them in and let them stay), they will die. (= If they return home, they will die.)

A.   [They don't want to die.]

∴   3.   They should not insist on cultural integrity.

Each of these arguments, instead of presenting evidence and reasons for a position, involves an attempt either to persuade by a threat or use of force, or to silence by threatening an undesirable state of affairs. In the first case, the implicit threat to withdraw advertising dollars is not relevant nor is it a reason for not running a particular story. Legitimate reasons might be that the story is not newsworthy, has been improperly researched, or is old news. In the second example, refugees are being threatened with being returned to homelands they have fled unless they relinquish their cultural identities, instead of reasons being provided for why they should integrate into the mainstream.

QUICK QUIZ 7.3   Appeal to Force or Threat

Which of the following arguments is an appeal to force or threat? For those that are, explain how the criteria for this fallacy apply in the example. For those that are not, formulate the argument and explain why you do not consider it to be a fallacy of appeal to force or threat.

1. *A professor to a student who has challenged her argument:* "I suggest that you remember who is marking your paper before you continue this line of reasoning."
2. *Spoken by a Canadian cabinet minister:* "If the United States continues to engage in unjust and unfair restrictions on Canadian softwood lumber imports, Canada will have no choice but to take the issue to arbitration and to impose countervailing restrictions on U.S. imports to Canada."
3. *Manager to an employee:* "I don't care if you think the 1-2-3 accounting program will do a better job and cost less. Remember that you are working for me, and if you don't support it, I will give you a bad performance appraisal."

2. Appeal to Emotion, Pity

Another way an arguer commits a fallacy is by **appealing to emotion** (pity, shame, flattery, disgust, sympathy, or some other emotion) instead of to reasons as a way of persuading someone to believe or to do something.

Consider the following:

Example 1   You should hire Mae. She has a disability and hasn't been able to get a job. I know that she is quite depressed, and giving her a job would really boost her self-esteem.

Example 2   I need an *A* to get into law school; I know that I didn't show up for class and turned in only some of my assignments, but if I don't get into law school, my parents will be heartbroken, and my father, who has a serious heart condition, will be terribly crushed.

Formulated as arguments, both of these examples have as a major premise an appeal that one should have pity on someone and take action based on feelings rather than on solid reasons. Analyzing example 2, we get the following:

1. If I don't get into law school, my parents will be heartbroken.

2. My father has a heart condition and will be crushed.

A.   [You don't want these things to happen.]

_____

∴   3.   You (the professor) should give me an *A*.

The appeal is to consider the possible consequences for the student's family and the fact that the professor would not want these on his or her conscience. However, if grades are based on performance, then this is an irrelevant appeal to an individual's personal circumstances. More specifically, it is an appeal to the professor to have pity on the student's parents, innocent parties to the situation.

Emotions are not good reasons because they are usually irrelevant to the issue. The potential law student is asking for an *A* not because of her accomplishments but because of the effects of her not getting an *A* will have on her parents. The possible effects on her parents are irrelevant to whether the student deserves an *A* in the course. Emotions can be useful in motivating one to pursue an issue; they can also serve as the basis for exploring an issue further. If one believes strongly that Mae should be hired, emotion can serve as the basis for exploring better reasons than the ones given. However, by themselves, emotions are not reasons and when offered as reasons, they are fallacious.

QUICK QUIZ 7.4   Appeal to Emotion

Which of the following passages are appeals to emotion? For those that are, explain how the criteria for this fallacy apply in this example. For those that are not, portray the argument and explain why you do not consider it to be a fallacy of appeal to emotion.

1. *Tenant to landlord:* "I know that I am six months behind on my rent, but I lost my job and then my wife left me. You've got to let me stay until I can get back on my feet."
2. I know that my client has admitted killing his parents, but consider the effects of sending him to prison for this. This poor, homeless orphan, without anyone to turn to, will wither and become a shell of himself. Do you want that on your conscience?
3. Children are dying in Africa everyday. Just pennies a day can help save a child from malnutrition. Send your money today.

3. *Ad Hominem*

Ad hominem literally means "to the man." An arguer commits this fallacy by attacking an individual rather than the individual's arguments. Often such attacks misrepresent the person's character. However, even those that do represent the person accurately violate the basic rule of argumentative discourse. We are assessing the person's arguments, not character. Even someone of poor character and judgment can give good arguments. The assumption of the *ad hominem* is that someone who is evil or ignorant or otherwise flawed cannot present a sound argument. This is, of course, a faulty assumption. There are several versions of this type of argument:

- **Abusive *ad hominem* fallacy:** In this version, one makes a personal attack on another person's expertise, character, intelligence, good faith, or other personal characteristic to demonstrate that that person's argument or position should not be considered.

Example   Why do you accept Professor Richards's claims that most men seriously abuse women? She's one of those man-hating radical feminists who want to castrate all men. How could she have anything unbiased to say on this?

The attack here is on a person, not the arguments she has presented. The speaker is trying to get the listener to accept that Professor Richards's arguments are faulty. This appeal is not based on an examination of her arguments but on the claim that she is a feminist. (The arguer is also trying to discredit all feminists by portraying them as man-hating. This may be a form of straw person, discussed in Section 7.2. Even without this attack on feminists, the argument is an *ad hominem* fallacy because it attempts to discredit Professor Richards based on her politics.)

- **Circumstantial *ad hominem* fallacy:** In this variant, the person arguing holds that the argument of another should be rejected because of the person's relationship with the subject of the argument. It suggests that the person being attacked has a personal interest in the matter and hence is not objective, trustworthy, or sincere.

Example   The officer in command of the West Coast naval detachment has argued in favour of an increase in the personnel under his command and the addition of new equipment. He has presented a detailed case with statistics that seem to show that he needs these in order to fulfill his mandate. In response, his challenger replies that this is all a smoke screen; the officer's real motive is to increase his own importance and stature in the military. Therefore, his argument should be rejected.

The challenger seeks to discredit the officer by pointing to his personal reasons for advancing his arguments and suggesting he has a personal stake in the outcome. This is intended to discredit his arguments. However, the arguments themselves have not been addressed. A basic principle of rational dispute is that we evaluate claims on the basis of evidence given for them, not on the characteristics of the person offering the claim.

In some situations, what appears to be an *ad hominem* is justified. If someone is testifying based on his or her experience and there are good grounds for doubting the person's powers of observation, memory, or truthfulness, then such a challenge would be legitimate. For example, if a person who has been convicted of perjury is testifying in a criminal trial, that would be a relevant fact to offer for consideration in judging his testimony. Similarly, if a medical doctor was called to testify on the medical competence of a colleague, then their relationship may indicate bias in the testimony and may be a legitimate challenge.

QUICK QUIZ 7.5   *Ad Hominem*

In the following, identify whether an *ad hominem* fallacy has been committed. For those that are *ad hominem* fallacies, explain how the criteria for this fallacy apply in the example. For those that are not, portray the argument and explain why you do not consider it to be an *ad hominem* fallacy.

1. *George Bush speaking about John Kerry in the 2004 U.S. presidential election campaign (paraphrased):* "My opponent is simply repeating the liberal tax-and-spend ideas that have proved bankrupt in the past." (Implication: You should not vote for him.)
2. *John Kerry speaking of George Bush (paraphrased):* "I would urge you to look at George Bush's policies over the past four years. He has taken the nation from a substantial surplus to a massive deficit. He is the first president since the Depression to preside over a net loss of jobs. He has led

the nation into an unjustified and costly war that is taxing the American economy. He has enriched the wealthiest 10% at the expense of the middle class and poor. This is the policy of a compassionate conservative? Are these the policies you want continued for another four years?"

3. Dr. Khan was a member of the committee who authored the report. I doubt that we can accept anything he has to say in favour of it.

4. Poisoning the Well

An arguer commits the fallacy of ***poisoning the well*** by attempting to put the opponent in such a position that anything he or she says is dismissed; the arguer does this by discrediting the opponent before he or she is able to say anything.

Example 1	Anyone who disagrees with our position is (a) obviously repressed (Freudian); (b) a running-dog lackey of the capitalist imperialist warmongers (communist); (c) a male chauvinist; (d) an irrational women's libber; (e) an uptight prude; (f) a foe of the family; (g) a friend of big business; and so on.
Example 2	My opponent is not noted for his fondness for the truth.

The arguer in example 1 labels those who disagree with the position as a way of discouraging criticism. The arguer in example 2 attempts to discredit the opponent by accusing him or her of being a liar. Both serve to discredit the opponent prior to their arguments being considered or even presented.

These may not appear as arguments in themselves. However, in context, they can be portrayed as such.

1. x has a particular characteristic or is associated with a certain position or people.

A. This characteristic or association is disreputable.

∴   x's position should not be considered.

Since this strategy is designed to discredit what an opponent says before he or she has a chance to present an argument, it is an illegitimate argumentative move.

QUICK QUIZ 7.6   Poisoning the Well

In the following, identify in which of the passages a poisoning the well fallacy is committed and explain how it is committed. If a poisoning the well is not committed in the passage, explain how it might be confused as one.

1. My opponent is a vulgar opportunist who will say and do anything to get elected and in so doing corrupts the entire electoral process.
2. *Lawyer in summation to a jury:* We need to carefully consider anything that the witness has to say. She has already been shown to have lied under oath on numerous occasions to serve her own interests.
3. Anyone who doubts the president's approach to the war on terror is only helping the terrorists.

5. Shifting the Burden of Proof

The person who introduces a claim has the obligation to defend that position. When the person defending the position shifts the burden of proof to the critic, he or she has committed the fallacy of **shifting the burden of proof.**

Example   Aleksandra has introduced the claim that pornography causes harm and therefore should be banned. When Mikko challenges her to show that pornography causes harm, she replies, "Can you prove it doesn't?"

If successful, Aleksandra has shifted the burden of proof. She is the one who has introduced the position and therefore has an obligation to defend her claims. Her move here suggests Mikko must instead show that her claim is false. When the arguer demands that a critic provide a reason for not accepting the claim, the arguer has reversed the burden of proof.

The fallacy is not committed if someone points out that the person advancing a claim has not supplied evidence or support for the argument and needs to.

> **QUICK QUIZ 7.7   Shifting the Burden of Proof**
>
> In the following, identify whether or not one of the persons involved has shifted the burden of proof and explain how it is done. If the burden of proof has not been shifted, explain why the argument might be confused with a shifting the burden of proof fallacy.
>
> 1. The advocates for gay marriage keep claiming that the legalization of gay marriage is necessary to ensure civil rights. Yet they have not shown what these rights are nor how legalizing gay marriage ensures them. Before we can continue, they must support those claims.
> 2. You will have to show me why I shouldn't believe in astrology before I will consider giving it up.
> 3. I don't believe that man ever went to the moon. What evidence have you got to show that he did?

6. Self-Evident Truth

In the fallacy of **self-evident truth,** the arguer presents his position as self-evident and not in need of defence.

Example   Women should not be in decision-making positions. Isn't it obvious that they are more emotional than men? And since women are more emotional, they are likely to make decisions based on emotions rather than reasons.

In this case, a contentious claim is presented as obvious and not in need of defence. The person assumes it is obvious that women are more emotional than men. No reasons are given. He then uses this to conclude that women should not be in decision-making positions. The self-evident truth fallacy violates the argument principle and the reason principle.

Terms such as the following *may* signal an appeal to self-evident truth:

It is self-evident that . . .

It is obvious to everyone that . . .

No one can deny that . . .

The implication is that anyone who fails to see the statement's self-evident nature is deficient in some way. It is only when these terms are used as substitutes for arguments that they become a fallacy.

However, we must be careful because the terms above can also be legitimate inference indicators that may simply signal a conclusion of an argument. Contrast the previous argument with the following:

> Example   Women go through far more hormonal swings than men do.
> They have periods once a month at which time their hormones
> vary widely. They go through menopause, when again their hor-
> mones vary widely. Men do not suffer from such variations in
> their hormone levels. It is obvious that women are therefore
> more emotional than men.

The phrase *It is obvious that* is used in this context as an inference indicator. Reasons have been given for the claim that follows. Since reasons have been given, it is not an appeal to self-evident truth. The argument, however, is not cogent.

QUICK QUIZ 7.8   Self-Evident Truth

In the following, identify whether or not one of the persons involved has committed a fallacy of self-evident truth and explain how it is done. If there is no fallacy, explain why the argument might be confused with a fallacy of self-evident truth.

1. Evolution is clearly true. No one doubts that.
2. The evolutionists either ignore or can't answer the basic questions of origin. It is obvious that their theory is incomplete and therefore false.
3. I am absolutely convinced that God made the world in six days. I don't understand why others don't accept this.

7. Appeal to Ignorance

The fallacy of **appeal to ignorance** uses an opponent's inability to prove something as evidence for the truth of the arguer's own conclusion. There are two versions of this: (1) If you can't prove it is wrong, it must be right, and (2) if you can't prove it is right, it must be wrong. Either way, no evidence has been given for the conclusion. The argument rests entirely on the fact that no evidence has been offered.

> Example 1   There must not be any intelligent life in outer space, for no
> one has been able to prove that there is.

> Example 2   No one has proven to me that the company wasn't responsible
> for the Westray coal mine disaster. Until someone does, I stick
> by my claim that it was the carelessness of the company that
> led to the deaths of those miners.

These arguments amount to "There is no evidence, so I will hold as true whatever claim I want to." One basic principle of argumentation is that we accept claims only if argument or evidence is provided to support them.

The fallacy of appeal to ignorance is sometimes confused with the fallacy of shifting the burden of proof. See Section 7.5 for more on distinguishing these.

> **QUICK QUIZ 7.9**   Appeal to Ignorance
>
> Which of the following arguments are appeals to ignorance? For those that are, explain how the criteria for the fallacy apply in this example. For those that are not, portray the argument and explain why you do not consider it to be a fallacy of appeal to ignorance.
>
> 1. You haven't shown me that abortion is wrong, so it must be OK.
> 2. You need to show me that passive euthanasia is wrong. So far, I haven't seen an argument against it.
> 3. Nessie [the Loch Ness monster] must exist. No one has been able to show that she doesn't.

8. Loaded Presupposition

An arguer commits the **fallacy of loaded presupposition** (also called *fallacy of many questions, fallacy of loaded questions,* or *fallacy of complex questions*) when he or she makes a claim or asks a question that has a contentious presupposition buried in it. It occurs when someone presents several issues together and assumes that an answer to one implies an answer to another. In effect, this presents a false starting point in the argumentation. An arguer can think that he or she is addressing one question or assessing one claim, assuming a prior one has been answered when it hasn't been. This fallacy consists of presenting a claim with a highly doubtful, false, or misleading presupposition. It is often committed by asking a question with one or more debatable assumptions.

> Example 1   Why is it that children of divorce are less emotionally stable than children raised in unbroken homes?

This complex question presupposes a questionable claim — that children from divorced homes are emotionally less stable than children from intact homes. The rush to answer the stated question may commit us to a false presupposition.

Often this rule is violated by hidden presuppositions that are not explicitly stated and defended. Consider the following:

> Example 2   The scandalous Goods and Services Tax introduced by the Liberals needs to be rejected if the country is to regain its economic health.

This claim asserts not only that the Liberals introduced the tax but that it was scandalous. Normally such adjectives are not defended. The claim also presupposes that the country had economic health (whatever that means) before the Liberals introduced the tax.

Notice that the fallacy of presupposition does not have to occur in the argument as a whole. Each of our examples has illustrated the use of the fallacy in individual claims. Accepting the claim requires accepting the presupposition within it.

QUICK QUIZ 7.10   Loaded Presupposition

Which of the following arguments are fallacies of loaded presupposition? For those that are, explain how the criteria for this fallacy apply in the example. For those that are not, portray the argument and explain why you do not consider it to be a fallacy of loaded presupposition.

1. We cannot accept the fiscally unsound and morally bankrupt policies of the opposition. They would only lead us down a path we should not take.
2. The objectionable notion that intelligence is genetically determined is one of the central tenets of sociobiology.
3. When did you stop beating your wife?

9. Begging the Question (Circular Argument)

An arguer commits the fallacy of **begging the question (circular argument)** by assuming what he or she has set out to prove. Typically, an arguer proves a conclusion by giving reasons; however, in developing the argument using the fallacy of begging the question, the arguer takes as an undefended premise the conclusion that he or she originally intended to prove. This is sometimes called "circular reasoning" because the arguer starts and ends with the same basic claim. When trying to prove a given claim, *a*, he or she offers as a reason for *a* some variant of *a*, in effect offering no independent premise for the conclusion.

> Example   All claims of the Bible are true because they are the words of
> God himself. We know that the Bible represents the word of
> God, for its writers were divinely inspired. The Bible makes it
> clear that the Biblical writers wrote "at direction" and that the
> truth of Biblical statements is beyond doubt.

Paraphrasing this makes the circularity of the argument clear. What this claims is that the Bible is true because the Bible is true. But what the arguer has to show is that the Bible is true.

There are several variants of this:

- **Logical equivalence (or definitional) form:** The premises and conclusion say the same thing but in different words.

> Example 1   Socialism is wrong because it is government control of the
> means of production.

"Government control of the means of production" is a definition of socialism, not a reason against it. The logical equivalence form of begging the question may, as it does in this case, involve substituting a definition for a concept as though one is giving a reason.

> Example 2   A: Pornography degrades women.
>
> B: Why do you say that?
>
> C: Because I define pornography as anything that
> degrades women.

The definition that pornography degrades women is used to support the (presumably empirical) claim that pornography degrades women. The claim "pornography degrades women" has been made true by definition. Yet that is what needs to be established.

- **Interdependence form:** The premises are acceptable only if we have already accepted the conclusion or some important aspect of the conclusion.

Example

Customer:	"You can be assured that any money you lend to me will be repaid because I am a trustworthy person."
Bank manager:	"How can I be assured of that?"
Customer:	"Well, Frank Lucci will vouch for me."
Bank manager:	"How do I know he is to be trusted?"
Customer:	"That's easy. I will vouch for him."

In this case the customer's trustworthiness is vouched for by Mr. Lucci, and Mr. Lucci's trustworthiness is vouched for by the customer. In order to accept the conclusion, we must accept the claim offered as a reason. But that requires accepting the conclusion. The claims depend mutually on one another for support. No independent support has been given.

QUICK QUIZ 7.11   Begging the Question

Which of the following arguments are fallacies of begging the question? For those that are, explain how the criteria for this fallacy apply in this example. For those that are not, portray the argument and explain why you do not consider it to be a fallacy of begging the question.

1. Euthanasia is wrong because it involves helping someone to end his or her life.
2. Women are less rational than men because they can't reason as well as men.
3. Democracy is a form of government in which the leaders are elected and represent the will of the people. Using that definition, the government of Vulcan is not a democracy. The so-called elections are shams, and the leaders represent only the will of the power brokers.

10. Common Practice/Popularity

The *fallacy of appeal to popularity, common belief,* or *common practice* rests on making the claim that something is true and should be accepted because it is widely believed, accepted, or done. A number of different kinds of appeals are included under this label. We could separate them as different fallacies or focus on the commonalities. What unites the various versions is that the attempt at justification is made through an appeal to the common practice or popularity of a belief rather than through an attempt to establish that it is true for particular reasons.

The versions of this fallacy include the following:

- **Appeal to popularity:** Based on the simple claim that something is popular; therefore, it must be acceptable or true.

Example 1   Everyone knows that polygamy is unacceptable.

OR

Example 2   No one agrees that polygamy is acceptable; therefore, it must
be wrong.

The latter is an inverse version of the appeal to popularity. If something is not commonly accepted, then it must be false or unacceptable.

- **Appeal to tradition:** Based on the simple claim that we have always done something a certain way or have always believed something to be a certain way.

    Example   Music has always been part of the curriculum. How can the government even think of removing it for fiscal reasons?

- **Appeal to common belief:** A variant of the appeal to tradition but slightly more specific in that it focuses on belief; based on the idea that if something is commonly believed, then it must be true.

    Example   Everyone knows that the world is flat, so it must be flat.

- **Appeal to common practice:** Can easily blur into an appeal to tradition or past practice; based on "We have always done it this way."

    Example   Everyone uses formal logic in teaching critical thinking. It must be the best way for students to learn critical thinking.

- **Appeal to group membership/patriotism:** Based on membership in a particular group.

    Example   Every right-thinking Canadian knows . . .

- **Appeal to novelty or change:** Opposite of the preceding but is still a form of appeal to popular opinion; based on the idea that if something is new or different, it is better.

    Example   That's old-fashioned and must be wrong.

Sometimes, the arguer simply dismisses the idea or position with a claim — "That's sixties thinking" — without giving the conclusion, which is left implied.

- **Appeal to dislike of eccentric, unusual, or uncommon habits, beliefs, lifestyles, clothes, et cetera:** Based on the idea that if something is unusual or uncommon, it must be false.

    Example   These untried ideas . . .

- **Appeal to racial, religious, social prejudices:** An appeal to common preconceptions and ideas on the assumption that others share them and that they don't have to be argued.

    Example 1   All true Canadians believe . . .

Example 2   All true Muslims support . . .

Example 3   We all know that homosexuals are . . .

The fallacy is an appeal to common positive values (e.g., safety, loyalty) for a group of insiders, and common beliefs, negative emotions, or values (e.g., fear, greed, shame) about outsiders. Often, the negative appeals are based on social and economic prejudice against the outsider. The positive appeals are based on a sense of belonging. Rather than presenting arguments, the arguer appeals to the in-group or out-group status of the arguments being supported or challenged.

The contraries — that since everyone believes or does *x*, *x* must be wrong — are also included in the fallacy of appeal to common practice. They are based on the contrarian notion that whatever the majority believes must somehow be wrong. Whereas the typical version of this fallacy involves appealing to popular sentiments, to common practice, to the way things have always been done, the contraries involve the dismissal of tradition and common belief as wrong simply because they are traditional or common.

Example 1   Immanuel Kant wrote his philosophy in the eighteenth century; therefore, his ideas are dated and wrong. [Although simplified for illustration, I encounter this commonly in some of my philosophy courses.]

OR

Example 2   Although Thomas Aquinas's views on marriage may have been correct for his time, they are dated and don't fit the twenty-first century.

The only reason given for Aquinas's or Kant's ideas being wrong is that they are from a different time and place. This is a contrary version of the appeal to common belief.

QUICK QUIZ 7.12   Common Practice/Popularity

Which of the following arguments are appeals to common practice or popularity? For those that are, explain how the criteria for this fallacy apply in this example. For those that are not, portray the argument and explain why you do not consider it to be a fallacy of appeal to common practice or popularity.

1. You're an essentialist? No one believes in essentialism anymore.
2. The Canadian legal system is based on the core values of tolerance, equality, respect, and social justice. This proposal violates all of these and should be rejected.
3. I don't see how you can argue that pornography is beneficial. Society disagrees and rightfully bans it.

11. Faulty Appeal to Authority

The *faulty appeal to authority fallacy* is called such because some appeals to authority are legitimate. Module 3 outlines the conditions for a legitimate appeal to authority. Appeals to authority are justified when

1. there is an identifiable field of knowledge;
2. the person appealed to is an authority in that field;
3. the authority's knowledge of the field is current;
4. there is general consensus within that field on the topic being appealed to;
5. the authority is clearly identified; and
6. the authority's testimony does not put the authority in an obvious conflict of interest.

These criteria are arranged in order of importance. If there is no field of knowledge, there can be no appeal to authority. Not identifying the authority is a lesser charge that could be corrected. When one or more of these conditions are not met, the appeal is a faulty appeal to authority.

> Example   Linus Pauling, a double Nobel prize–winning chemist has argued
>   that mega doses of vitamin C will increase a person's life span.
>   Surely if such a noted scientist claims this is true, it must be true.

Linus Pauling may be a double Nobel laureate, but he is not an authority in the field of medicine and vitamin C. This violates condition 2.

> Example   J. Philippe Rushton, a noted Canadian psychologist, argues that
>   head size and IQ are strongly correlated and that black people
>   have smaller head sizes than white people.

What the arguer fails to note is that the claim about the relationship between head size and IQ has been substantially disproved by many scientists for over 100 years. This appeal violates condition 4 — this statement is not the consensus in the field. Unfortunately, as in this case, we are not always able to determine whether some of the conditions are met without further investigation.

Although ideally all of the conditions should be met for the appeal to authority to be legitimate, in practice, usually some of the conditions are not explicitly stated. Whether the absence of a condition within a passage indicates a faulty appeal or simply a concise presentation of a case is something we have to judge in context. For example, rarely is it stated that a purported expert does not have a conflict of interest. The challenge of determining that is often left to those questioning the appeal.

QUICK QUIZ 7.13   Faulty Appeal to Authority

Which of the following arguments are faulty appeals to authority? For those that are, explain how the criteria for this fallacy apply in the example. For those that are not, portray the argument and explain why you do not consider it to be a fallacy of faulty appeal to authority.

1. Don Cherry, a noted hockey announcer, appears as a spokesperson for a leading auto insurance company, claiming that it has the lowest rates in the industry.
2. My art history professor says that the *Mona Lisa* is the most beautiful painting in the Western world. I guess it must be.
3. A: There are only about 30,000 genes in the human genome.
   B: How do you know that?
   A: I read a study that claimed that.

12. Hasty Generalization

Review the criteria for a good generalization in Module 5, Section 5.4. An arguer commits the fallacy of **hasty generalization** when he or she violates the criteria for a good generalization, usually by using a small or unrepresentative (biased) sample, or by generalizing beyond the limits of the population.

Example   The notorious serial sex killer Paul Bernardo viewed pornography. So did Ted Bundy, another notorious serial sex killer. This shows that all serial sex killers view pornography.

In this example, the arguer generalizes, stating that since Paul Bernardo and Ted Bundy both viewed pornography, all serial sex killers view pornography. (Do not confuse a hasty generalization with a false cause, in which the inference would be that pornography is the reason that the individuals became serial sex killers. That is a different kind of argument.) The arguer is assigning to all cases the attributes of two probably unrepresentative cases.

QUICK QUIZ 7.14   Hasty Generalization

Which of the following arguments are hasty generalizations? For those that are, explain how the criteria for this fallacy apply in the example. For those that are not, portray the argument and explain why you do not consider it to be a fallacy of hasty generalization.

1. Book prices sure have gone up. I bought my texts for the fall, and they were double the cost of last year's.
2. I have asked six of the ten support staff what they would like for lunch. They all agreed on the salmon. Since everyone wants it, we should order salmon for everyone.
3. People who support euthanasia also support abortion. Liz supports euthanasia, so she must support abortion.

13. False Cause

Review the criteria for a good causal inference in Module 5, Section 5.5. An arguer commits the fallacy of **false cause** when he or she fails to establish all of the conditions for a causal connection. The most common kind of false cause argument involves mistaking a correlation or spatial or temporal connection for a cause.

Example   Ever since capital punishment was abolished, the crime rate has been increasing. The abolishment of capital punishment is the reason there's more crime.

In this example, a simple correlation has been confused with a causal relationship. Two things occurred around the same time; therefore, one must have caused the other. However, many factors can affect the crime rate. Capital punishment is only one. Demographers know that crime rates fluctuate systematically with the number of unattached (unmarried or not bound by strong family ties) and underemployed males in the population. As their numbers vary, so, too, do rates of violent crimes and crimes against property. If the percentage of unattached, underemployed males has been on the rise in the same time period, then that may account for the increase in crime.

A common strategy for challenging a possible false cause is to show that there is another possible cause for the result. This does not prove that the alternative is the cause, but only that another possible, reasonable cause could explain the result and that the offered cause has not been established.

QUICK QUIZ 7.15 False Cause

Which of the following arguments are fallacies of false cause? For those that are, explain how the criteria for this fallacy apply in the example. For those that are not, portray the argument and explain why you do not consider it to be a fallacy of false cause.

1. A recent government study has found that smoking and education are inversely related. The lower a person's education, the more likely he or she is to smoke and the more difficulty that person has in quitting smoking. Obviously, being less educated causes people to smoke. The solution to getting people to stop smoking, therefore, is to develop a more educated populace.
2. When the city repaved the street in front of my house on Monday, severe vibrations shook my house. Tuesday it rained, and the foundation of my house started leaking. The vibrations obviously cracked the foundation in my basement. The city should be held responsible for damaging the foundation of my house.
3. Several South Korean scientists have announced that they have found a prevention for stomach cancer. They fed kim chi (pickled cabbage) to a test group of subjects and compared their rates of stomach cancer with those of people who did not eat the kim chi. Those fed the kim chi had a twenty-five percent lower rate of stomach cancer than those who did not eat the cabbage. The scientists have concluded that kim chi has an inhibiting effect on the development of stomach cancer.

14. Slippery Slope

The *slippery slope fallacy* suggests that one action sets off a sequence of others that will lead to an inevitable end result, which is usually seen as undesirable. This fallacy rests on the idea that if you take the first step, you are committed to a "slippery slope" of unspecified intermediate steps and a far-off, harmful outcome. While pointing out the long-term effects of an act can be a legitimate argument strategy, slippery slope is a fallacy because the consequences are distant, questionable, suggested to be inevitable, and usually unconnected to the first step.

> Example   Professor to class: "I do not permit questions in my class because if I allow one student to ask a question, then everyone starts asking questions, and the first thing you know, there is not enough time for my lecture."

The professor jumps from the allowing of one question to the result that everyone will ask questions, and from there to the result that she will be unable to give her lecture. It is not certain that allowing one question will lead to a barrage of questions. Furthermore, the instructor is not helpless to say no if there are too many questions. The causal connection is neither inevitable nor obvious.

QUICK QUIZ 7.16   Slippery Slope

Which of the following arguments are slippery slope fallacies? For those that are, explain how the criteria for this fallacy apply in this example. For those that are not, portray the argument and explain why you do not consider it to be a fallacy of slippery slope.

1. We can't allow abortion. Once we start killing innocent babies in the womb, there is nothing to stop us from killing the elderly, the disabled, or anyone deemed undesirable. We become no better than the Nazis with their gas chambers!
2. I can't take that first drink. I'm an alcoholic. I know that if I have one drink, I will be in the gutter tomorrow. I can't stop myself.
3. *Argument given in response to a proposal to fund a school exclusively for black students who are at special risk of dropping out of the school system:* We can't fund schools exclusively for black students. If we do, then every ethnic and religious group will want its own school, and that will be the end of public education. And we don't want that to happen.

15. False Dichotomy

An arguer commits the fallacy of **false dichotomy** (also called *false dilemma* or *false alternative*) when he or she presents only two alternatives, as though they exhaust the range of possibilities, and then forces a choice between the two.

> Example   A person has to choose between the Bible and evolution. There is no need of salvation if man never fell. (TV televangelist)

The arguer is presenting the alternatives as mutually exclusive and forcing a choice between them when they are not mutually exclusive options. In this situation, one could choose both, or neither.

A fallacy is not committed if there are only two legitimate logical or practical alternatives. This is called an *exclusive alternative* — a person can choose only one or the other. If a student is faced with two alternatives — studying for an exam or going to a party — and these are the only two practical alternatives, then the choice between staying home to study for the exam or going to the party is a legitimate exclusive alternative. It is also a *practical exclusive alternative*, in which, practically speaking, a person cannot do both. A *logical exclusive alternative* is one in which a person cannot logically do both: either I study for the exam or I don't. A false dichotomy presents alternatives that are neither practically nor logically exclusive. The basic way to challenge a false dichotomy is to show that there are other viable alternatives.

QUICK QUIZ 7.17   False Dichotomy

Which of the following arguments are fallacies of false dichotomy? For those that are, explain how the criteria for this fallacy apply in the example. For those that are not, portray the argument and explain why you do not consider it to be a fallacy of false dichotomy.

1. *George Bush in a speech to the American people:* "If you are not supporting us, then you are supporting the terrorists. Democratic opposition in Congress is only helping the terrorists in Iraq."

2. Either we save for a down payment on a house by cutting out all luxuries or we allow ourselves the luxuries of lattes, new clothes, and vacations and forgo saving for a house. I, personally, can't forgo the little luxuries of life. So it looks like we won't get the down payment for a house.

3. Either we raise taxes and break an election promise or we don't raise taxes and keep an election promise. However, we need the additional revenue from taxes. So it looks like we'll have to break an election promise.

16. Equivocation

An arguer commits the ***fallacy of equivocation*** when he or she uses one word or phrase that has two different meanings, and this shift of meaning affects the reasoning. The fallacy of equivocation usually occurs when a term used to mean one thing in a premise is used to mean something different in another premise or in the conclusion. The shift in meaning can make the claims appear to be true and the argument, cogent. However, when the term is paraphrased or the difference in meaning identified, it becomes clear that the claim is not true.

Example   I don't see any reason for us to listen to the superintendent of schools on the textbook issue. We need to hear from someone who has authority in the field of education. Our superintendent doesn't have enough authority to keep students or teachers in line. Nobody respects her orders.

This example equivocates between *authority* meaning an expert in a particular discipline and *authority* meaning the power to influence others' behaviour. If we paraphrase this portion of the argument, we get the following:

1.   The superintendent does not have the power to influence the students' or teachers' behaviour.

2.   We should listen only to someone who is an expert on the textbook issue.

∴ 3.   We should not listen to the superintendent of schools about the textbook issue.

With this paraphrase, it is clear that the premises do not support the conclusion. Premise 1 and premise 2 use the term *authority* in two different senses.

QUICK QUIZ 7.18   Equivocation

Which of the following arguments are fallacies of equivocation? For those that are, explain how the criteria for this fallacy apply in the example. For those that are not, portray the argument and explain why you do not consider it to be a fallacy of equivocation.

(continued)

1. Men and women are clearly not equal. They differ in various attributes. Men are stronger; women, more verbal. So how can one say that we ought to treat them equally?
2. Active euthanasia is morally justified. When a doctor administers a lethal injection, he or she is not killing the patient. Rather, the disease is killing the patient. If a person is responsible only when he or she actually kills someone, then the doctor is not responsible for the death. The disease is.
3. We shouldn't teach critical reasoning because critical reasoning teaches people to argue and arguments create conflict and dissent between people.

17. Faulty Analogy

An arguer commits a fallacy of **faulty analogy** when he or she draws an inappropriate comparison. An *analogy* is used to show the similarities between two things — *a* and *b*. *a* has certain properties — *p*, *q*, *r*, and *s*; because *b* has some similar properties — *p* and *q* — it is inferred that *b* has one or more of the remaining properties — *r* and/or *s*. Schematically, it is as follows:

1. *a* is like *b* in some respects.

2. *a* has properties *p, q, r, s*.

3. *b* has properties *p* and *q*.

_____

∴ 4. *b* must have property *r* and/or *s*.

Analogies can be a good way of developing and generating ideas. However, analogical arguments can commit the fallacy of faulty analogy if the stretch is too great between the items being compared — that is, if the properties being compared are superficial or if the stated similarities do not apply.

Consider the following:

The world is like a machine.

It has many intricate parts that fit together.

Machines have inventors.

_____

∴ There must be a supreme being who invented (created) the world.

This argument compares two things:

- the world
- a machine

Machines have properties: *a* many intricate parts that fit together
                             b creators (inventors)

The world has properties: *a* many intricate parts that fit together

Therefore, the arguer states, the world has the other property of the analogy: *b*.

In a faulty analogy, the properties of the first half of the analogy either are superficial (i.e., the *analogues* — the items being compared — do not have much in common) or do not apply to the second half of the analogy. The argument is consequently not sufficient to establish the conclusion.

Analyzing an analogy requires

1. **identifying the two things being compared;**
2. **identifying the properties characterizing the first analogue;**
3. **identifying the properties characterizing the second analogue; and**
4. **identifying the inference from the properties of the first analogue to the properties of the second.**

Our natural tendency is to focus on the similarities between the analogues. One way to challenge an analogy is to point out important differences between them and explain why, as a result, the analogy does not work. In the above analogy, we might call attention to the fact that we have seen machines designed and constructed. We have no such clear evidence that the world has been similarly designed and constructed.

Consider the following argument:

Example   No one objects to the practice of a physician looking up a diffi-
               cult case in medical books. Why, then, shouldn't students taking
               a difficult examination be permitted to use their textbooks?

This can be diagrammed as follows:

1.   Students' textbooks are like physicians' medical books.

2.   Physicians use their reference books to look up difficult cases.

∴   Students should be allowed to use their textbooks on difficult
       examinations.

The two analogues are

- students' textbooks
- physicians' medical reference texts

Students' textbooks are being compared to physicians' reference books.

The problem is that the similarity between physicians and students is superficial. The doctor's knowledge has already been tested and certified. The students' has not. The functions of referring to a text are therefore different. For this argument to work, the arguer would have to establish that the two functions do not significantly differ. This is a faulty analogy.

Having analyzed the analogy, exposing a faulty one further involves showing

5. **the ways in which the two items are different; and**
6. **how that difference affects the conclusion being drawn.**

Which of the following arguments are faulty analogies? For those that are, explain how the criteria for this fallacy apply in the example. For those that are not, portray the argument and explain why you do not consider it to be a fallacy of faulty analogy.

1. The state is like a ship. Just as a ship needs a strong captain — one who insists on unyielding obedience — to command it, the state requires a strong leader whom all the citizens must obey.

2. Business is a struggle for survival in which only the most competitive should survive. For this reason, the government should not provide support to businesses. If businesses cannot survive on their own, they should not be supported by government handouts.

3. Nature is a book open to everyone to read. If we do not understand it, it is simply because we have not read it carefully enough. And like a book, nature requires an author. Its author is God.

18. Straw Person

A **straw person** (originally "straw man") fallacy refers to a dummy argument being set up in place of another. By substituting a weak or distorted argument or position for a stronger one, the arguer can instead challenge the weaker one. This fallacy can be committed by caricaturizing a position or argument; by misrepresenting an argument; by distorting it in subtle or not so subtle ways; or by picking the weaker or weakest of the arguments for a position when there are stronger ones available.

> Example   In a tract called "Six Bridges No Evolutionists Can Cross," a fundamentalist preacher attempts to refute the theory of evolution. He argues that Darwin cannot explain individual variation—for example, why some people have blue eyes and others have brown ones. He concludes, therefore, that there is no reason to believe that evolution took place.

Although it is true that Darwin himself could not explain individual variation (because he had an inadequate theory of heredity, as he himself knew), modern biology *can* explain the variations in traits. Attacking Darwin's original theory is not a refutation of evolutionary theory as it now stands but only a challenge to an early stage of the theory. Scientific theories develop over time. As our knowledge advances, we often discover that earlier versions of a theory are false. However, later versions usually address and correct its weaknesses. More recent arguments and statements in evolutionary theory are stronger and not subject to this same criticism.

Detecting this fallacy requires knowing the original claim and being able to show that it has been modified or distorted in the discussion. A variety of moves can produce a straw person fallacy, including simplification of a claim, exaggeration of a claim, generalization beyond what is reasonable, omission of nuances and qualifications, changing the meanings of terms, and making a relative claim absolute.[1]

---

[1] van Eemeren, Frans H., and Rob Grootendorst. *Argumentation, Communication and Fallacies: A Pragma-Dialectical Perspective.* Hillsdale, N.J.: L. Erlbaum, 1994.

Original claim:	Mary was upset at her mother's funeral.
Simplification:	Mary is emotional.

In the above case, the simplification omits the qualifications and context — that this occurred at her mother's funeral. The conclusion suggests that Mary is often, usually, or always emotional, which is not supported by the context.

Original claim:	Mary gets emotional when she thinks about her mother's death.
Exaggeration:	Mary is always emotional.
Original claim:	Some men are insensitive.
Generalization:	All men are insensitive.

In the generalization above, the claim changes from one that is qualified to one that is not.

Original claim:	If you want to graduate with honours and stand a good chance of getting into graduate school, you will have to get almost all *A*'s.
Omission of nuances:	My advisor told me I need all *A*'s to graduate.
Original claim:	Voluntary passive euthanasia is allowed by the Canadian Medical Association's Code of Ethics.
Changing the meaning of terms:	The Canadian Medical Association encourages euthanasia. [Usually this is not done quite so obviously. In this example, two terms have been changed—allowed to encourages, and voluntary passive euthanasia to the unqualified euthanasia.]
Original claim:	The Canadian Medical Association allows voluntary passive euthanasia under certain exceptional circumstances.
Making a qualified claim absolute:	The Canadian Medical Association allows euthanasia.

The final example omits the qualifications *voluntary passive euthanasia* and *under certain exceptional circumstances*, thereby turning a limited claim into an absolute one. Whenever a claim seems a bit too easy to challenge and involves some kind of overly general claim or seems a bit ludicrous, it is worth checking the original source to see if a straw person has been used.

Some straw person fallacies occur intentionally: the original position is deliberately distorted. However, many are the result of sloppy scholarship, poor listening skills, inattention to the position of the other, or the attempt to develop a strong challenge to a strong position.

QUICK QUIZ 7.20   Straw Person

Which of the following arguments are straw person fallacies? For those that are, explain how the criteria for this fallacy apply in this example. For those that are not, portray the argument and explain why you do not consider it to be a fallacy of straw person.

1. *Original source — biology text:* Although we have many transition fossils for the large families, we have not yet found such transition fossils for many specific species. And we have none for the soft-body species. Nor are we likely to find any, since these creatures do not produce fossils. *Argument:* Even evolutionists admit that evolution is impossible. If evolution were true, then we should find many fossils for transition species. Yet a noted biology text claims that we don't have fossil remains showing any transition species, nor are we ever likely to.

2. Lara: "Unless we construct a nuclear power plant in this area within the next ten years, we will not be able to meet the significantly growing demands for electrical power in the province." Arkadi: "What you are saying is that you don't care what happens to the plant life and wildlife in the area or even to human lives that might be dislocated by the building of this plant."

3. The core claim in evolution is that species evolve over time. Yet we have no direct evidence of this. The best we have is fossil evidence or DNA evidence. But neither establishes that evolution has occurred. Both are compatible with the hypothesis that species are fixed and do not change.

19. Red Herring

An arguer commits the **red herring fallacy** when he or she introduces an irrelevant issue into an argument to confuse or sidetrack discussion of the issue. The image is taken from fox hunting, where a red (salted and cured) herring (a smelly fish), which was used to train hounds, would be dragged across a trail to throw the dogs off a scent. In the case of argumentation, a red herring is the introduction of information that is seemingly related to the topic at hand but is, in fact, irrelevant and used simply to distract the listener from the issue.

Example   My opponent has claimed that I have stolen from the public purse and enriched myself. Ladies and gentlemen, I have introduced and passed bills that have benefited this community; I have opposed unscrupulous developers and those who would destroy family values; I have opposed video parlour games.

Instead of addressing the issue of whether the speaker has stolen from the public purse, the argument points to his or her contributions, about which everyone can probably agree. By focusing on this positive aspect, the speaker diverts attention from the original charge. A red herring can be used both in response to a challenge and to defend a position.

QUICK QUIZ 7.21   Red Herring

Which of the following arguments are red herring fallacies? For those that are, explain how the criteria for this fallacy apply in the example. For those that are not, portray the argument and explain why you do not consider it to be a red herring fallacy.

1. Eugenics is a failed science. After all, it was used by the Nazis as a justification to eliminate over six million people — Jews, gypsies, homosexuals, and the mentally challenged.

2. In response to the charge that she has mismanaged the union, been ineffectual as chair, played partisan politics, and been ineffectual in negotiations, Chandra Johnson argues that the charges should be dismissed because they are merely an attempt to discredit her because she is a woman and the members obviously don't believe a woman should run a union.

3. My opponent has argued that we should implement a national child care program that would ensure that all parents have access to universal child care for all children up to the age of six. While there are good reasons for a program like this, and my opponent has advanced them, there is one critical and overwhelming objection — the cost. We, as a society, simply do not have the resources to fund this project and, therefore, we can't introduce such a program.

20. Genetic Fallacy

The *genetic fallacy* attempts to show that a claim or idea is false or should be discounted because of its origins. Because the source of the idea is tainted or disreputable, the idea is deemed to be such also. Various kinds of origins can potentially discount an idea — historical, ideological, and psychological (e.g., needs and motivations).

> Example   Astrology is patently false; after all, it originated in the superstitious mumbo-jumbo of ancient Greek religion, something none of us believe now.

In the above argument, astrology is being dismissed because of its origins in "superstition." That an idea may have once been part of folk knowledge or superstition does not prove that there is no evidence for it now. A variant of this fallacy is the attempt to justify a belief or practice because of its origins.

> Example   Astrology is true. It originated with the ancient Babylonians and has existed for centuries.

QUICK QUIZ 7.22   Genetic Fallacy

Which of the following arguments are genetic fallacies? For those that are, explain how the criteria for this fallacy apply in the example. For those that are not, portray the argument and explain why you do not consider it to be a genetic fallacy.

1. Sergei: "As a rule of thumb, you can convert miles to kilometres by multiplying miles by 1.6." Pravar: "Don't you know that you shouldn't say "rule of thumb?" It's a sexist term. It refers to a nineteenth-century English law that says a man can beat his wife as long as he uses a stick no bigger than the diameter of his thumb. By using it, you are condoning wife abuse."

2. Liberalism as a political philosophy and guide for social policy is a nineteenth-century idea. How could it possibly provide guidance in the twenty-first century?

3. We have to rethink liberalism. It was founded in the nineteenth century as a guideline for social reform. However, many of the assumptions on which it was based no longer stand.

For more practice with identifying and critiquing fallacies, do the exercises in Module 7 in the Student Manual.

7.4 NEUTRALIZING FALLACIES

To *neutralize a fallacy* means to identify the fallacy, indicate what is wrong with the argument's reasoning, and explain how the criteria for the fallacy apply to a particular argument.

The following process has been designed to be used when dealing with an audience unfamiliar with fallacies and needing to be shown the full process of reasoning that neutralizes the fallacy. If the audience knows the fallacies, a shortened form of this process will suffice. To illustrate the method, we will use the following passage:

> Since my opponent has not clearly indicated his opposition to the new federal gun-control bill, he must be in favour of it.

Neutralizing a fallacy:

1. **Identify the conclusion or main point in a fallacy.** Identify the conclusion and relate it to the overall structure of the argument. If the fallacy occurs in the main argument of a complex argument, identify the main conclusion. If it occurs in a sub-argument, identify the argument in which the fallacy occurs and how the fallacy relates to the main point or conclusion of the overall passage. If the fallacy is in the context or the process of reasoning (e.g., a straw person fallacy), identify that.

> Conclusion: My opponent must be in favour of the new federal gun-control legislation.

2. **Identify the reason being given for that main point.**

> Reason: He has not indicated he is opposed to it.

The argument, thus, is:

> A.   [If people do not indicate they are opposed to something, they are in favour of it.]
>
> 1.   My opponent has not indicated he is opposed to the new federal gun-control legislation.
>
> _____
>
> ∴   2.   He must be in favour of it.

Although supplying the missing premises can sometimes be helpful in identifying the fallacy, it is not always necessary.

For fallacies that depend on the context, such as straw person, in which a challenger distorts the position and then attacks the distorted position, we need to *identify the argument move being made*. With a straw person fallacy, for example, we would identify the position being attacked and the original position.

3. **Name the fallacy.** Give the name of the fallacy if it is one that you know.

> Name of fallacy: Appeal to ignorance.

4. **Identify the criteria for the fallacy.** Identify the criteria for the fallacy explicitly.

> Criteria for   The appeal to ignorance occurs when a disputant uses the
> the fallacy: opponent's inability or failure to disprove something as the
>   sole reason for his or her own position.

5. **Show how the criteria for the fallacy fit this particular argument.** Demonstrate for the audience how the criteria for the fallacy relate to the features of the argument.

> How the argument   In this argument, the arguer is asserting that
> fits the fallacy criteria: because the opponent has not said anything
>   against the new federal gun legislation, he or she
>   must be in favour of it.

6. **Challenge the fallacy.** Show what is wrong with the argument. Some fallacies commit a variety of errors in reasoning. At this stage, we use the criteria in #4 and the application in #5 to explain why this particular argument should not be accepted because of the fallacy.

> Challenge: Not saying anything about the legislation may mean that the
>   person has no opinion or is still considering the relevant argu-
>   ments. The person may even be opposed but simply has not
>   made his or her stand public.

QUICK QUIZ 7.23   Neutralizing a Fallacy

In each of the following, use the six-step method for neutralizing a fallacy.

1. A number of peace activists are challenging the war on terrorism. People who challenge the government in a time of war are not true Canadians. We shouldn't listen to them.
2. The government is hiding the remains of several UFO crashes, including alien bodies, in "Area 51," a top-secret section of an air-force base in the Southwest. While the government has denied this claim, it has never proven that it is false. So I am inclined to believe that it is true.
3. Look, if you allow euthanasia of people even in irreversible comas, the next thing you know, they will be euthanizing anyone in a coma. Then it will be people with terminal illnesses, and, before long, they will be wanting to kill anyone who has become an inconvenience.

Putting It All Together: Presenting the Critique as Prose

We might present our critique in an essay, translating the step procedure into fluid prose, as in the following:

> In this argument, the author is trying to show that because his opponent
> has not indicated his opposition to the new federal gun-control legislation,
> he must be in favour of it. This is an appeal to ignorance, which occurs
> when one party uses the other's failure to disprove something as evidence of
> its truth. In this case, the author is claiming that his opponent is in favour of
> the federal gun-control legislation because he has not opposed it (i.e.,
> because he has failed to disprove his opposition). In fact, he may have said
> nothing about the legislation. If he has said nothing about the legislation,
> then using this form of reasoning, we could conclude that he must be both
> in favour of it and opposed to it.

In some situations, we will need to lay out all six steps for the fallacy and lead the audience through the reasoning process. In others, simply providing the "Putting It All Together" summary is sufficient for showing an audience what is wrong with the argument. Most important in critiquing a fallacy is identifying it and demonstrating what is wrong with the pattern of reasoning *as a pattern of reasoning in that particular argument.*

QUICK QUIZ 7.24   Putting It All Together

For each of the three questions in Quick Quiz 7.23, write a prose paragraph that puts the critique together.

7.5 LOOK-ALIKES

Look-alikes are fallacies that look similar to and/or are often confused with one another. Frequent confusion occurs because some of the criteria for fallacies are similar and require further differentiation. Of the various fallacies that can be confused, the following are two examples:

Cluster 1

    Hasty generalization

    False cause

    Slippery slope

These fallacies are similar in various ways. False cause and slippery slope are both causal fallacies. In the case of false cause, because two claims are associated, we infer that one causes the other even when no causal connection has been clearly established. Slippery slope, also a form of causal argument, says that if a person does a, then another event, z, will inevitably follow. That is, doing a causes z. Whereas false cause establishes a causal relationship between two things based on their appearance, slippery slope claims that a cause exists when none has been established. Further, in slippery slope, an arguer is not just invoking a cause but invoking a causal sequence: a causes something, which causes something else, which causes z. A third difference between the two is that with slippery slope, the causal outcome is an undesirable one: Taking the first drink causes one to become an alcoholic. The slippery slope is used in an argument to get another person to reject the initial step — the a: Don't take that first drink. A false cause does not have these conditions.

    Hasty generalization is more commonly confused with false cause than with slippery slope. A hasty generalization draws a general conclusion from an unrepresentative or insufficient sample. On the basis of one corrupt politician, I conclude that all are corrupt. This is often confused with false cause because some people are unclear on the difference between generalizing and attributing cause. To further confuse things, passages can commit both the fallacy of hasty generalization and the fallacy of false cause.

Paradigm Cases

Hasty generalization:	You have been late for work twice now. You are always late.
False cause:	I went to the show the night before my exam and failed my driver's test the next day. Going to the show caused me to fail the driver's test.
Slippery slope:	If you take one drink, you will become an alcoholic. Therefore, you shouldn't take the first drink.

QUICK QUIZ 7.25   Hasty Generalization, False Cause, Slippery Slope

Identify and explain which fallacy is committed in each of the following. Explain how each might be confused with one of its look-alikes.

1. *Said in a campaign for mayor:* "My opponent is opposed to increasing the number of police officers, yet there have been an increased number of crimes, especially crimes involving guns, this year in the city. If we don't put more police on the street, then the streets will degenerate into disorder and chaos with the thugs running everything. We don't want the criminals and thugs running this city. We have to put more police on the street."

2. We have proof that marijuana causes violent behaviour. In a murder trial in Alabama, the prosecution established that the defendant, previously a model young man, had been smoking marijuana. He became inflamed — nay, possessed — by overwhelming lust and slew a rival for his girlfriend's affections. This is not the only case like this. In New York, several young children were smoking marijuana. They went on a rampage, smashing everything in their apartment. In San Francisco, an arsonist torched several buildings — this, after he became a regular marijuana user.

3. *A newspaper report of a scientific research study:* Psychologists have discovered that most male scientists make their major discoveries in their late twenties and thirties, which is also the period when their sexual interest is at its peak. Therefore, the psychologists concluded, male scientists strive to achieve to attract the attention of women. Scientific inquiry is driven by sexual desire.

Cluster 2

Ad hominem

Poisoning the well

Genetic fallacy

An *ad hominem* occurs when an arguer attacks the person rather than the person's arguments. A poisoning the well occurs when an arguer attempts to discredit someone or someone's arguments before they have been given. A genetic fallacy occurs when an arguer attempts to discredit a claim by showing that its origins are suspect.

All of these are fallacies of irrelevance — each attempts to discredit a claim or a person based on irrelevant criteria. Rather than examining the claims and arguments, the arguer attacks the person's character, the origins of the idea, or something the idea or person is associated with. What these fallacies have in common is a misguided target. The *ad hominem* is a direct criticism of the opponent and his or her circumstances. The genetic fallacy is a condemnation of either the person's claims or ideas, not because of the content but because of their origins. Poisoning the well is more contextual. While it is an attack on the person and thus similar to an *ad hominem*, its context is different. It tries to discredit not a specific claim or argument but anything the opponent might offer by undermining the opponent before he or she has the opportunity to say anything.

Paradigm Cases

Ad hominem: All I need to do to show that my opponent's arguments are not acceptable is to point out that he is constitutionally incapable of telling the truth.

Poisoning the well: My opponent is not known for his integrity. I don't think we need to consider what he has to say on the issue.

Genetic fallacy: We shouldn't engage in trick-or-treating on Halloween. After all, Halloween started as a pagan holiday.

QUICK QUIZ 7.26   *Ad Hominem,* Poisoning the Well, Genetic Fallacy

Identify and explain which fallacy is committed in each of the following. Explain how each might be confused with one of its look-alikes.

1. Aristotle's comments on women can safely be ignored, for they simply reflect the patriarchal society of the fifth century B.C.E.
2. We should reject the arguments in *The Bell Curve* that blacks have lower IQs than whites and are disproportionately involved in social problems, because the authors are known racists.
3. Pravar: "Martina Lieberman in the biology department claims that gay men are born that way. She claims that the evidence shows that brains of gay men are structurally different from the brains of straight men. So we do have proof that there is a biological basis to being gay." Sergei: "Of course she's going to say that. She's a lesbian, isn't she?"

7.6 WHEN IS A FALLACY NOT A FALLACY?

Once we learn about fallacies, we tend to see them everywhere, including where there are none. Sometimes in looking for fallacies, we identify anything that meets part of the criteria for a fallacy as a fallacy; for example, we confuse name calling with an *ad hominem*, or a general claim with a generalization. In some cases, we confuse other kinds of faulty arguments with fallacies — arguments with faulty premises or invalid arguments.

Avoiding this requires that we hone our understanding of the criteria for the fallacies and pay attention to the context of claims and arguments. The following identifies some of the ways in which we mistakenly cry, "Fallacy!"

Faulty Arguments and Fallacies

Not all faulty arguments are fallacies.

1. If I study hard, I will pass the exam.

2. I studied hard.

   _____

∴ 3. I should have passed the exam but didn't.

This is a faulty argument but not a fallacy. The first premise is false. Studying hard is no guarantee of a pass. A student must also understand the material and be competent in test-taking.

Simply being a poor argument does not make an argument a fallacy. It must have a pattern of poor reasoning that violates one of the constitutive rules of argument. Not all faulty arguments meet that condition. A faulty argument may simply have a false premise.

Ad Hominem, Poisoning the Well

Fallacies are failures of argumentative communication and of reasoning. If I am intending to discredit someone or heap invective on them, and I am not in an argumentative situation, then it is not a fallacy. It may be disrespectful; it may be poor manners; it may even predispose me not to listen to what the person says later in an argument. However, none of these make it a fallacy.

> The prime minister's press secretary says in a private conversation with a colleague that George Bush is a moron. She is overheard by a reporter, and the comment is publicized.

Some might suggest the press secretary's words are a *fallacy of abusive ad hominem* because she utters something discrediting and disrespectful about George Bush. Since fallacies are errors in reasoning and this is not an argument but just name-calling, there is no fallacy here. In this context, even the fact that the press secretary's comment may predispose me not to listen to the U.S. president when he gives an argument does not make it a fallacy. But if I prejudge George Bush and use this comment as a reason for dismissing his arguments, then I would commit the fallacy. Therefore, the following is a fallacy:

> George Bush's taxation policies shouldn't even be considered because George Bush is a moron.

In this case, the arguer dismisses George Bush's taxation policies without presenting an argument against them by attacking George Bush as a person. It is an *ad hominem* fallacy.

Context can make a critical difference in whether an utterance is a fallacy. Calling George Bush a moron in a situation in which his arguments are being considered, even if not directed to a specific argument, might be a form of poisoning the well, since it sets up a predisposition within that context to discredit whatever Bush has to say. If reasons are given, however, the same claim may not be a fallacy:

> Look, we all know that George Bush is a moron. We all know that his taxation policies are simple-minded and should not be accepted. Let me show you what I mean. His policies will increase the differential between the poor and middle class and the wealthy. They benefit only the wealthiest one percent and put the burden on the poorest in society. The policies are based on a discredited theory of trickle-down economics that will only increase the national debt, not diminish it as he thinks. And they are likely to stall economic growth and put us into a recession, if not a depression.

In this context, the claim "George Bush is a moron" is not a fallacy of any sort. The arguer in this passage has provided reasons (whether one accepts them or not) suggesting why Bush's economic policies are unacceptable ("simple-minded"). Although the arguer is trying to discredit Bush's position, he is doing so by presenting arguments (which themselves need to be evaluated and considered) relevant to dismissing Bush's position, indicating that he is taking Bush's arguments seriously and not employing a poisoning the well fallacy.

Fallacies are committed in arguments and in reasoning. Simple name-calling or labelling does not constitute giving an argument and normally does not involve a fallacy. However, there are some borderline cases. Rush Limbaugh, a radio/TV commentator, tends to label and dismiss anyone he dislikes. Feminists have become "feminazis," for example. Since Limbaugh's job is to comment on people's views and since he is, at least implicitly, inviting us to dismiss those views solely on the basis of the labels he uses, his labels do amount to a form of poisoning the well. It is a slightly different kind than the one discussed earlier in this module. Whereas the original form of poisoning the well refers to uttering a specific claim usually directed to a specific issue of a specific opponent, the way Limbaugh commits the fallacy, he establishes a **hostile climate,** in which anything said by the opponent (and in the case of our example, the opponent is a whole class of people — all feminists) is automatically dismissed. He sets up a we–they dichotomy: Everything "we" say and accept is accepted unquestioningly, and everything "they" say is rejected simply because "they" are they. In effect, Limbaugh develops an environment for feminists and their supporters in which their views cannot be considered fairly or objectively. Since his behaviour involves a rejection of their positions and, implicitly, their arguments before they can even be expressed, an argument context exists and, hence, this is a fallacy — specifically, a poisoning the well fallacy.

This differs from the "George Bush is a moron" situation above because there the prime minister's press secretary states an opinion or vents her frustration. However, it does not occur in an argument context and does not obviously involve a wholesale dismissal of anything or everything George Bush says. At least, it is not obvious that it does. By the principle of charity, we ascribe the best interpretation to an utterance. We do not select a possible worst-case scenario and treat that as the norm.

General Claims and Hasty Generalizations

A general claim is simply a claim; a generalization is an argument. A general claim that is false is not a fallacy. A generalization is a result of an inference and can be a fallacy of hasty generalization.

> All politicians are corrupt.
>
> Mark is a politician.
>
> ─────────────────────
>
> ∴   Mark is corrupt.

While the general claim "All politicians are corrupt" in the above argument is false, it is not a fallacy of hasty generalization.

An example of a hasty generalization would be the following:

> I have known three politicians.
>
> They were all corrupt.
>
> ─────────────────────
>
> ∴   All politicians are corrupt.

In this example, the arguer makes a generalization from cases both too few and unrepresentative.

There is also a difference between showing that a generalization is false and showing that it is unsupported. Claiming that a statement is unsupported tells us nothing about the truth of the claim. It simply says that in this context, it has not been sufficiently backed up.

Appeals to Authority

In making an appeal to authority, we should examine all of the criteria for a legitimate appeal to authority, defined in Module 5, Section 5.5. As arguers, we do not always specify that all relevant criteria have been met. We rarely identify and defend something as a legitimate field of inquiry or show that the authority is not in a conflict of interest. Unless that is in question, we simply take it for granted.

Arguer:	Carl Sagan, the noted astronomer, claims that Venus, although hot compared to the earth, is no hotter than one would expect it to be given its closeness to the sun and the greenhouse effect.
Challenger:	You have not shown that Sagan is current in his field nor that astronomy is a field of knowledge. You have committed a faulty appeal to authority.

The arguer has not presented all of the criteria for a proper appeal to authority and shown that they apply to his appeal in this particular case. In an attempt to discredit the argument, the challenger has invoked two of the criteria that have not been demonstrated. Yet in this case, something seems inappropriate about the challenges. The arguer is relying on background knowledge about both Sagan and the field of astronomy. The challenger may be ignorant of that background, in which case he or she simply needs to be informed.

If we challenged all criteria that are not explicitly defended in an appeal to authority, we would rarely end up with a legitimate appeal to authority. We rely on background knowledge and, to some extent, goodwill in practical argumentation. I don't need to defend that astronomy is a field of knowledge unless there are grounds for doubting some aspect of it. Although there may not be consensus (a different criterion) about some claims or theories in astronomy, the field itself does constitute a body of knowledge. For many audiences, it is well known that Carl Sagan is an astronomer. For audiences that do not know of Carl Sagan, it would be wise to establish his credentials.

There is a difference between the blind imposition of the criteria for a fallacy and the reasoned application of them in context. Insisting that the arguer identify and defend all of the criteria for a proper appeal to authority in every case where there is an appeal to authority would more likely hinder the process of argumentation and inquiry than advance it. The rules of argumentation imply that when we challenge something, we should have good reason and the challenge should be central to the process. Although the constitutive rules hold that anything may be challenged, our challenges need to be relevant to the task at hand.

Slippery Slope

The slippery slope fallacy rests on the idea that taking the first step commits a person to a series of further actions that will result in some distant, undesirable consequence. The fallacy occurs when the steps are not obvious and it is not clear how the end result is likely to follow from the initial steps.

On the other hand, in some situations, the steps are obvious and relatively inevitable, or the mechanism is fairly clear. In such cases, a slippery slope has not been committed. The fallacy relies on large, unspecified gaps in the causal connection. An arguer jumps in the causal linkage from cause *a* to effect *m* without filling in the intermediate steps *b*, *c*, *d*, et cetera.

Contrast the following:

> You should never try marijuana, even once. One joint will get you hooked and lead to a life of crime and degeneracy.

> Getting involved in the drug culture often leads to individuals trying harder drugs and then resorting to illegal means to support their habits. People are better advised not to get involved in the first place.

The first argument is clearly a slippery slope. The second looks similar in that it identifies an action and the likely consequences. However, the mechanisms are more obvious, and the consequences not presented as inevitable for everyone. While there may be various ways of challenging the second argument, it is not a slippery slope.

Genetic Fallacy and Provenance

A genetic fallacy occurs when a person dismisses a position or argument based on the origins of the position or argument. In some conditions, an appeal to the origins of a position or story may be relevant in assessing the account.

The term **provenance** literally means origins or source. When used in the art world, it means tracking the piece of art back to the artist who made it and establishing its authenticity. A failed or questionable provenance indicates we cannot establish the connection between the work of art and the purported artist. We can also examine the provenance of a story or position.

The story of Atlantis as a lost continent is widely known. Various authors have written books claiming that Atlantis existed. However, by tracing the provenance of the story, we discover that there is a solitary source of the story — the philosopher Plato. Not only was Plato writing about something that allegedly happened 10,000 years before he lived, he also introduces the story as a myth to make a philosophical point. In this case, identifying the provenance of the story can cast doubt on its truth, and challenging the provenance is not a genetic fallacy.

Another example is the story of flying saucer crashes at Roswell, New Mexico, in 1947. Tracing the story's provenance, we discover that until 1980 there was no story of crashed saucers or recovered alien bodies, and that the story was promulgated by the same individual who manufactured the mystery of the Bermuda Triangle. While this looks like a form of genetic fallacy — we are discrediting a story or argument based on its origins — in this particular case, it is not. The provenance of the story is directly relevant to establishing the truth of the claims of flying saucer crashes at Roswell.

Force/Threat vs. Warning

Not all threats or warnings are fallacies. In the fallacy of appeal to threat or force, an arguer tries to coerce someone through the use of force or a threat of use of force. This may include depriving someone of something he or she has a legitimate right to or abusing a position of power:

> I want your support at the board meeting. Remember, I am doing your performance appraisal.

On the other hand, we often issue legitimate warnings to change someone's behaviour:

> Supervisor to tardy employee: "If you continue to come in late, I will have to report it on your next performance appraisal."

In such circumstances the supervisor is issuing a warning quite within his or her role.

Part of the difficulty in sorting out the difference between an improper appeal to force or threat and a fair warning is in determining whether the appeal is legitimate based on the roles, obligations, and duties of the parties involved. It may also depend on the options available. Whether someone is given a choice and allowed to make a decision (even if the options are not fully open) or forced into a situation where there are no options also helps us distinguish between an appeal to threat or force and the issuance of a legitimate warning about behaviour.

Summary

Not everything that appears to be a fallacy is one. Sometimes what appears to be a fallacy isn't one because a key criterion for that fallacy is not met or the context indicates that a fallacy is not being committed.

In general, a passage is not a fallacy (1) if it is not an argument or not part of an argumentation context; (2) when the context indicates that there is further information that needs to be considered in making a charge of fallacy; or (3) when the criteria for the fallacy are not fully met.

QUICK QUIZ 7.27   Fallacy . . . or Not?

In each of the following, identify whether or not a fallacy is committed. If a fallacy is committed, explain and neutralize the fallacy. If it is not, explain how the argument might be confused with a fallacy.

1. Yan is insensitive to the suffering of animals because he eats meat. And all meat eaters are insensitive to the suffering of animals.
2. Unless we find a way to stop the indiscriminate use of guns by gang members, violence on the streets is likely to increase. And the increase in violence will likely mean that more bystanders will be injured or killed, and we don't want that. We must stop the violence.
3. Professor Harrison is a convicted sex offender. He has been convicted twice of sexual assault. I do not believe he should be allowed to teach in a school where he will come into contact with teens and others who could be at risk of being his targets.
4. Carl Sagan, an astronomer who researched global warming on Venus and has investigated the effects of global warming on the Earth, has claimed that unless we limit automobiles and industry, human life as we know it will be seriously threatened by 2030. Although other experts disagree, we need to consider Sagan's arguments.
5. George Bush lied to the American people and the world when he said that he had proof that Saddam Hussein had weapons of mass destruction. He lied to the American people and the world when he claimed that he had proof that Saddam Hussein was part of the axis of evil that was fueling terrorism. He lied to the American people about his war record in the Vietnam War. He lied about his involvement in various financial scandals. [Take all of this as true for the sake of argument.] Now he is asking us to trust him when he says that U.S. intentions in Iraq are honourable. I say all that we have to do is look at his record.

MODULE SUMMARY

Fallacies are patterns of false appeals and arguments that often are mistaken for good arguments. They violate one or more of the basic principles for good argument, the constitutive rules of argumentation. This module identifies a number of common fallacies. Fallacies can be neutralized by identifying the pattern of reasoning for the argument, showing that the argument meets all of the criteria for a given fallacy, and explaining why that fallacy is a form of bad reasoning. Some fallacies commonly mistaken for one another — look-alikes — can be distinguished by noting what their similarities and differences are and by paying close attention to the criteria for each of the look-alikes. Some arguments that appear to be fallacies may not be fallacies upon closer examination of the arguments, the criteria for the fallacy, and the context in which the arguments appear.

KEY TERMS

abusive, *ad hominem*
appeal to force or the threat of force
appeal to ignorance
appealing to emotion
begging the question (circular argument)
circumstantial, *ad hominem*
fallacy
fallacy of equivocation
fallacy of appeal to popularity, common
    belief, or common practice
fallacy of loaded presupposition
false cause
false dichotomy
faulty analogy

faulty appeal to authority fallacy
genetic fallacy
hasty generalization
hostile climate
look-alikes
neutralize a fallacy
paradigm case
poisoning the well
provenance
red herring fallacy
self-evident truth
shifting the burden of proof
slippery slope fallacy
straw person

MODULE 8

ANALYZING AND ASSESSING EXTENDED ARGUMENTS

8.1 LEARNING OBJECTIVES

After completing this module, you should be able to

1. analyze and portray the logical structure of an extended passage;
2. clarify meaning of key terms and phrases within that passage;
3. assess the specific arguments within the passage for cogency and acceptability;
4. assess the overall acceptability of a passage;
5. develop a critical strategy for critiquing a passage; and
6. present a written critique of your analysis of a passage.

8.2 INTRODUCTION

Many arguments are embedded in extended passages ranging from the length of a paragraph to the length of an entire book. Because instructors often ask students to write critical essays that require the analysis and evaluation of one or more texts and because longer passages often involve multiple arguments and sub-arguments, we need a strategy for analyzing and critiquing them. The skills learned in identifying, structuring, and evaluating arguments in Modules 3 through 7 can be used to analyze such texts. This module integrates the material from those modules, provides an overall strategy for analyzing extended texts, and shows how to turn an extended argument analysis into a critical analysis essay.

8.3 OUTLINE OF THE MODEL

Portraying the Structure

Step 1: Read and Annotate the Passage

a. **Read the passage quickly to get the gist of it.**
b. **Read the passage a second time, actively, annotating and asking questions.** Circle inference indicators and box key concepts and unclear terms. Attend to each sentence. What does it do in the overall context of the passage? See Module 3, Section 3.9 for some functions of sentences in prose. If the article is long, provide in the margin a one-sentence summary that captures the main point of each paragraph. These can help in identifying the overall structure of the passage.
c. **Formulate what you see as the main point of the passage** in one sentence by imagining that you are writing a headline for the piece. Make it a substantive claim — not "The passage is about abortion" but, rather, "Abortion should be allowed under exceptional circumstances." Check your formulation against the passage. Can most of the statements in the passage be seen as supporting that claim or in some way related to that claim? If not, consider an alternate paraphrase unless much of the material is extraneous.

Step 2: Clarify Meaning

d. **Clarify the meaning of key concepts, phrases, and claims.** Use a dictionary, do a conceptual analysis (see Module 9), or look for materials within the passage, such as examples or applications of the concept, that will help you. If there are several possible ways to interpret the concept and the text does not make clear which is intended, provide various paraphrases using the alternative meanings and consider the effects of each on the overall passage and the argument.

Step 3: Portray Argument Structure

e. Using the key concepts, inference indicators, and the thesis sentence, **formulate the main argument in your own words.** If the argument hinges on the precise language used by the author, then use that.

f. Once you have identified the main lines of argument, **develop the sub-arguments.** Work systematically. Start from the main conclusion, the bottom of the *argument tree,* and work upward one line at a time into the sub-arguments and supporting arguments. If you get stuck, try to find a basic reason that supports a given line of argument and work down from there. Paraphrase each line of argument to get the gist of what each says.

Not all claims may fit into your initial analysis. Put aside the claims that do not fit. Once you have identified the main structure, see how the claims contribute to the passage. If they are extraneous material, ignore them.

g. **Give each line of argument a name that captures its main reason.** This helps you both to remember the line and to summarize the reasoning in that line.

h. **Reread the passage and check your reconstruction against the text.** Ensure that the central features of the original are captured in your paraphrase *and* that the paraphrase does not add additional materials *without justification.* If necessary, go back and reformulate and fine tune the reconstruction. Is everything you have given necessary for understanding the argument? Is there anything that is not clear? If so, is it because it is unclear in the passage or because you have not captured some important information?

At this point, you should have an analysis of the argument in the passage. You can now move to assessing the arguments.

Assessing the Arguments

In determining whether an arguer has made his or her case, we need to examine each of the lines of argument. If the arguments are deductive, each line stands on its own. If the arguments are inductive, some of the lines may mutually support one another. Analyze each line and assess how each supports the main conclusion.

Step 4: Assess for Soundness

i. **Supply missing premises and hidden assumptions.**

j. **Assess the specific arguments for soundness.** Start the assessment with the main sub-arguments, the ones that directly support the main conclusion. If those are good arguments, then move to the sub-arguments. Examine each of the lines of argument independently. Each line or sub-line that supports a conclusion needs to be examined. If there is a major problem at any level, then you do not need to examine the higher sub-arguments in that line of argument. Review Modules 4 through 6 for the specific tools for argument assessment.

Step 5: Give an Overall Assessment

k. **Assess the overall passage.** Once you have an analysis of the individual arguments, provide an overall assessment of the case the arguer has made in the passage. Minimally, this
is a summary of the acceptability of each main line of argument and whether or not the
arguer has made a good case for his or her conclusion. It may also include suggestions on
how the argument could be improved, additional arguments that might help in developing
the case, and any important insights that have emerged from the analysis.

l. **Present your assessment.**

The remainder of this module applies this model for analysis to the passage in the next
section. The passage is reprinted in the Student Manual so that you can annotate and analyze it before reading the material in each section. Another passage is provided as the basis
for the Quick Quizzes. You can find additional passages for analysis practice in the Student
Manual.

8.4 PASSAGE FOR ANALYSIS

The following passage will be used to illustrate the techniques in this module. This passage is
reprinted in the Student Manual for you to analyze on your own before proceeding with each
step in this module. The Quick Quiz provides an additional passage for you to analyze in conjunction with each of the steps outlined in this module.

Gay Marriage Is Bad for Everyone

1. Although the Canadian government has legalized gay marriage, we believe that this is a
mistake and should be rescinded. The legalization of gay marriage will harm the entire population. Sanctioning such unions will be harmful on three grounds: It will undermine the concept
of marriage as a permanent commitment; it will harm the children of gay marriages; and it will
harm society by changing its view of marriage as an institution for procreation.

2. Allowing gay marriage will undermine the very notion of marriage. Since the time of the
Old Testament, marriage has meant the lifelong union of one man and one woman making a
commitment to create a family. That is what it means today. Changing the definition of marriage to include homosexuals will fundamentally change the nature of the commitment. Most
people recognize that homosexuals are far more promiscuous than heterosexuals. They will
bring this into their unions, and this will affect heterosexual marriages by weakening the commitment that partners are expected to have to one another. Moreover, if we allow the term *marriage* to apply to homosexual unions, then there is nothing to prevent it applying to unions of
more than two people.

3. Allowing homosexual unions will be unhealthy for the children in gay families. Some lesbian couples will have children through anonymous sperm donations, and this will deprive the
children of knowing one of their biological parents. More significantly, the homosexual lifestyle
is one that is characterized by high rates of drug use, depression, suicide, promiscuity, and sexually transmitted diseases. Children will be exposed to these situations, affecting their sense of
self and increasing the likelihood of their becoming homosexual, drug dependent, depressed,
and sexually promiscuous.

4. Finally, allowing gay marriage sends the message that marriage is about intimacy, not the
development of family. In all western societies, the government supports the family as the basis of

perpetuating society by treating marriage as the legitimate means for raising children. Redefining marriage as a union of intimacy rather than one for the purpose of procreating and raising children will undermine the stability of marriage and the commitment to propagating future generations, and will thereby undermine the stability of society as a whole.

8.5 STEP 1: READ AND ANNOTATE THE PASSAGE

The first time you read through the passage, skim it, looking for the main points and the main conclusion — the overall meaning of the passage. Read actively by asking questions of the text, thinking about it, and summarizing it. What is the passage about? What is the author trying to accomplish? You will often read the text differently on subsequent readings than on the first.

First read:

- Read with a pen or pencil (not a highlighter) and annotate the text as you go. Use the margins of the text to make notes about the argument. Using a pen or pencil forces you to summarize and integrate the ideas and look for the relations.
- Start by skimming the text, noting titles and headings.
- Look at the introduction and conclusion for cues to the main line of argument.
- Look for the *topic sentence* (the sentence containing the main point) in each paragraph. How does each relate to the overall topic?
- Make a list of questions about the argument in the text that you wish to explore on further readings.
- Look for and circle *signposts* to the passage. These are both logical cue words and other indicators that authors use to identify the structure of the text. "Three considerations for this proposal are . . .," "It might be argued that . . .," "For example . . ."
- Look for key concepts that are central to understanding the passage. Draw a box around these.
- For longer texts, make summaries periodically of each section of the argument. It is often helpful to do this paragraph by paragraph. After the first read, summarize the main conclusion and the main arguments of the entire text.
- For a short text, read through it and then try to formulate and record a brief summary of the main point and argument.
- Treat your summary as a hypothesis for further reading and then try to disconfirm that hypothesis when you read more closely. You may discover that you will need to revise your hypothesis about the text.

On your second and further readings, study the passage more carefully, testing your initial hypothesis. Is there anything in the passage that will disconfirm your hypothesis about what the main arguments are? What questions do you have of the text that you hope to answer with a closer read?

Before continuing, do your **active reading** *of "Gay Marriage Is Bad for Everyone" in the Student Manual.*

In the passage "Gay Marriage Is Bad for Everyone," the authors indicate their main position — that the legalization of gay marriage should be rescinded — in the title and in the first sentence. (Because I was unsure of the term *rescinded*, I looked it up: It means "repealed.") They identify three lines of argument in the opening paragraph: that it will undermine marriage as a commitment; that it is harmful for children; and that it will change what society has always known to be the purpose of marriage. Each of the remaining three paragraphs (2, 3, and 4) develops one of those lines of argument.

The following key concepts in the passage need to be clarified: "marriage," "the homosexual lifestyle," "stability of marriage," and "stability of society." The following claim also needs to be clarified: "the government supports the family as the basis of perpetuating society."

Based on a *first* reading of the passage, I have the following questions:

1. Is the author arguing that changing the meaning of the concept will change the nature of the institution?
2. Is the author arguing that homosexuals will encourage their children to be homosexual?
3. How will allowing allegedly promiscuous people to marry undermine marriage?

QUICK QUIZ 8.1   Read the Passage

The following passage will be the basis for the Quick Quizzes in this chapter. It is reprinted in the Student Manual so that you can do the analysis there. Read the passage, and then answer the questions below.

1. Write a brief summary of the main point after the first reading (don't reread yet).
2. What is your hypothesis about the main point (conclusion) of the passage?
3. What questions do you have about the argument of the text?

An Idea Whose Time Has Come

The government has no choice but to legalize the possession and sale of marijuana. First, individuals have a right to engage in whatever activities they choose as long as they don't harm others. This is a basic assumption of our society. We allow people to ingest alcohol and nicotine, to eat unhealthy foods, and to engage in risky behaviour such as hang-gliding and scuba diving. The use of marijuana puts no one but users at risk. Therefore, we should allow people to use marijuana.

Second, no one has conclusively established it is harmful.

Third, legalizing it will make money for the government through taxes and will curtail various evils, such as the proliferation of grow-ops and the use of illegal marijuana profits to fund other criminal activities.

It might be argued that using marijuana can harm others. For example, it might be claimed that people will use marijuana and then drive. However, drunk drivers kill people, yet we don't ban alcohol. Rather, we try to prevent people from driving while impaired.

Answers for all Quick Quizzes in this text are provided in the Student Manual. After doing the Quick Quizzes, consult the Student Manual to check your understanding of the material.

Annotate the Passage

Read the passage actively. Identify the relevant statements and note any inference indicators.

1. Circle all inference indicators.
2. Bracket and number all statements in the text. (You can delete irrelevant ones later.) A single sentence may contain several statements. The sentence "Although the government is committed to improving health care, it is not willing to fund this initiative at this time" contains the separate statements "the government is committed to improving health care" and "the government is not willing to fund this initiative at this time."

3. Rewrite any fragments and referential indicators (*this, it*) into complete statements. Rewrite any rhetorical questions and other grammatically problematic sentences into statements.
4. Identify buried claims and write them as explicit claims. A **buried** or **implicit claim** is one that is contained within another assertion: "The unfeasible idea that the government can fund all medical care and not go bankrupt should be dismissed." The author appears to be making one claim. However, he or she is actually making two claims — the claim that "the idea that the government can fund all medical care and not go bankrupt should be dismissed" and the claim that "this idea is unfeasible."
5. Supply any obvious cue words.
6. Use square brackets to identify anything you have supplied or changed — for example, cue words added, claims rewritten, missing premises identified.

In the following, square brackets [ ] are used to identify claims, curly brackets { } to indicate supplied or changed text, and arrow brackets < > to indicate terms that need to be clarified.
Before continuing, annotate "Gay Marriage Is Bad for Everyone" in the Student Manual.

Gay Marriage Is Bad for Everyone

1
Although [the Canadian government has legalized gay marriage], [we

2   3
believe that this is a mistake] and [{the legalization of gay marriage} should

4
be rescinded]. [The legalization of gay marriage will harm the entire population.]

5   6
[Sanctioning such unions will be harmful on three grounds]: [It will undermine

7
the concept of marriage as a permanent commitment;] [it will harm the children

8
of gay marriages;] and [it will harm society by changing its view of marriage as an

institution for procreation.]

9
[Allowing gay marriage will undermine <the very notion of marriage>.]

10
[Since the time of the Old Testament, marriage has meant the lifelong union of one

11
man and one woman making a commitment to create a family.] [That is what it

12
<means> today.] [Changing the definition of marriage to include homosexuals will

fundamentally change the nature of the commitment.] [Most people recognize that

13

homosexuals are far more promiscuous than heterosexuals.] [They will bring this

14

15

into their unions,] and [this will affect heterosexual marriages] [{this will affect

16

heterosexual marriages} by weakening the commitment that partners are expected

17

to have to one another.] Moreover, [if we allow the term *marriage* to apply to

homosexual unions, then there is nothing to prevent it applying to unions of more

than two people.]

18

[Allowing homosexual unions will be unhealthy for the children in gay

19

families.] [Some lesbian couples will have children through anonymous sperm

20

donations], [{having children through anonymous sperm donation} will deprive

the children of knowing one of their biological parents.] More significantly, [<the

21

homosexual lifestyle> is one that is characterized by high rates of drug use,

depression, suicide, promiscuity, and sexually transmitted diseases.] [Children will

22

be exposed to these situations,] thereby [{being exposed to these situations will

23

affect} their sense of self] and [{being exposed to these situations will increase} the

24

likelihood of their becoming homosexual, drug dependent, depressed, and sexually

promiscuous.]

25

(Finally), [allowing gay marriage sends the message that marriage is about

intimacy, not the development of family.] [In all western societies, <the government

26

supports the family as the basis of perpetuating society>] by [{the government

27

treats} marriage as the legitimate means for raising children.] [Redefining marriage

28

as a union of intimacy rather than one for the purpose of procreating and raising

children will undermine <the stability of marriage>] and [{redefining marriage as a

29

union of intimacy rather than one for the purpose of procreating and raising

children will undermine} the <commitment to propagating future generations>,]

and [{redefining marriage as a union of intimacy rather than one for the purpose of

30

procreating and raising children} will thereby undermine the <stability of society as

a whole>.]

QUICK QUIZ 8.2   Annotate the Passage

Annotate the marijuana passage:

 1. Circle all inference indicators.
 2. Number and bracket all claims.
 3. Rewrite any fragments, referential indicators, and rhetorical questions.

8.6 STEP 2: CLARIFY MEANING

Identify key terms, phrases, and sentences in the marijuana passage and highlight them for easy reference. Box terms and phrases that need clarifying. Put a question mark in the margin next to the line on which the term, phrase, or sentence needing clarification occurs.

Method of clarification:

 1. Read the whole passage before trying to clarify anything.
 2. Look up and, if necessary, replace unknown or unfamiliar terms by using a dictionary. Make sure that the dictionary definition you choose fits the meaning of the term in context. See Modules 2 and 9 for more on determining meaning in context.
 3. Rewrite any unclear parts, using clearer language where the meaning of the text allows. Demand a reasonable level of clarity from the passage. Some authors simply do not express their ideas clearly. Your goal is to make the claims in the passage as clear as possible without reading meaning into the passage. If the passage's lack of clarity affects the argument, say so and show how.

In particular, identify vague or ambiguous terms that you suspect the argument of exploiting — e.g., by shifting from one meaning to another. Translate each clause or sentence containing these terms into other language that conveys the correct meaning (or possible or probable meaning) of the term in each context.

4. Write out any important unstated but clearly intended implications or suggestions of the premises, conclusions, and argument as a whole. (What is the passage trying to get across that isn't actually spelled out?)

Be careful not to confuse your assumptions about the argument or the issue with what the author is claiming. Ask yourself if you really understand how everything fits together; if you have a "feeling" for the argument or passage as a whole (even if you don't accept the claims made in it). Don't let any hostility you have for the position expressed mislead you into misrepresenting the argument (e.g., by making it sound more stupid than {you think} it already is).

5. Look over the results of 1 through 4 and criticize the passage for clarity and precision where appropriate. Most of this is laying the ground for later analysis, at which time we may modify some of the results of this stage.

Not every vague, imprecise, unclear, or ambiguous term or phrase in a passage is necessarily central to the argument. One common error is to criticize as unclear a term or phrase that is inconsequential. Don't waste time criticizing what is not central to the argument.

Before continuing, clarify meaning in "Gay Marriage Is Bad for Everyone" in the Student Manual.

In the gay marriage passage, the following concepts need clarification:

- marriage
- the homosexual lifestyle
- stability of marriage
- stability of society
- the government supports the family as the basis of perpetuating society

Although the argument appears to be framed as an issue about the meaning of a term, the reasons suggest that the real issue is the nature of the institution of marriage. The authors mention "the very notion of marriage" and "changing the definition of marriage" in paragraph 2. Yet most of their argument involves not the word but the institution itself and practices relating to the referent of the term. What the writers see as the core features of marriage — reproduction, lifelong commitment to procreate and raise children, and monogamy — are their central concerns.

Based on the text, the authors characterize "the homosexual lifestyle" as one involving promiscuity, drug use, suicide, and depression, and appear to assume that everyone with a gay orientation lives like this.

By "stability of marriage" the authors appear to mean that the institution and practices associated with heterosexual marriage in contemporary society do not (and should not) change. However, they seem to have a normative and fairly narrow idea of contemporary heterosexual marriage, depicting it as monogamous, lifelong, and solely for the purpose of procreation. Many heterosexual marriages do not meet some or all of these conditions.

The claim that "the government supports the family as the basis of perpetuating society" might mean several things. It could mean that the government sanctions marriage by making marriages legal and recognizing only legal marriages. We could expand this with the following: "It is only through legally protecting marriage that we can ensure the survival of society." But this does not address the idea of "perpetuating society." The basic idea the authors seem to be getting at, both through this claim and the rest of the passage, is that the stability of marriage is necessary for the stability of society. We might paraphrase this as follows. In order to perpetuate society, we need to ensure that the traditional idea of marriage is protected. And the only (or best) way of doing this is by having the government protect it.

QUICK QUIZ 8.3   Clarify Meaning

1. Examine the text for clarity and precision of meaning. Are there concepts whose meaning is unclear? Does a dictionary help in the clarification of the meaning? If not, can you paraphrase to clarify the meaning or come up with alternative possible meanings?
2. Are there any hidden implications in the premises?

8.7 STEP 3: PORTRAY ARGUMENT STRUCTURE

We need to work systematically to portray the structure of a passage. The central problem most students have in critiquing a longer passage is in not working through the passage systematically. Instead they select bits and pieces for critique and ignore how these fit together into a whole.

As you go through the text, look for both explicit and implicit connections between the claims.

1. **Identify the main conclusion.** Find, formulate, or paraphrase a sentence that as clearly as possible states what you take to be the argument's main conclusion.
   a. Use cue words, position, and meaning to help you identify conclusions and distinguish them from premises.
   b. Sometimes the main conclusion will be stated in several different ways in the passage. Usually you will have to piece together parts of sentences or paraphrase to get the most appropriate, and precise meaning, for the argument. Focus on the central meaning of the claim, not the specific expressions.
2. **Identify the main lines of argument,** noting the reasons and conclusions in each.
   Before portraying the structure of the argument, writing a synopsis of it can help you clarify exactly what is being argued. A *synopsis* is a brief characterization of the conclusion and the main line(s) of development of the argument written in your own words. Once you have identified the main conclusion and the basic reasons, you can then try to fit in the other reasons that contribute to the argument.
   In writing the synopsis, you may find that the rhetorical organization of the text is not a reliable guide to the logical structure of the argument. Repetition, extraneous material, irrelevant background information, digressions, and sloppy writing may obscure the logical structure. Note these, but do not include them in your standardization of the argument. They may be included in a critique of the argument; however, they should not appear in the synopsis. Stylistic and rhetorical features are not relative to the logic of the argument.
3. **Develop the structure of the argument.** Once you identify the conclusions, ask yourself, "What reasons in the text support these conclusions?" Search the passage for premises for each claim that acts as a conclusion. Ignore anything that does not contribute to the logical structure of the argument: examples, repetitions of claims, rhetorical flourishes. Sometimes the argument of a long passage may be quite simple.

Using inference indicators and other cues, mechanically structure as much of the passage as you can. As you go through it, note reasons and conclusions, and then diagram them. Once you have done that, consider the content of the claims to determine if any further logical connections can be identified.

Once you have identified the preliminary structure of the argument, test your analysis against the passage, reading it claim by claim to determine whether you have left out anything crucial.

In some cases, we may have choices to make in the construction of the argument diagram. Generally we try to construct a diagram that reflects the logical structure and relations in the text, portrays the strongest argument of the alternative possibilities, and incorporates as many of the contributing statements and sub-arguments as possible. Sometimes it is not possible to succeed in all of these. A simpler formulation may omit substantial parts of the passage but still capture the core argument structure.

The structure of the argument may still be ambiguous or indeterminate after diagramming. To the extent that the intended inferences are unclear in the original text, the responsibility lies with the author and not with you.

One strategy when confronted with an unclear passage is to indicate that the passage is ambiguous and show why it is. Addressing this ambiguity may involve (a) selecting one interpretation of the passage and using that in your analysis, or (b) articulating the alternative possibilities and showing how each possibility fits into the larger argument. In choosing (a), select the strongest version of the argument, and give reasons for your selection — for example, demonstrate that it generates a better argument or that it is more consistent with other things that the author says either within the passage being analyzed or in other texts. In choosing (b), if in the course of identifying alternate possibilities for interpretation, one creates a better argument, you can argue for that one being the best interpretation whether intended by the author or not.

4. **Formulate the missing premises** of the argument. All that can legitimately be supplied to an argument as a missing premise are those claims that are being assumed by the argument and are necessary to make the argument work (i.e., to establish relevance and sufficiency, or validity). We can supply one of three types of possible missing premises:

   a. **The arguer's assumptions:** What the author consciously assumed or would accept as an assumption if asked — statements that are faithful to the author's beliefs and intentions, insofar as these are known. Often this requires background knowledge about the author and other texts the author has written.

   b. **The minimal assumptions:** What is, logically speaking, necessary to establish criteria of relevance and sufficiency between the premises and the conclusion.

   c. **The optimal assumptions:** Claims that are both logically adequate and independently well supported — these are usually stronger than minimal assumptions and sometimes stronger than the author might accept. These assumptions help in constructing the best argument possible given the materials you have to work with.

The basic rationale behind supplying missing premises is to establish clearly the logical structure of the argument by filling in the assumptions the arguer is making. The types of missing premises above, in some cases, may conflict. If, for example, the arguer has made a basic blunder in his or her argument or presentation of it, adhering to the first option, the arguer's assumption, may yield an invalid argument. Adhering to options b or c may yield a good argument but one that is inconsistent with the author's statements or intentions. Which approach you adopt in such an instance will depend on your purposes in analyzing the text. If you are trying to determine what the arguer meant, the reconstruction of the argument should be as faithful to the author's beliefs and intentions as it can be. But if you are trying to determine how good a particular line of reasoning is, regardless of who authored it or what he or she had in mind, then the minimal and optimal assumptions are more important than fidelity to a particular author's intentions or text.

When analyzing an argument, always be careful to indicate where you have supplied missing premises (or rewritten premises) and why you have supplied them. (Just saying "because it was needed" is not enough. You need to be specific, explaining why what you have supplied is required by this particular argument.)

Test your argument analysis by comparing it to the text. Is there anything in the text that is not reflected in the argument diagram? Is your analysis true to the argument in the text?

Before continuing, portray the structure of the arguments in "Gay Marriage Is Bad for Everyone" in the Student Manual.

An Argument Paraphrase of the Passage

We can portray the structure of the arguments in the passage by using either a literal reading or a paraphrase. In a literal reading, we reconstruct the arguments in such a way as to keep them as close as possible to the original text, using the original claims and paraphrasing only where necessary. Although this method produces a detailed analysis of the passage, it may overanalyze it and actually hide its core structure. A literal reading is useful in a closely written, well-argued passage such as can be found in some philosophy texts. A paraphrase reconstruction is more useful for texts that contain a good deal of extraneous and redundant material.

In a paraphrase reconstruction, we identify the main lines of the argument and then use a combination of paraphrase and original claims to portray its structure. This method is usually better for outlining the core structure of the passage. The following is an argument paraphrase:

The main conclusion is that we should not legalize gay marriage. The passage has three main lines of argument — the meaning of marriage, the harm to children and the harm to society lines — with several sub-lines. The following arrow diagram displays the main structure of the argument, using short-form names for each of the lines and sub-lines.

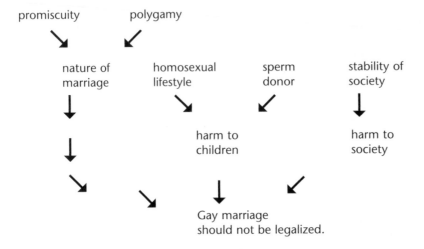

These will be fleshed out into full arguments with missing premises and assessed in the next section.

8.8 STEP 4: ASSESS THE SOUNDNESS OF THE ARGUMENTS

Assessing the argument follows the basic principles we have already encountered, with some additions. First, we assess the logical adequacy of each argument; then we assess the truth of the claims. Each line of argument must be assessed.

If we have diagrammed the argument with the conclusion at the bottom and the various independent arguments stemming from the conclusion, the argument structure will look like a tree. The main conclusion is its trunk, and the main arguments and sub-arguments, its branches. To assess a multiline argument, we start at the bottom of the *argument tree* and work up. Each main argument with its sub-arguments is called a **line of argument** or an **argument branch.**

If the argument fails in a fundamental way at the bottom of the tree, then we do not have to go higher in the tree unless we are interested in exploring the kinds of reasons that have been developed for this argument.

As you progress, evaluate each argument in the argument tree for soundness. Then assess the claims, including presuppositions and corollaries, for adequacy. In most cases, adequate evaluation of the truth of the premises requires some knowledge of the subject matter. There is no single set of rules or criteria, no test or procedure, for deciding the truth or even the plausibility of premises. However, the following guidelines can help in this task:

1. Read each premise critically. Think about what it is claiming. Even if you think you agree with it, would the intended audience?
2. Examine and evaluate the evidence for key claims. Where the claims are questionable, have evidence or sub-arguments been provided? Examine those. Consider the different kinds of claims — empirical, conceptual, normative — and the kinds of challenges that can be raised for each of those. Look for disconfirmations rather than confirmations.
3. If there are general claims in the premises, can they be challenged by counterexamples? Would limiting them in scope make them more defensible?
4. Check for problematic presuppositions or corollaries.
5. When offering a challenge or counterexample, consider possible responses the defender of the argument could give. Is it possible to limit the scope or qualify the claim to give the arguer a better argument?

Before continuing, assess the adequacy of arguments in "Gay Marriage Is Bad for Everyone" in the Student Manual.

In the following analysis, we have used the numbers from the annotation on pages 158–60. Where the original claim is used, the number appears before the claim; where the claim has been paraphrased, it appears after the claim. Letters are used to indicate paraphrased claims or supplied missing premises.

Argument 1: The Meaning of Marriage

This main line of argument can be formulated as follows:

    A.   If we change the meaning of marriage by legalizing gay marriage, we will undermine marriage. (9)   If a then b

    B.   [We should not undermine marriage.]   not b

∴ C.   Gay marriages should not be legalized. (3)   not a

This denies the consequent and is valid.

This argument rests on the ambiguous "meaning of marriage." The authors seem to assume that changing the linguistic definition will change the institution. Constructing the argument around this idea, though, will produce a fairly weak argument. Changing the definition alters who may get married, but that does not mean that it changes the fundamentals of the institution. I will treat the claim as meaning that changing the institution undermines the institution. How this would happen is detailed in the sub-arguments that support A — the nature-of-marriage argument, the promiscuity argument, and the polygamy argument.

B is a missing premise, supplied to make the argument valid.

Three sub-arguments support A:

    1.   The nature-of-marriage sub-argument can be formulated as follows:

    E.   The definition of marriage is one man and one woman making a lifelong commitment to create a family. (10 + 11)

    12.   If we change the institution of marriage to include same-sex partners, then we will undermine the commitment between marital partners.   If a, then b

    D.   If we undermine the commitment between marital partners, we will undermine marriage.   If b, then c

---

∴ A.   If we change the institution of marriage by legalizing gay marriage, we will undermine marriage. (9)   If a, then c

This is a conditional chain argument and is valid.

Support for E is given by the following claims:

    10.   Marriage has traditionally been defined as the lifelong union of one man and one woman to create a family.

    11.   The meaning of marriage in contemporary society is the lifelong union of one man and one woman.

Neither guarantees E. Both rest on a form of the common practice fallacy: This is the way marriage has traditionally been defined or is currently defined; therefore, it should continue to be defined in this way. Claim E is a stipulative definition that restricts marriage to lifelong commitment for the purpose of procreation. It means that marriages of convenience or marriages in which individuals do not intend to procreate are not "true" marriages. The definition does not reflect the fact that many contemporary marriages do not fit this definition.

Claim 12 is supported by the promiscuity-of-homosexuals sub-line:

13. Homosexuals are more promiscuous than heterosexuals.

14. They will bring this into their marital unions.

15. This promiscuity undermines the commitment partners have to each other.

16. This promiscuity will undermine heterosexual marriage.

F. [Promiscuity undermines marriage.]

∴   12. If we change the meaning of marriage to include gay marriage, then we will undermine the commitment between marital partners.   If b, then c

The premises of this inductive argument only weakly support the conclusion, and several are false. The argument rests on the assumption that because some members of a group have a characteristic (promiscuity), allowing them to marry will extend that characteristic to all married people. That this is false can be seen by the parallel arguments. At one point in time, blacks and whites were forbidden to marry. Most black people were poor. Allowing them to marry white people did not thereby make all married white people poor. The author's assumption is a form of slippery slope here: that allowing individuals with one characteristic to be married will spread that characteristic to all or most persons who are married. Even if it were true that some homosexuals remain promiscuous after marrying — a highly contentious claim — the argument presupposes that heterosexual couples will imitate these alleged sex patterns. This seems highly unlikely.

The argument also rests on a number of false claims. It is not obvious that all or most homosexuals are more promiscuous than all or most heterosexuals. Like heterosexuals, some homosexuals are celibate; some are involved in or searching for committed relationships; and some are promiscuous. Someone who is promiscuous when dating will not necessarily be so once he or she has formed a relationship. The argument is based on the false presupposition that people cannot or do not change when they enter into permanent relationships. Additionally, within existing heterosexual marriages, some couples — swingers — engage in consensual extramarital sex. That such couples exist, are married, and have not "corrupted" those who choose to remain monogamous present a problem for this argument. If swingers have not caused others to become promiscuous and thereby undermined marriage, then it is not apparent why homosexuals would.

The polygamy sub-line supports claim A.

17.   If we allow same-sex marriage, then nothing will prevent polygamy. [If a, then b]

G.   [If we allow polygamy, we will undermine the institution of marriage.] [If b, then c]

∴   A.   If we change the meaning of marriage by legalizing same-sex unions, we will undermine marriage. (9)   If a, then c

This is a valid conditional chain argument.

Although valid, this argument, is not cogent. Claim 17 is a slippery slope fallacy. There are many things that can be done to prevent legalizing polygamy. Extending marriage to include same-sex couples does not mean we extend it to include all possible combinations of people. Premise G is also false. Some religions recognize polygamy and that has not undermined the institution of marriage. The claim would be true only if "undermine the institution of marriage" means "undermine monogamous marriage." But that would beg the question, and the argument would rest on yet another fallacy.

Overall, this line of argument is not sound. A is not supported by its sub-arguments and is false. The arguments given do not support the claim that allowing same-sex couples to marry will undermine the institution of marriage.

Argument 2: The Unhealthy for Children Line

This main line of argument can be formulated as follows:

7.   If we legalize gay marriage, we will harm children.   If a, then b

H.   [We should not do anything that will harm children.]   not b

---

∴   C.   Gay marriages should not be legalized. (3)   not a

This denies the consequent and is valid.

Claim 7 is supported by two sub-arguments: the homosexual-lifestyle and the sperm-donor arguments.

The homosexual-lifestyle sub-argument can be formulated as follows:

22.   If we legalize gay marriage, children will be exposed to the homosexual lifestyle.   If a, then b

24.   If exposed to the homosexual lifestyle, they will become homosexual, drug dependent, depressed, and sexually promiscuous.   If b, then c

J.   If children become homosexual, drug dependent, depressed, or sexually promiscuous, then they will be harmed.   If c, then d

---

∴   7.   If we legalize gay marriage, then we will harm children. If a, then d

This is a valid conditional chain argument.

This line of argument is not cogent. It rests on the presupposition that the "homosexual lifestyle" is characterized by high rates of drug use, depression, suicide, and sexually transmitted diseases, and that children exposed to such a lifestyle will be adversely affected. Even if, for the sake of argument, we grant that exposure to such a lifestyle can and often does adversely affect children, that does not establish the conclusion. The problem is threefold: (1) The line of argument assumes that all or most homosexual individuals participate in what the authors call "the homosexual lifestyle," whereas only some do. (2) A small minority of heterosexuals participate in a similar lifestyle. Given that some heterosexuals engage in similar activities, the authors need to show why we should prohibit only homosexuals and not also heterosexuals from marrying, since the latter may pose the same threat of harm to their children. (3) Moreover, many heterosexuals who engage in such a lifestyle in their dating years change their behaviour when they marry. No reason is offered for believing that would not be true of homosexuals. The argument presupposes that same-sex individuals who marry will have children yet still engage in the "homosexual lifestyle." While this may be true of a few, it is not obvious that it would be true for all or even most. Prohibiting marriage for all because of what some or a few might do is unreasonable. Some heterosexuals who marry might do the same thing, yet we don't prohibit them from marrying.

The sperm-donor argument can be formulated as follows:

19. If gay marriage is legalized, some lesbians will have children through anonymous sperm donors.

20. If lesbians have children through anonymous sperm donors, children will be deprived of knowledge of one of their biological parents.

K. [If children are deprived of knowledge of one of their biological parents, they are harmed.]

∴ 7. If we legalize gay marriage, then we will harm children.   If a, then d

This is an invalid conditional chain argument.

The only way of making this argument valid is by modifying the conclusion to apply only to lesbians or only to lesbians who have children through anonymous sperm donation. The premise that children will be deprived of knowledge of one of their biological parents justifies only a conclusion forbidding lesbians who intend to have children by anonymous sperm donation from marrying. In addition, it would have to apply to any heterosexual couple who intend to have children by anonymous sperm donation as well. The scope of the premises does not match the intended scope of the conclusion. Furthermore, the argument rests on the missing premise that not knowing his or her biological parents in some way harms a child (K). That is not necessarily true. Many adopted children do not know their biological parents and are not harmed by that lack of knowledge. This sub-line is not cogent.

Argument 3: Harmful to Society

This main line of argument can be formulated as follows:

8.   Legalizing gay marriage will be harmful to society   a
     as a whole.

L.   If something is harmful to society as a whole,   If a, then b
     it should not be made legal.

∴ 3.   Gay marriage should not be legalized.   b

This affirms the antecedent and is valid.

The central issue is whether 8, which rests upon one argument, the stability-of-society sub-argument, is true.

25.   Legalizing gay marriage inherently redefines marriage
      as based on intimacy rather than on the commitment   a
      to raise bear and children.

28.   If marriage is redefined as being based on intimacy
      and not on the lifelong commitment to   If a, then b
      procreate and raise children together, then this
      undermines the stability of marriage.

29.   If marriage is redefined as being based on intimacy
      rather than on the lifelong commitment to procreate   If a, then c
      and raise children, then this undermines the
      commitment to future generations.

30.   If we undermine the commitment to future
      generations, then we undermine the stability   If c, then d
      of society.

∴ M.   Gay marriage undermines the stability of society.   d

N.   If something undermines the stability of society, then it
     is harmful to society.   If d, then e

∴ 8.   Legalizing gay marriage will be harmful to society as a whole.   e

Although the argument is valid — it is a complex form of affirming the antecedent — the falsity of several premises makes it not cogent. Premise 25 commits a false dichotomy fallacy by claiming that marriage is about either intimacy or the bearing and raising of children. It clearly can be, and often is, both. The argument works only if the proposal for gay marriage is seen as an attempt to define marriage solely in terms of intimacy and to deny the childbearing and child rearing aspects. Yet many homosexual couples want both. And some heterosexual couples marry for intimacy, not children. We don't deny marriage to heterosexuals who marry for intimacy.

Premises 28 and 30 are probably false for similar reasons. It could be argued that a commitment based on intimacy is a stronger foundation for a couple's staying together than having a child together. And if couples' staying together is the basis for a stable society (a dubious assumption, but one seemingly presupposed by the argument), then marriages based on intimacy might be better for society than those based on breeding.

The arguers have not established that claim 8 is true. Their sub-arguments supporting it rest on a false dichotomy and other dubious premises.

QUICK QUIZ 8.5   Assess Cogency

1. Supply missing premises for the arguments in the marijuana passage.
2. Using the topics model or the argument patterns, assess the arguments for validity.
3. Assess the arguments for cogency.
4. Explain and justify your assessments.

8.9 STEP 5: GIVE AN OVERALL ASSESSMENT

We now need to integrate the assessment of the individual arguments into an overall assessment of the case that has been presented.

Examine each line of argument to see if it is sound. If the arguer has one or more sound lines of argument supporting the conclusion, then the arguer has made his or her case. For the arguments that are not sound, consider how devastating the weaknesses are. Could someone who supports the position reasonably defend against the challenges by modifying the argument in minor ways? If so, develop those possible responses and consider what further challenges might be made. Consider ways in which the argument might be improved.

Examine other relevant considerations. What we have developed thus far are arguments for a particular position. Are there other relevant arguments or considerations that could be brought to bear on this conclusion? (This leads us into issue analysis, the subject of Module 10.) Some of the questions you might want to ask yourself include (1) Are there other arguments that support the same conclusion? (2) Are there other arguments that point to a different conclusion? (3) What are the implications of this argument and the basic reasons that have been given in related areas? An argument may seem impeccable when considered by itself, but it may have implications that are inconsistent with other beliefs, ideas, or values.

Ask yourself what you can learn from the argument in the passage. Even when you don't accept an argument, you can often learn from it. Are there interesting or relevant considerations that are poorly developed and might be developed better? What can you suggest that might improve the arguments given?

Go back to your criticisms and give an overall evaluation of the argument in this passage. Look at the strongest criticisms you have. Do they address all of the lines of argument or only some? Could some of your challenges be stronger if you had more information or evidence to support them? Does the argument in this passage make a very strong, moderate, inconsistent, or weak case for its conclusion?

Virtually every argument with an interesting and controversial conclusion is open to criticism. This does not mean that virtually every such argument is a poor argument. An argument may be strong even though it has flaws and even though we may have strong reasons for opposing its conclusion. A fair overall assessment involves identifying those strengths as well as the weaknesses.

On Diagrams and Notation

Notation symbols can help us quickly identify our assessment of an argument. Using the symbols below and combining them with a more complete arrow diagram, we can present a visual representation of the overall argument.

✓   A check mark beside a claim indicates that the claim is acceptable.

✓g   A check mark with a small *g* beside it indicates that we are granting the claim for the sake of the argument.

F   An *F* beside a claim indicates that it is false. [Alternatively, you could put an *X* through the number or letter of the claim to indicate that it is false.]

?   A question mark beside a claim indicates that the claim is doubtful in some key way.

V   A *V* beside an inference arrow means that the inference is valid.

X   An *X* beside an inference arrow indicates that the inference is invalid.

X/F   An *X/F* beside an inference arrow indicates that the inference is based on a fallacy.

C   A *C* beside an inference arrow indicates the argument is cogent.

NC   An *NC* beside an inference arrow indicates the argument is not cogent.

S   An *S* beside an inference arrow indicates the argument is sound.

NS   An *NS* beside an inference arrow indicates the argument is not sound.

Using these and the analysis above, your arrow diagram with assessment annotations would look like this:

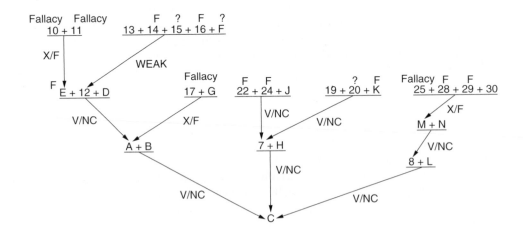

A diagram is useful as an analytical tool. When we try to write out each of the arguments and what is wrong with them, it is very easy to get lost in the details and the verbiage and miss a strategic analysis of the argument. While it is important to be able to articulate and explain the reasons for our assessment, the diagram provides us with a way of seeing the whole argument and, in conjunction with our bracketing and numbering and writing out the missing premises, provides us with specific and strategic assessments of the overall case being made.

Before continuing, assess the overall adequacy of the arguments in "Gay Marriage Is Bad for Everyone" in the Student Manual.

An Overall Assessment of "Gay Marriage Is Bad for Everyone"

The gay marriage passage presents three lines of argument, none of which are sound. The sub-arguments are based on either false claims or fallacies.

In the first line of argument, the authors need to show how changing the definition of marriage will change the practices and values associated with it. The authors might be able to make a better argument if they could show how this specific change will have a detrimental effect on the institution of marriage. To do that, they will need to identify and defend the key features of the institution of marriage.

The definition they give has some serious problems in that it tends to focus on certain things (childbearing and rearing) and to denigrate others (intimacy). Marriage has a number of characteristics. These are not mutually exclusive, nor are they all essential to defining marriage. A more careful analysis of marriage, both the meaning of the concept and the nature of the institution, might give the arguers a better case for their argument.

A key problem that emerges in argument 1, and is expanded upon in argument 2 is scope. The arguments given apply either to only a subset of homosexuals or to heterosexuals as well as homosexuals — or both of these. If a person is going to argue for the prohibition of gay marriage, then the reasons should apply to all (or most) heterosexuals and to no (or few) heterosexuals. I don't see a way of salvaging the second line of argument.

The basic premise of argument 3 — that if something is harmful to society and it is more harmful than beneficial, then it should not be made legal — is a fairly strong consideration. The main problem with the harm to society argument, however, is that it rests on a false dichotomy between marriage based on intimacy and marriage based on procreation, as well as faulty claims on what creates stability in society.

Present Your Critique

The purpose of giving a critique is to identify the strengths and weaknesses of an argument so that your reader can determine whether the argument should be accepted. In presenting your critique, you are making a case — an argument — about the argument in the passage. You need to not simply present your conclusions about the passage but also demonstrate your reasoning so that the reader can make his or her own assessment of your assessment. This means that in developing a critique for an audience, you need to focus your writing around the needs of your audience: What do they already know? What do they need to know in order to assess your conclusion? How can you present what they need to know in a way that they can easily understand?

To do this effectively, you need to do the following:

1. **Give your overall assessment of the passage,** preferably in one sentence — in effect, this is your conclusion about the passage.

2. **Make your case to support that conclusion by**
   a. **identifying clearly the structure of the argument you are critiquing.** The audience may not be familiar with the passage, but, even if they are, they may not reconstruct the argument as you have. In structuring the argument, pay attention to the specific parts you are going to critique. It helps to identify and label the separate lines of argument. Make the logic of the argument clear by using cue words and ordering the argument. If there is anything problematic in your reconstruction — for example, possible alternate reconstructions of the argument — indicate that and justify your preferred reconstruction. Identify supporting arguments, but provide details only if relevant to your critique.
   b. **identifying the strengths and weaknesses of the arguments systematically.** Focus on the key strengths and weaknesses. If you critique a relatively minor point and ignore a major problem, the reader is likely to think that you have not properly understood the argument. Order the critique in terms of severity of criticism, and be as precise as possible: "The second premise has a false presupposition" rather than "There is a weakness in the argument." Simply saying that there is a problem without identifying what exactly the problem is does not provide the reader with any way of determining how you are critiquing the argument.
   c. **providing reasons to justify your analysis, which should include your strategic assessment of the main arguments in terms of cogency, validity, and meaning:** "The second premise in this sub-argument is false because . . ." If it is not obvious, explain how the deficiency affects the argument. The more explicit you can be in presenting and supporting your critique, the more likely the reader is to follow and accept your critique.
   d. indicating the significance of your critique of the specific pieces on the overall argument.
3. **Conclude by providing your overall assessment of the argument, possibly together with observations on how the argument could be improved.** Simply providing a laundry list of challenges doesn't provide an overall assessment of the argument. Is the line of reasoning completely flawed? Are there some insights but poor argument development?

Much of the critique has already been done in the preceding work. The task now is to put it into a format to present to your reader.

The Critique of the Passage

A Poor Defence of Marriage

The authors of "Gay Marriage Is Bad for Everyone" present three lines of argument to support their conclusion that gay marriage should not be legalized: (1) It will undermine marriage, (2) it is unhealthy for children, and (3) it will be harmful to society as a whole. None of the main lines of argument provide adequate support for the conclusion. Although all of the arguments are valid, none are sound. This paper examines each of the lines of argument and shows their major problems. At the end, I will point out how some of the considerations might be used as the basis for a better argument on the issue.

In the first argument, the authors argue that legalizing gay marriage will undermine marriage and that if something undermines the institution of marriage, it should not be legal. The conclusion is that gay marriage should not be legal. The sub-arguments—that homosexuals are promiscuous and will bring this into marriage and that legalizing same-sex unions will open the door to legalizing polygamy—are both based on fallacies. The first sub-argument, that allowing gay marriage will change marriage by introducing promiscuity into it, rests on three unproven and false assumptions: (1) that homosexuals are more promiscuous than heterosexuals, (2) that homosexuals when they marry would continue to be promiscuous, and (3) that their promiscuity would influence heterosexual married couples and undermine heterosexual partners' commitments to one another. The author has not shown that homosexuals, as a group, are more promiscuous than heterosexuals. Some heterosexuals—for example, swingers—are married and engage in what can be considered promiscuous behaviour without this undermining their marital commitment or influencing the whole class of heterosexual married couples. The authors fail to show why they believe homosexuals' alleged promiscuity would have an effect on heterosexual couples' marriages.

The sub-argument that allowing gay marriage will lead to allowing polygamy rests on a slippery slope fallacy. The author does not show how taking the step of allowing marriage between two individuals who are homosexual will necessarily lead to allowing polygamy.

The second line of argument holds that gay marriage should not be legalized because legalizing gay marriage will be unhealthy for children and anything unhealthy for children should not be legalized. This argument is valid, but the premise that legalizing gay marriage would be unhealthy for children is based on two faulty sub-arguments. The first sub-argument holds that legalizing gay marriage would lead to more lesbians using anonymous sperm donation to have children, that this would mean that children would not know their biological parents, and that not knowing one's biological parents is harmful. Therefore, gay marriage should not be allowed. The premises do not adequately support the conclusion that gay marriage should not be legal. The reasons, at best, might support the conclusion that lesbians or lesbians who intend to have children by anonymous sperm donation, should not be allowed to marry. It would not support banning gay men from marrying. Furthermore, accepting the premises would lead either to banning anonymous sperm donation for any couple, heterosexual or homosexual, or to prohibiting anyone who intends to have children by anonymous sperm donation from marrying. The claim that a child not knowing his biological parents causes harm is challenged by the fact that many adoptees don't know their biological parents and are not harmed.

The second sub-argument, the adverse effects sub-line, concludes that gay marriage is bad for children because the homosexual lifestyle is characterized by high rates of drug use, depression, suicide, and sexually transmitted disease, that children in gay marriages will be exposed to these, and that this exposure will adversely affect them. This argument presupposes that all or most individuals who are homosexual participate in what the authors call "the homosexual lifestyle." This is neither argued nor true. Many homosexuals do not participate in the presumed lifestyle but instead lead fairly quiet lives. The argument also has a problem of scope, similar to the previous one. Granting the premises would be grounds for prohibiting heterosexuals who engage in a party-type lifestyle from marrying as well, something that I doubt the authors intend and that would be difficult if not impossible to enforce. Such a restriction would impinge on individual autonomy in an unacceptable way.

The third main line of argument holds that legalizing gay marriage will be harmful to society as a whole and that if something is harmful to society as a whole, then it should not be done. Therefore, gay marriage should not be legalized. The argument affirms the antecedent and is valid. However, the sub-argument that seeks to establish that allowing gay marriage would be harmful to society as a whole is based on a false dichotomy. The sub-argument holds that allowing gay marriage would be harmful because it would undermine a married couple's commitment to procreate by redefining marriage as a union based on intimacy rather than a lifelong commitment to bear and raise children. Such a redefinition would have, according to the authors, a harmful effect on the stability of society. This argument is based on a false dichotomy between defining marriage as being based either on intimacy or a commitment to bear and raise children. In fact, marriage can be based on either or both.

Although none of the arguments the authors offer supports their conclusion, we can learn from the argument how a better case might be made for this position.

In the first line of argument, the authors need to show how changing the definition of marriage will necessarily change the practices and values associated with marriage. A more careful analysis of marriage, both the meaning of the concept and the nature of the institution, might give the arguers a better basis for their argument.

Both the harm-to-children and harm-to-society arguments provide fairly compelling reasons for banning something. The main difficulty with the arguments presented here is that they do not show how legalizing gay marriage would cause harm to children and society. If they were able to do that in a way that does not also apply to heterosexual relationships, a stronger case could be made for banning same-sex marriage.

The underlying considerations presented in this argument include the following: preserving stability in society, ensuring that children are properly cared for and raised, and preventing harm to children. The authors have not been able to show that allowing same-sex marriage would undermine any of these. Were they able to, they might succeed in making a stronger case.

QUICK QUIZ 8.7   Write Your Own Critique

Write your critique of the marijuana argument using the criteria outlined in this section.

MODULE SUMMARY

Longer passages, more complex arguments, and extended passages with lots of extraneous material or confused and muddy reasoning require more systematic analysis. We can use the arrow diagrams and paraphrase to analyze and critique such passages. This module outlines ways of diagramming and assessing the arguments in complex passages in systematic ways, using both arrow diagrams and argument paraphrase. Much of this builds on the skills developed in earlier modules. Although we can develop the technical skill for analyzing, a key requirement of doing such analyses is to fully understand our and our argument partners' positions, arguments, and considerations and be able to address these.

KEY TERMS

active reading
argument branch
argument tree
buried or implicit claim

line of argument
signposts
synopsis
topic sentence

MODULE 9

CONCEPTUAL ANALYSIS

9.1 LEARNING OBJECTIVES

After completing this module, you should be able to

1. explain what conceptual analysis is;
2. identify a question of concept in a text;
3. generate various kinds of cases — paradigm, contrary, borderline, imaginary;
4. use the techniques of reasoning by cases, similarities and differences, and conjectures and refutations to analyze the cases and develop the criteria for the meaning of the concept;
5. use challenge cases to test and refine your analysis; and
6. write up and present a conceptual analysis.

9.2 INTRODUCTION

Conceptual analysis is a method of analyzing the meaning and use of concepts. It goes beyond dictionary definitions to provide an analysis of the way a concept is used in the language or in a given passage. It uses a form of reasoning — "reasoning by cases" — that is a central part of law, ethics, social policy, philosophy, nursing, and everyday reasoning, among other areas.

Conceptual analysis helps us analyze an author's use of a particular term as well as the meanings of complex ideas and concepts. In its latter use, it can be an excellent aid in working through an issue. This module identifies some of the techniques and uses of conceptual analysis as a tool for the clarification of meaning in everyday disputes and inquiries.

Consider the following cases:

1. Is artificial insemination by a donor (i.e., the fertilization of a woman's egg using the sperm of someone other than her husband) adultery? Because she has become pregnant by someone other than her husband, in some legal jurisdictions, it is. And according to the Roman Catholic Church, it would constitute adultery. Should we call this adultery? What do we mean by adultery?

2. Catherine MacKinnon claims that women in a patriarchal society are unable to consent to have sex with men. Is she using the same notion of consent that we use?

3. Is Data on *Star Trek* a moral agent? Can androids be moral agents? What makes someone a moral agent?

4. Albert Carr claims that bluffing is perfectly acceptable in business. Isn't bluffing a form of lying? What might Carr mean by saying bluffing is acceptable?

5. I have read several articles that claim that pornography degrades women. What exactly does *degrade* mean? Does it apply to pornography? What makes something degrading?

6.   What does it mean when someone says homosexuality, or any form of
     sexual activity, is "unnatural?" Does that necessarily mean that it is
     immoral?

In all of the above questions, our first response is likely "That depends on what you mean
by . . ." The answer to each hinges on the meaning of a concept.

Other factors may influence our responses — for example, there are ethical issues about
abortion and homosexuality. However, the central issue in each of these cases is a **question of
concept.** A question of concept is a problem that hinges on the meaning of a concept, the relation of one concept to another, or the application of a concept to a specific situation. Before
we can address any of the other issues, we have to clarify the meaning of the central concept —
for example, adultery, consent, moral agent, bluffing, degrading, or unnatural.

Consider a specific case:

Robert Latimer had a fifteen-year-old daughter, Tracy. She had cystic fibrosis, was unable to
talk, walk, or attend to her bodily functions, and was in constant pain. One night, Robert
put Tracy in the cab of his truck, ran a hose to the cab from the exhaust, and killed her. He
claimed he could no longer stand to see her suffer. Latimer claimed that what he did was
euthanasia. Although euthanasia is illegal, a substantial number of people consider it
morally justified. His critics claimed that he had murdered his daughter. Did Robert Latimer
"euthanize" or "murder" his daughter? Is there a difference? Are they mutually exclusive?

The facts of the situation are not in doubt. What is in doubt is the meaning of the concept. What do we mean by *euthanasia*? How is it related to murder? And does it apply in this
particular case? These are three separate questions, and they are all issues of concept.

Although we can initially address a question of concept by looking up the word(s) in a dictionary, that is rarely satisfactory. The dictionary provides the following definition for euthanasia:

euthanasia *n.*   The act or practice of ending the life of an individual suf-
                     fering from a terminal illness or an incurable condition.
                     [Gk., a good death : *eu*-, eu- + thanatos, death.][1]

This doesn't help distinguish between euthanasia and murder. Nor does it help with the
Latimer case. A dictionary definition often is just a report of how the term is used in the language and does not cover new uses or uses in specific contexts.

9.3 WHY USE CONCEPTUAL ANALYSIS?

We have already seen the major reasons we would want to use conceptual analysis:

- Dictionary definitions are sometimes inadequate.
- We want to analyze the meaning in context, and the dictionary accounts are not pre-
  cise enough to help us.
- Meanings vary, and dictionaries do not always capture these variations.
- Some concepts are relatively new, and their meanings are either not yet fixed or not
  yet recorded.
- We want to establish clear boundaries where there aren't any yet, for reasons of policy
  or ethics.
- The meanings of existing concepts are sometimes stretched and used in quite different
  ways from their main meanings; we need to be able to detect such shifts in meaning.

[1] "Euthanasia." Def. *ITP Nelson Canadian Dictionary of the English Language,* 1997.

- We want to see how various concepts relate to one another.
- It is a means of exploring an issue and helping us discover our reasons and thoughts on that issue.

Using conceptual analysis can improve our reasoning skills in a variety of fields where it is used — ethics, law, policy, philosophy, most humanities and social sciences, and the developing of theory.

9.4 DOING CONCEPTUAL ANALYSIS

This section provides an overview of the process of conceptual analysis. Section 9.5 identifies the kinds of cases used and relates them to the Latimer example.

1. **Identify the concept and why it needs clarifying.** For an inquiry, this can include the role the concept plays in the inquiry, or for a passage analysis, the role the concept plays in the passage.

    In the Latimer case above, the concepts of euthanasia and murder need conceptual analysis to determine which concept his actions fall under. This can help us decide whether we hold him morally accountable or excuse his actions.

2. **Identify specific cases (concrete instances of the use of the concept).** Use different kinds of cases to develop the analysis — paradigm, contrary, mixed, borderline, related, and imaginary (see below). Normally we start with a paradigm case, analyze that, move to a contrary case, analyze that, and then use the others. None of these cases should be the one being analyzed. See Section 9.5 for the various kinds of cases and how to analyze them to develop criteria.

3. **Analyze the cases for criteria of meaning/use.** To develop the criteria of meaning/use that are inherent in the cases, we make conjectures about the possible criteria, challenging those criteria with new cases, and comparing cases for similarities and differences.

    Cases are used both to generate and critique criteria. Examine each case to identify the criteria that make it an example of the concept being analyzed. Ignore prior definitions and see what there is about the case itself that makes it an instance of the concept. The aim is to *generate* a set of criteria, not confirm a preexisting one. Usually, if you start with a prior set of criteria, you will tend to confirm that and not be able to see the weaknesses in it.

    Conceptual analysis relies on cases, not examples, the difference being in how they are used. An ***example*** is used to illustrate something we already know, while a ***case*** becomes the basis for analysis to discover something new. We use the case as a concrete referent and then extract the relevant criteria of meaning from it.

    Use the principle of similar cases. How are two cases alike? If we want to treat them differently, what is the relevant difference between them?

    Use counterexamples to challenge the criteria. Counterexamples, in this situation, are other cases or variants of a case that are used to test the specific criteria we have arrived at.

    Vary the features of a case to test and expand the proposed criteria. If you have derived the criteria from a paradigm case, how would varying the conditions of the case affect the criteria? Would varying certain conditions in the original case change it from a paradigm to a contrary or borderline case? If so, how does that affect your statement of the criteria?

    Test and revise your criteria as necessary. Try taking the criteria you have arrived at and systematically varying the existing cases so that they fit all but one of the criteria. What would you say about the new case? Is it an example of the concept? If not, why not? Work through all of the criteria sequentially. Are the individual criteria necessary for the use of the concept? Test the criteria as a whole. Are they sufficient for the concept? Can you think of something that fits the criteria and is not an example of the concept?

4. **Examine how the concept is related to other concepts.** This may require doing a conceptual analysis on the other concepts.

   Euthanasia is related to such concepts as murder, suicide, assisted suicide, death, and suffering. Others may arise in the course of analysis. What criteria do these concepts have in common? In what criteria do they differ?

5. **Test your analysis**

   - **by examining whether and how it clarifies the situation.** What is the meaning of the passage or issue now with the concept elucidated? Does this clarify the passage or issue? If not, you may need to redo part of your analysis.
   - **by examining the meaning of the concept in the language.** Do the proposed criteria require significant changes to the way in which we use the concept? If your analysis requires us to dramatically modify or abandon many of the ways we use the concept, reconsider your analysis.

9.5 KINDS OF CASES

The core of conceptual analysis involves identifying and analyzing various kinds of cases. In the Latimer case described above, we are faced with the questions (1) What do I mean by *euthanasia?* (2) What do I mean by *murder?* (3) How are the two concepts related? (4) Does the concept of euthanasia apply in this particular case? There are three different kinds of questions here: two about the meaning of concepts, one about the relation between concepts, and one about the application of the concept to a specific case.

The kinds of cases we can use for analysis include the following:

Model or Paradigm Cases

A *paradigm case* is an ideal, perfect, or model case of the concept you are analyzing. It is a case that no one would challenge as an instance of the concept, and it need not be real.

In analyzing the concept of euthanasia in order to address the Latimer case, we would choose a clear example of euthanasia. (We can't start with the Latimer case because it is the one in question.) To illustrate, let's use a modified version of a real case — the Sue Rodriguez case — although if we didn't know of this case, we could use an imaginary one.

Sue Rodriguez was a woman in her early forties who had contracted Lou Gehrig's disease (ALS), a wasting disease that slowly paralyzes various muscles until those necessary to keep them alive (lungs and heart) fail. It is progressive and always kills. After a certain stage, death is fairly quick but not painless. Sue Rodriguez had made various attempts to get the law changed to allow euthanasia. Although unsuccessful in this, as she began losing control of all her functions, she managed to get a doctor to help her die by injecting her with a lethal combination of drugs.

Virtually everyone would recognize this as a clear case of euthanasia. Now we need to analyze it. What is it that makes this a paradigm case of euthanasia? What criteria are we using that enable us to call this *euthanasia?* What is there about this case that is (a) typical and (b) essential of euthanasia?

Examining the case, we can extract the following possible criteria:

Criteria for the meaning of *euthanasia:*

1. The person being euthanized is suffering from a terminal illness.
2. The person is close to death.
3. The person wants to die.
4. The person takes action to die.

This is our initial hypothesis about the criteria for the use of the concept. Are these four criteria sufficient? That is, if they are met, would we say that the case is one of euthanasia? A criterion is *sufficient* for something being x, if, together, they constitute x. Are the individual criteria necessary? A criterion is *necessary* if the phenomenon could not occur without it. For example, if we can call something euthanasia without the person's having consented to it, then consent to being euthanized is not a necessary condition for the concept of euthanasia. Ideally, we want to identify the set of necessary and sufficient conditions for the use of a concept.

The criteria we develop should clearly emerge from the cases and not go beyond them. Based on the Sue Rodriguez case, were we to propose a fifth criterion — for example, the intention of the person who helped the person die is to ease her pain and suffering — we would be extending the criteria beyond the case's given characteristics. We could, however, rewrite the case to include this. As we develop our cases and extract the criteria from them, we elaborate and refine our criteria to meet our needs.

The criteria above are not satisfactory, because we can imagine a case that fits the stated criteria in which Sue Rodriguez, instead of having a physician help her, takes an overdose of sleeping pills, thus committing suicide. We need to distinguish between the two concepts by modifying criterion 4. This is one of the ways in which we develop criteria: imagining situations that would meet the criteria but not be instances of the concept. These counterexamples, or what can be called, in this context, **challenge cases,** are detailed cases that challenge a specific set of criteria. Addressing the issue with criterion 4, we get the following:

Criteria for the meaning of *euthanasia:*

1. The person being euthanized is suffering from a terminal illness.
2. The person is close to death.
3. The person wants to die.
4. Another person assists the person to die.

We can continue with other paradigm cases and try to challenge these criteria, or we can move on to other kinds of cases and use those to test and extend our criteria for euthanasia. Normally, it is best to examine at least three cases of each kind to develop a final set of criteria. If we look at only one or two cases, we may fix on one set of criteria that do not adequately characterize the concept.

QUICK QUIZ 9.1　　Paradigm Cases

For the next series of Quick Quizzes, we will use the following case for analysis:

I am talking with a friend and say that since I have been in the country for thirty years, I no longer feel like an immigrant and am going to apply for my citizenship papers. My friend says, "You will always be an immigrant. The only people who aren't are First Nations people."

1. What is the issue?
2. Identify the question(s) of concept in this passage.
3. Generate three paradigm cases of each concept and identify the possible criteria that emerge from those cases.

Answers for all Quick Quizzes in this text are provided in the Student Manual. After doing the Quick Quizzes, consult the Student Manual to check your understanding of the material.

Contrary or Opposite Cases

Contrary or *opposite cases* are clear examples of something that shares a key characteristic with the concept being analyzed but is contrary to the concept being analyzed. A bank robber kills someone in the commission of a robbery. That is clearly not euthanasia. A person dies of natural causes. That is clearly not euthanasia. Both of these would be contrary cases. A person riding a bicycle is not a contrary case, nor is it a case of a similar type. Euthanasia has to do with dying. That is the general type.

What is it about the bank robbery and natural causes cases that clearly make them not examples of euthanasia?

1. In both cases, there is a lack of consent. The individual did not consent to his or her death.
2. In neither case, as described, was the person suffering from a terminal illness.
3. In neither case was it clear that the person wanted to die.

Comparing these with our original criteria, they seem to confirm them as well as add to them. We now have the following:

Criteria for the meaning of *euthanasia:*

1. The person being euthanized is suffering from a terminal illness.
2. The person is close to death.
3. The person wants to die.
4. The person consents to having someone help him or her die.
5. Someone else takes direct action to assist the person to die.

Suppose the situation of the Rodriguez case were as described above, except that while she is nearing death, she hasn't found a medical doctor to assist her. One night, a burglar breaks into the house; she wakes, and he kills her. Would that be euthanasia? We would likely say "no." That is murder, not euthanasia. Even though she was terminally ill, was in a great deal of pain, was close to death, wanted to die, wanted to be euthanized, and someone else took action to kill her, she did not consent to this particular act by this person at this time and place. This is a clear contrary case.

To accommodate this, I would modify the criteria as follows:

Criteria for the meaning of *euthanasia:*

1. The person being euthanized is suffering from a terminal illness.
2. The person is close to death.
3. The person wants to die.
4. The person consents to having someone help him or her die.
5. Someone else who has been designated takes direct action to assist the person to die.

We have modified criterion 5 to rule out murder. Sometimes it is useful to contrast paradigm cases and contrary cases to see what about the contrary cases prevent them from being examples of the concept. What distinguishes the two cases in this situation is that the person did not consent to that particular person killing her, nor did she consent to the circumstances. Would it make a difference if the burglar knew she wanted to die and decided while he was there to do her a good deed by helping her to die? This is a variation on the contrary case. We would probably still say that it was murder. Even though his intent in this last variant of the case is different, his killing her is not euthanasia.

QUICK QUIZ 9.2   Contrary Case

For the case in Quick Quiz 9.1, generate three contrary cases and identify their possible criteria. Compare these criteria with those developed in Quick Quiz 9.1 and modify the criteria if necessary.

Mediant or Mixed Cases

Not all cases are clear examples of the kind of thing we are trying to analyze. Some cases fulfill only part of the criteria for the concept, and some cases have features of several different concepts. These are **mediant** or **mixed cases.** Examining such cases can help us sharpen our criteria and determine what is essential for the concept and what is not.

Imagine a slightly different scenario. A doctor, knowing that Sue Rodriguez wants to die but fearing repercussions, breaks into her home at night and gives her a lethal injection while she sleeps. Again, the specific consent is not there. What would we say now? Some of us might say it is euthanasia, and others might say it is not. We tend to get hung up here on two competing issues: (1) whether the form of killing is euthanasia and (2) whether it is morally justified. Sometimes we answer that the killing is not morally justified and, therefore, we want to say that it is not euthanasia.

This is a difficult case. We've said euthanasia involves a person in specific circumstances consenting to a specific other person doing something to bring about the first person's death. Although Sue Rodriguez may have wanted to die and may even have asked this specific doctor to euthanize her, the doctor has done it in a way that is not clearly in accord with her wishes. For that reason, we might be hesitant to call it euthanasia.

Would it make a difference if the doctor, unknowingly to Sue Rodriguez, changed her medication in such a way that she would end up taking an overdose? Again, using the reasoning in the previous case, we might be hesitant to call it euthanasia. This is a mixed case because it meets some of the criteria but fails to meet others. On the basis of the reasoning we have given, the criteria it fails to meet are essential and thus the mixed case, although having characteristics of euthanasia, is not euthanasia.

However, let us look at a parallel case. A nurse in a hospital deals with aged and chronically ill individuals. Some of them are near death and in considerable pain. On her own, she decides to give them lethal injections of morphine and potassium (which will stop their hearts). When she is caught, she claims that she was simply providing them a "peaceful death"—euthanasia. Is this euthanasia or murder? While we are tempted to say murder, it may be both.

We have assumed that euthanasia must be voluntary—something the patient requests and consents to. However, there is precedent for using the term *euthanasia* for *involuntary euthanasia.* We euthanize our pets when they are terminally ill, and they can't consent. Further, the Nazis had a program they called "euthanasia" for the seriously ill and people with mental problems.

The problem is that involuntary euthanasia violates our basic moral principles. We consider that in order to be justified, euthanasia must be voluntary. In the case we are examining, Robert Latimer claims he did nothing morally wrong because he was simply providing a peaceful death for his pain-racked daughter. That justification works for voluntary euthanasia, which is what most of us think of as *euthanasia*. Having discovered that we are analyzing voluntary, not involuntary, euthanasia, we can adjust our criteria further.

Criteria for the meaning of *voluntary euthanasia:*

1. The person being euthanized is suffering from a terminal illness.
2. The person is close to death.
3. The person wants to die.
4. The person consents to having someone help him or her die.
5. Someone else who has been designated takes direct action to assist the person to die . . .
6. . . . in a time and place of his or her choosing.

QUICK QUIZ 9.3   Mixed Cases

For the case in Quick Quiz 9.1, generate three mixed cases and identify their possible criteria. Compare these criteria with those developed in Quick Quizzes 9.1 and 9.2 and modify the criteria if necessary. Explain what makes these cases mixed cases.

Borderline Cases

Borderline cases are unusual or interesting cases that straddle the concept. If we imagine that there are a number of clear examples or instances of the concept and a number of clear examples or instances of things that are not the concept, then for many concepts, there is a fuzzy boundary between the clear cases of *x* and the clear cases of not *x*. These are the borderline cases. By examining them and asking questions such as "Why would it be included or not included?" and "How are we going to deal with the borderline case?" we can sharpen the criteria of what does and does not fit.

Consider another case (loosely based on a real case in Halifax). A man is dying of throat cancer. He will die sometime within the next four to twenty-four hours, during which time he will be in unbearable pain. Although not fully coherent, several times he cries out, "Stop the pain! I want it to end." However, he has not made a prior declaration that he wants to have increasing amounts of morphine, even if it will stop his breathing. He's been given the maximum safe dosage of morphine, but it is not enough to relieve the pain. The attending physician gives him a combination of morphine and potassium, which stops his heart. Potassium has no other function than to stop the heart. Is this euthanasia? Is it voluntary or involuntary?

This is a difficult case. My intuitions and those of the deputy coroner for Ontario — Dr. James Cairns — differ on this one. He believes this is murder. I think it could be justified as euthanasia, although it is a borderline case. It has some of the characteristics of euthanasia but not others and is on the boundary of the use of the concept. That Dr. Cairns and I do not agree does not mean that we have different criteria but that we apply them differently in the borderline areas.

Part of the problem with this case is that the patient has given what can be taken as ambiguous consent. He has asked to have the pain stopped and said, "I want it to end." Should that be interpreted as consent to euthanasia or simply a request for more of the painkiller? The maximum amount of morphine he can have without it stopping his heart is not working. He will die within hours and knows it.

Would the situation be different (variation of the case) if the attending physician had simply given increasing amounts of morphine to ease the pain, knowing it would bring about the patient's death? There are times when a physician will increase the amount of morphine to ease pain and it inadvertently stops the heart. Is that euthanasia? Whether one answers yes or no, the critical feature is how the answer is defended. Personally, I would suggest that this is not euthanasia. The physician does not intend to end the life of the patient. The patient's death is an unintended but foreseeable possible consequence of the action. This means that I am using the following as one of my criteria for euthanasia:

7. The person performing the act that results in euthanasia intends the death of the other person.

The case of the attending physician administering potassium and morphine fits this condition. However, it is still clearly a borderline case. It ambiguously fits one of the other conditions: The person being euthanized must consent to the act. It is not clear from the situation that the person has consented. We have to make a decision about how to treat such a case. To understand the problems involved, let us look at the next kind of case.

Criteria for the meaning of *voluntary euthanasia:*

1. The person being euthanized is suffering from a terminal illness.
2. The person is close to death.
3. The person wants to die.
4. The person consents to having someone help him or her die.
5. Someone else who has been designated takes direct action to assist the person to die . . .
6. . . . in a time and place of his or her choosing.
7. The person performing the act that results in euthanasia intends the death of the other person.

QUICK QUIZ 9.4   Borderline Cases

For the case in Quick Quiz 9.1, generate three borderline cases and identify their possible criteria. Compare these criteria with those developed in Quick Quizzes 9.1, 9.2, and 9.3, and modify the criteria if necessary. Explain what makes these cases borderline cases.

Related Concepts

Related concepts throw light on the concept being examined and on the criteria being developed for that concept. Concepts get their meaning, partially, through their relation to other concepts in the language. The concept of "rights" is related to other concepts such as obligation, duty, responsibility, and to kinds of rights — human, civil, et cetera. Examining related concepts helps us understand the concept in question.

One way of identifying related cases is simply by brainstorming other concepts associated with the one we are trying to clarify. Other concepts related to euthanasia include death, suicide, murder, accidental death, as well as some of the concepts that appear in the criteria, such as consent, terminal illness, pain, and suffering.

I might also consider phrases and statements that use the term and analyze those to see what light they shed on the concept. This can lead me to other possible concepts. For example, if I were clarifying "right," I might generate the following list of phrases and statements using the term:

My rights entitle me to . . .

I have a right to . . .

You have no right to . . .

Animal rights . . .

Smokers' rights . . .

These might lead me to the related concepts of "having a right," "entitlement," holding rights in virtue of a characteristic one has (being a smoker, human, or animal), and possibly others. I might remember the phrase "a right, not a privilege" and contrast those two notions. What is the difference between a right and a privilege?

Let us look at a couple of other cases. The seven criteria work for the Sue Rodriguez case. However, instead of giving her, for example, a lethal injection, the physician provides her with a lethal drug cocktail and then leaves the premises. She takes the drug cocktail on her own. Is this euthanasia? I would say no. The other person has facilitated her dying by providing the means. But she is the one who actually undertakes the action that leads to her death. She has, in effect, committed suicide, although she has been assisted in that by someone else. We, in fact, have a concept for this—*assisted suicide,* which involves a second party helping the ill person to die. Although assisted suicide is related to euthanasia, the two are not the same. The critical difference is in whether a person directly causes the death or simply provides the means for suicide. The border between these two concepts can sometimes be murky.

Some related concepts help us draw the boundaries between concepts (e.g., murder versus assisted suicide), while others are necessary in elucidating the concept (e.g., if euthanasia involves consent, then there are situations where we will need to know something about consent in order to determine whether a given case is an example of euthanasia).

We might also consider possible ways of qualifying the concept. The nurse example above gave us a related concept — involuntary euthanasia. In talking about euthanasia and consent, we have determined that euthanasia with the patient's consent would be voluntary euthanasia. So the concept of euthanasia can be divided into voluntary and involuntary. The paradigm case of Sue Rodriguez would be an instance of voluntary euthanasia; the nurse case, involuntary euthanasia. The case of the patient with throat cancer would seem to straddle the borderline between the two.

Part of the reason we concern ourselves with clarifying the meaning of "euthanasia" is so we can determine whether it is morally justified or morally unjustified — two other related concepts. One of the clusters of meaning that "euthanasia" belongs to is that of moral discourse. We want to distinguish the assigning of moral responsibility. A person who supplies the means for a suicide has, at worst, assisted in a person's dying; he or she has not actually ended the person's life. The patient could still decide not to go through with the suicide. The person committing euthanasia is physically killing another person. The moral responsibility is different.

Another way of generating related concepts is by thinking of the various applications of the concept. Although we use the term *euthanasia* to apply to situations such as the Rodriguez case, we also apply it to our pets. This suggests a related use of the concept. When we have a veterinarian "put down" a beloved pet that is suffering and in pain, we call it "euthanasia" although the pet has obviously not given consent. Alternatively, there are cases where people murder pets — for example, by putting out poison to kill the neighborhood cats. So we can draw a distinction between euthanasia and murder for pets as well as for humans.

Now for a hard case. The Nazis developed a program to "euthanize" the seriously ill and those with mental problems, using some of the strategies they would later use in the mass extermination of Jews, gypsies, homosexuals, and others. Was this a proper use of the term *euthanasia,* or is it an example of "concept stretching?" In **concept stretching,** we take a concept with a reasonably well-agreed-upon use and extend the meaning far beyond its original use to validate something not normally justified by it. Concept stretching can occur when the boundaries of the term are not clearly defined, when the term is misunderstood, or when the boundaries of the concept are deliberately stretched for specific purposes. This often happens in heated controversies and political contexts. The terms *sexual harassment* and *pornography* are two examples of terms that have been stretched in the context of a controversy. For example, *pornography*, originally meaning sexually explicit material, has been expanded to include portrayals that degrade or objectify women even if not sexually explicit.

The Nazi "euthanasia" program was, minimally, one of involuntary euthanasia since consent was neither sought nor given. However, I am reluctant to extend the term *euthanasia* to the Nazis' program for the following reason: In the context in which we use *euthanasia*, the term, whether voluntary or involuntary, applies to individual cases — not a state policy enforced on whole categories of people. Moreover, the point of the Nazi program was not to relieve patient pain and suffering but to rid the state of unwanted individuals. These differences are sufficient for us not to count this as euthanasia. Since the issues involved in each differ significantly, I would rather not conflate them under one concept. For these reasons, I would not call the Nazi policy a legitimate use of the concept "euthanasia."

QUICK QUIZ 9.5   Related Concepts

For the case in Quick Quiz 9.1, generate three related concepts and identify their possible criteria. Compare these criteria with those developed in Quick Quizzes 9.1, 9.2, 9.3, and 9.4, and modify the criteria if necessary. Explain what makes these related concepts.

Invented or Imaginary Cases

Invented or **imaginary cases** are made-up situations that help us clarify the logical criteria of a concept. There are two kinds of invented cases. One kind simply requires inventing a detailed case from features of the world we experience. My example of the nurse above is an invented case. Although my Rodriguez case is based on a real case, it did not have to be, and some of the variations — the burglar, for instance — were imaginary. We might better describe this kind of made-up case as an **invented situation.**

The second kind involves changing the features of the world in important ways and then asking what we would say about them. For example, if we have clarified the concept of person and understand it to mean a bearer of rights, then we might construct an imaginary situation to test our criterion. A Martian lands on earth. This Martian has desires, communicates with others of its species and with humans, reasons, feels pain, and has a host of other characteristics. Is it a person? Most people would probably say yes. Suppose now, however, that we discover that this "person" is a well-crafted android; that is, it reproduces not through transmission of genetic material to offspring but through manufacturing processes. What would we say of it then? Alternatively, imagine that we discover that porpoises share all of the characteristics of this Martian. Would we say that porpoises are persons? And what would this commit us to?

In such cases, we imagine fundamental changes in the reality we experience. If we know how to use the concept we're examining, then we should know how to apply it to novel situations and cases, as well as know when we are puzzled by its application to novel cases. We use imaginary cases (in the above examples, they also happen to be borderline cases) to stretch and test our understanding of the original concept. They might also be looked upon as sophisticated ways of generating counterexamples to test our initial criteria. This second kind of invented case we can call **science-fiction cases** to differentiate them from invented situations based on real-world properties.

The following is an example of a science-fiction case that applies to euthanasia. Imagine a situation in which Data on *Star Trek* has been exposed to a lethal pathogen that will kill all the members of the Starship Enterprise. The only way of stopping the infection is to atomize Data. Once atomized, he cannot be reassembled; he will cease to exist. Because he is an android, his programming does not allow him to "kill" himself. He agrees. Would we call this *euthanasia?* This case raises at least two interesting questions: Can an android be euthanized? Is it euthanasia if someone asks to be killed not to prevent pain and suffering to himself or herself but to others? Other conditions for euthanasia are met: It is done by another, and there is consent. We can also consider a variation on this where the person infected with the pathogen was human, not an android. Is it euthanasia if a human consents to die to save others from pain and possibly death?

I would suggest that this particular case is not euthanasia. I might call the action *altruistic*. An essential feature of euthanasia seems to be that the person — in pain, suffering, and nearing death — seeks to die for him- or herself, not to benefit another.

Consider a parallel case: A man is fatally ill but not suffering. His sister needs a heart transplant and his is a match. He offers to sacrifice himself so that his sister can have his heart. This does not meet the conditions for euthanasia, nor would I want to call it euthanasia. His intent is not to ease his pain but to use the opportunity to ease his sister's. Likewise, I can imagine a state of affairs where the members of a tribe on a distant planet sacrifice themselves so that siblings and other tribal members can have live organ transplants. I would not call this practice euthanasia. The intent of the person dying is not to ease his or her own pain and suffering but that of others. The context of the case is quite different.

To generate a science-fiction case, we try to imagine a situation that is beyond the normal realm of experience. Imagining science-fiction situations, other possible societies, or variants in our reality is a way of generating such cases.

Invented cases can be any of the other kinds — paradigm, contrary, borderline, mixed, or related.

Criteria for the meaning of *euthanasia:*

1. The person being euthanized is suffering from a terminal illness.
2. The person is close to death.
3. The person wants to die.
4. The person consents to having someone help him or her die.
5. Someone else who has been designated takes direct action to assist the person to die . . .
6. . . . in a time and place of his or her choosing.
7. The intent is to ease the pain and suffering of the dying person.
8. The term applies to individuals, not state policy aimed at groups or classes of people.

We now have a preliminary analysis of euthanasia. To address our initial question of whether euthanasia is murder, we should do the same kind of analysis with the concept of murder.

QUICK QUIZ 9.6   Imaginary Cases

For the case in Quick Quiz 9.1, generate three imaginary cases, at least one of which is a science-fiction case, and identify the possible criteria found in those cases. Compare these criteria with those developed in Quick Quizzes 9.1, 9.2, 9.3, 9.4, and 9.5, and modify the criteria if necessary. Explain what makes these cases imaginary cases.

9.6 METHODS OF ANALYSIS

Generating cases is the starting point for conceptual analysis. Once they're generated, we must analyze the cases for the implicit criteria of their use. If we know how to use the term, we know how to use the concept, even if we cannot necessarily articulate its meaning. This means that we implicitly know the rules and criteria that govern the use of the concept. The point of generating cases is to provide us with clear examples (referents) for the concept.

Analysis involves several discrete elements. Some of the illustrations of these have been incorporated into the preceding section.

1. **Examine the cases, usually one by one to generate the criteria for the use of the concept.** This is why we want our cases to be as detailed as is reasonable. What is there about the details of the situation that lead me to say that, for example, this is a paradigm use of the concept? What are the features found in this case that are general and how do they apply to other cases? It is useful to analyze a few of each kind of case to help you abstract the concept. What are the similarities and differences among the cases? How do they affect the criteria?
2. **Synthesize the criteria.** Try to unify the criteria from the various cases. Reword and reformulate the criteria as precisely as possible.

QUICK QUIZ 9.7   Synthesize the Criteria

Examine the criteria developed in each of the cases for the analysis of the concept in Quick Quizzes 9.1 through 9.6 and synthesize them into one set of criteria.

3. **Critique your criteria.** (1) Compare them against the existing cases to see whether they fit. (2) Use counterexamples to challenge the criteria. Generate additional cases that fit the criteria but that may not be an instance of the concept. (3) Generate additional cases that fit some of the criteria but not all in order to test whether a given criterion or set of criteria are necessary and/or sufficient. Our discussion of euthanasia has used all of these methods of critiquing criteria.
4. **Revise your criteria and test again against the various cases.**

QUICK QUIZ 9.8   Critique Your Criteria

Identify possible challenges that might be made to the criteria you identified in Quick Quiz 9.7. Develop those challenges, and then respond to them by modifying your criteria.

By the time we have developed a variety of these cases and analyzed their criteria, we will have arrived at a set of criteria for the use of the concept — that is, we will have completed a conceptual analysis. We can continue to sharpen and refine our analysis with additional cases. However, we also need to know whether our analysis is useful. To determine this, we use the following steps:

1. **Test your criteria against the original context.** What is the situation or context in which the problematic term and the need for a conceptual analysis arose? That is, what is the purpose of doing this conceptual analysis? We started with a question about whether or not

the Latimer case was a case of euthanasia and whether or not euthanasia is murder. We now take the criteria we have developed and apply them to the original situation. Do the criteria help us understand the situation better? Do they help us develop an answer to our original questions?

If you are confused by a particular concept, but your analysis makes no sense of the text, then you may not have analyzed the correct concept, or your analysis may have somehow missed the point. For example, if you are puzzled about whether smokers have rights, but your analysis cannot be applied to smokers (as either having or not having rights), then you have not successfully analyzed the concept.

In the case of euthanasia, we have produced a proposed set of criteria for the concept. Applying them systematically to the Latimer case, we find that they do not fit on several grounds:

1. **The person being euthanized is suffering from a terminal illness.** Although Tracy Latimer had a disease that would ultimately kill her, the disease was not likely to do that in the next few years.
2. **The person is close to death.** Tracy was not near death.
3. **The person wants to die.** From the facts of the situation, we do not know this. Tracy was unable to speak, and there is no evidence that she had in any way indicated that she wanted to die.
4. **The person consents to having someone help him or her die.** There is no indication that she had given such consent, and no one has contended that she did.
5. **Someone else who has been designated takes direct action to assist the person to die.** There is no indication that she had designated anyone to take such action.
6. **. . . in a time and place of his or her choosing.** Since there is no indication that Tracy chose to die, she could not have chosen a time or place.
7. **The intent is to ease the pain and suffering of the dying person.** This was the intent of Robert Latimer, but we don't know if it was the intent of Tracy Latimer, nor was she dying. In the absence of evidence, we cannot assume this.
8. **The term applies to individuals,** not state policy aimed at groups or classes of people. This does apply to the Tracy Latimer case.

Based on these criteria and their application to the Tracy Latimer case, her death was not an instance of voluntary euthanasia. If 1 and 2 are essential for involuntary euthanasia (something we would have to establish through further analysis and argument), then it is also not a case of involuntary euthanasia.

There is a critical difference between analyzing the meanings of concepts and our beliefs about the concepts. The **_meaning of the concept_** is the common criteria for the use of the concept. They are what we imply when using the concept in the language. **_Beliefs about a concept_** are the specific beliefs we hold with respect to a given concept. These are not necessarily shared. Part of the meaning of the concept "cat" includes a furry, domesticated creature that purrs. Some of the beliefs about cats are that they are dirty; they are clean; they destroy flowerbeds by digging in them; and they chase mice. These are beliefs about cats, not part of the meaning of the concept. Some people believe that voluntary euthanasia is always morally wrong; others believe that it is often morally right. Some people believe that allowing it will lead to a wider use of euthanasia; others believe that it can be limited and strictly controlled. These are beliefs about the concept, not part of the meaning of the concept.

2. **What are the practical results of the conceptual analysis on the language?** If we have clarified a concept and it requires a major rewriting of how the term is used in the language — that is, most claims once thought to be true using that concept would now

be false, whereas many claims thought false would now be true; or most claims using the concept would now be meaningless — then we should reassess the analysis. If we are trying to clarify the concept as it is used in the language, then our results should not be drastically counterintuitive. If, for example, our conceptual analysis results in a meaning for the concept "euthanasia" that negates most of the claims made about euthanasia, then we have not clarified the ordinary sense of the term. If our analysis of the term conflates what are normally seen as distinct terms or applies only to a very few cases of what most people see as instances of that term or stretches the meaning of the concept to cover cases not normally thought of as instances of the term, then we have not clarified the ordinary concept of it as it is used in the language.

In some cases, we may want to argue for a technical or special use of a term (introduce a new concept). However, we should make this explicit and give the new concept a different name.

The above analysis of "euthanasia" seems to capture the way in which we use the term. It explains why the Nazis used the term (concept stretching), the euthanizing of pets (an extended use of the term), and the difference between voluntary and involuntary euthanasia.

In doing a conceptual analysis, we proceed only as far as necessary to clarify the concepts sufficiently for the purpose of the discussion or dispute we are involved in. Beyond that we may be trying to be overly precise. If we are simply engaged in clarifying the concept for our own understanding, then we can pursue it as far as necessary. After all, entire books have been written on the meaning of single concepts.

QUICK QUIZ 9.9   Results in Context and Results in Language

1. How well do your criteria in Quick Quiz 9.8 answer the question of concept from the original context in which it arose? Explain.
2. What are the practical results of your conceptual analysis on the way the concept is used in the language? Explain.

9.7 PRESENTING A CONCEPTUAL ANALYSIS

Once we have completed a conceptual analysis, we should, at least, summarize our criteria, apply them systematically and specifically to the conditions of the case or situation with which we began, and reach a conclusion.

Often we want to present our results to others, either as part of a paper, in which we clarify the meaning of a term before continuing to develop an argument based on it, or as an entire paper whose purpose is the presentation of the conceptual analysis.

The record of the process of inquiry, of arriving at our insights and ideas, is not usually the best format for presenting our ideas to an audience. This is true for virtually any material that we present. Offering the audience a blow-by-blow of our reasoning process is likely to be counterproductive. So to move from generating an analysis to presenting that analysis, we need to make a case for our results.

The basic strategy for making a case involves identifying the issue for the reader, presenting our position about that issue, providing the relevant arguments, and leading the reader through the arguments. For a conceptual analysis presentation, we must

1. **identify the issue or passage within which the question of concept arises.** Don't assume that the reader knows the issue or the passage. Provide a brief synopsis.
2. **identify the issue of concept within the passage and explain why it is an issue of concept.** Why is this issue of concept important to the inquiry, dispute, position, or argument under consideration? How does the lack of clarity about the concept affect the discussion?
3. **provide one or more cases that are central to the use of the concept being analyzed.** Imagine paradigm cases, contrary cases, mixed cases, et cetera, and choose which to present to the reader.
4. **identify the criteria for the use of the concept abstracted from the cases.**
5. **show how the cases support the criteria.** Using the methods of comparison and contrast as well as counterexamples to test our criteria can help us support the criteria.
6. **test our criteria using challenge cases.**
7. **argue why our criteria are the best criteria available.** Show that our criteria cover the hard cases, handle the mixed cases, make important distinctions, fit the meaning of the context, and fit the language.
8. **show how this clarification solves the issue of concept raised at the outset.**
9. **demonstrate that the criteria are justifiable.** Show either that these criteria for the use of the concept are those in use in the language or make an argument why these criteria should be adopted even though the criteria do not fit some of the uses of the concept in the language.

You can state your thesis at the outset or work toward it and state it at the end, depending on what you think will be more effective for your reader's understanding.

This pattern can be developed and expanded in a variety of ways. For example, steps 2, 3, 4, and 5 can be repeated a number of times before arriving at a final set of criteria. Step 2 can be developed and expanded using any of the types of cases we have identified. The central aim is to turn your detailed analysis into a presentation that the audience can follow and with which they are likely to agree.

9.8 SAMPLE CONCEPTUAL PRESENTATION: THE LATIMER CASE

Was It Euthanasia?

Robert Latimer's fifteen-year-old daughter, Tracy, suffered from severe cerebral palsy, was unable to talk or take care of basic bodily functions, and was in severe pain. Although the disease would eventually take her life, she was not likely to die for years. Robert Latimer killed his daughter by gassing her with carbon monoxide in the cab of his truck. He based his defence on the claim that he had committed euthanasia to ease her pain and suffering. Critics claimed that he had murdered his daughter. I will argue that what Robert Latimer did was not euthanasia, in either the voluntary or involuntary sense of the term, by examining the concept of euthanasia and showing that it does not apply to this case.

A clear and widely acknowledged case of euthanasia is that of Sue Rodriguez. Ms. Rodriguez suffered from Lou Gehrig's disease. In the last stages of that disease, a person's breathing and heart muscles are paralyzed, and he or she dies a painful and horrible death. When Ms. Rodriguez was near the end of the course of the disease, she arranged for a physician to give her a lethal injection that ended her life, since she was no longer able to do that for herself. She left a note saying that this was what she wanted. This is a classic example of what we call euthanasia. The person euthanized, suffering from a fatal illness, is near death, is in pain, and is suffering. She consents to someone assisting her to die. Based on this, we can suggest that the concept of euthanasia involves a person (1) suffering from a terminal illness,

(2) in the end stages of that illness, (3) who wishes to end her pain and suffering by dying, (4) consents to die at a time and place of her choosing, and (5) is assisted in dying by someone of her choosing.

The first and simplest objection to the Tracy Latimer case being euthanasia might be that, while Sue Rodriguez had a physician assist her, Robert Latimer was not a physician. However, euthanasia does not require the assistance of a physician. We often hear of a husband assisting his wife to die, a child assisting a parent. As long as the other conditions are met, we still call this euthanasia.

Having someone assist in a person's death is an essential element of euthanasia. If I simply take an overdose of sleeping pills, with all of the other conditions being met, I have not committed euthanasia; I have committed suicide. Even if someone has provided me the pills I use, it is suicide. We may call it assisted suicide, but not euthanasia. For it to be euthanasia, the person who assists must take an active role in bringing about the death. While we could analyze what "active role" means, that is not at question in the Latimer case, and I will not address it in this chapter.

Are all killings of people who are end-stage terminal and want to die euthanasia? I think not. The fact that someone wants to die under the conditions of euthanasia (1, 2, and 3, above) and does die under those conditions does not establish that it is euthanasia. Consider the following. Had someone broken into Sue Rodriguez's home the day before she had been euthanized, and, if while in the process of burglarizing the home, the intruder discovered her and killed her, we would say not that it was euthanasia but that it was murder. Although most of the conditions for euthanasia would have been met, she had not given her consent to die at this time or in this way. Moreover, it would not be the intent of the burglar to relieve her pain and suffering. Neither the consent condition nor intent condition would have been met.

However, let us consider a slightly different case. Sue Rodriguez has chosen the physician who will help her. She has specified the date and time of her death. However, the physician, unknown to the patient, gives Rodriguez a lethal injection six months before she had intended to die. He believes that her pain is becoming unbearable and acts to relieve her of it with a lethal injection. Is this euthanasia? It is clearly not voluntary euthanasia. Although Sue Rodriguez suffers from a terminal illness, is in the last stages of that illness, is in severe pain, is suffering, wants to be euthanized, and has given consent, she has not given consent for this time and under these conditions. The physician has acted independently. This case is closer to that of a care giver who kills his elderly patients without their knowledge and consent because he believes that they are suffering. Even though there had been knowledge and consent in the case of Sue Rodriguez, the physician has acted on his own and has not respected her wishes for a specific date of death. If anything, the physician has engaged in involuntary euthanasia. The intent condition is met but not the consent condition, which I consider a critical difference between voluntary and involuntary euthanasia.

Voluntary euthanasia occurs when an individual (1) has a terminal disease, (2) is in the end stages of that disease, (3) is in severe pain and is suffering, (4) wants to die, (5) consents to have someone assist him or her to die, (6) does so on his or her own terms, and (7) when the intent of the death is to ease the pain and suffering of the person with the disease. Involuntary euthanasia occurs when conditions 1 through 3 are met and condition 7 is met by the person doing the euthanizing.

Based on these criteria, Robert Latimer did not engage in euthanasia when he killed his daughter. Although her disease was terminal (1), she was not in the last stages of that disease (2). She had severe pain and suffering (3), but there is no indication that she wanted to die (4), nor that she consented to die (5). Although Robert Latimer claimed, and I accept his claim, that he acted to ease her pain and suffering (7), there is no indication that Tracy Latimer was willing to die to ease that pain and suffering. This was Robert Latimer's choice and not his daughter's. The Latimer case clearly does not meet the conditions for voluntary euthanasia.

Nor does it meet the conditions for involuntary euthanasia. Although conditions 1, 3, and 7 (for Robert Latimer) are met for involuntary euthanasia, condition 2 is not. (If necessary, an argument could be developed about why condition 2 is necessary to distinguish euthanasia from murder.)

Notes on the Essay

The analysis has been developed throughout the course of this module. In the essay, I made a number of changes to the analysis. I used neither all of the cases nor all of the criteria. I selected the cases and criteria needed to address the issue, omitting those cases and criteria that do not directly address the immediate issue. I also simplified and modified some of the cases and added new cases. As I developed my criteria, I was able to see new cases and variants of cases that helped me advance and defend my criteria. I used those in writing the essay. Sometimes we develop cases that better illustrate the criteria once we have worked through the criteria.

My intent in the essay is to defend the conclusion that I have arrived at. In the essay, I use the most relevant cases and criteria and eliminate those that are not relevant. For example, I do not have to establish that my criteria fit the use of the concept in the language. The imaginary cases and the Nazi case do not advance the argument substantially, although they helped in developing an understanding of the concept. I have, therefore, dropped them. A different kind of analysis might include them.

This essay does not address the separate issue of whether Robert Latimer was morally justified in killing his daughter. I could claim that what he did was not euthanasia, as I have done, but was nonetheless, morally justified, which I have not argued. That is a separate issue and a separate case. Many people were sympathetic to Robert Latimer's (and what they perceived to be Tracy's) plight and were willing to argue that he should not be held responsible because what he did was euthanasia. For them, euthanasia — the ending of terminal pain and suffering — would be sufficient grounds for excusing the action of killing his daughter (which everyone, including Robert Latimer) agreed he had done. Many others see his actions as horrific. This is a separate issue and needs to be argued separately.

QUICK QUIZ 9.10   Write Up Your Analysis

Briefly write a presentation of your conceptual analysis aimed at explaining it to other students who have not done this analysis. Follow the guidelines for presenting a conceptual analysis.

MODULE SUMMARY

Conceptual analysis is a method of analyzing the meaning and use of concepts that goes beyond dictionary accounts and helps provide us with a deeper understanding of key concepts and issues. The method of conceptual analysis involves generating specific cases that we then analyze, using the method of reasoning by cases. We generate a variety of different kinds of cases — paradigm, contrary, mixed, borderline, and imaginary — as the basis for analysis. We analyze each case for the underlying criteria governing the use of the concept in that particular case. By analyzing multiple cases and different kinds of cases, we can develop a deeper understanding of the concept, its relation to other concepts, its possible applications, and its use in the language. Through various techniques of analysis, we can develop and test the criteria for the use of the concept. These criteria then help us understand the issue more fully and help us resolve potential questions about the meaning and application of the concept both in the issue we are examining and in language in general.

KEY TERMS

beliefs about a concept
borderline cases
case
challenge cases
concept stretching
conceptual analysis
contrary or opposite cases
criteria for the use of the concept
example

invented imaginary cases
invented situation
meaning of the concept
mediant or mixed cases
paradigm case
question of concept
related concepts
science-fiction cases

MODULE 10

ISSUE ANALYSIS

10.1 LEARNING OBJECTIVES

After completing this module, you should be able to

1. explain what an issue analysis is;
2. identify and explain the key terms involved in issue analysis;
3. construct an issues map of a specific issue;
4. construct an issues map of the issues within a set of texts; and
5. use an issues map as the basis for constructing an argument essay on that issue.

10.2 WHAT IS ISSUE ANALYSIS?

Issue analysis is the study of a topic or body of literature with the purpose of identifying the issues, positions, reasons for the positions, challenges, and possible responses to those challenges. To analyze an issue, we use the techniques of argument analysis and development to expand those argument sketches (also called *considerations,* defined below) into more fully developed arguments. This system of issue analysis enables us to take a more strategic position on the issue than some other methods of developing an argument allow. It can be used either to develop our own position on an issue or to analyze the positions others take on an issue.

If we choose to develop an argument or paper on a specific aspect of a topic, we can strategically select an issue, positions, and arguments. Issue analysis gives us a greater appreciation of the significance of the positions and arguments we develop, allowing us to discover new things about the issue and move us beyond what others have said about it.

10.3 TOPICS, ISSUES, POSITIONS

To do an issue analysis, we work through the following steps:

1. **Identify the topic.** A *topic* is a *subject for discussion.* Typically, it consists of a single word or a phrase: "the hijab," "wearing the hijab in a secular society," and "prohibiting the wearing of the hijab in a secular society" are all topics.
2. **Identify the relevant background materials.** These include the context in which the issue arises, the players, their interests, and the history of the issue. Familiarity with the background helps us understand why the issue is controversial. Identifying the players can mean not only pinpointing the specific individuals involved (or those who should be involved) but also the typical positions taken.
3. **Identify and frame the issue.** An *issue* is a point of contention within a given context and between at least two disputants, inquirers, or points of view. It is normally stated as a question:

   What is the hijab?

This question, however, is not an issue. It is simply an inquiry, or request for information. There is no dispute or controversy (as far as I am aware) over what the hijab is.

Should all Muslim women wear the hijab?

Depending on the context, this may or may not be controversial. Asked within a certain sect of Islam, there may be no controversy; in a particular Muslim community, there may be. The moment that there are different positions on a question's answer, it becomes an issue.

Should the wearing of the hijab be prohibited in public schools?

Although this is not controversial in most of Canada, it would be considered so in Quebec, France, and Germany.

Should the wearing of an offensive religious symbol be prohibited in a secular society?

This framing of the issue has two potential difficulties. First, it biases the question by labelling certain religious symbols "offensive." Second, it is imprecise since it does not make clear what is meant by "offensive religious symbols."

The *framing of an issue* refers to how a person structures and presents an issue. It includes such things as *scope* (how broadly or narrowly we define the issue — e.g., the hijab vs. religious symbols), *focus* (what we emphasize and the perspective we take — e.g., moral, legal, practical), and the *language* we use in framing.

How we frame an issue is critical. Our framing of the issue should be controversial, precise (i.e., involve one central idea), and stated in neutral terms (i.e., in terms that do not favour one position over another).

QUICK QUIZ 10.1   Identifying Issues

For each of the following topics

   a. identify whether it is an issue and explain why it is or is not;
   b. if it is an issue, explain whether it meets the criteria for a proper framing of the issue; and
   c. determine what kind of issue it is (factual, conceptual, normative)?

1. The morality of abortion.
2. Abortions have been done illegally by people who are not licensed medical practitioners.
3. Is abortion ever ethical?
4. Should abortion be allowed?
5. Should abortion for the purpose of preventing the spread of defective genes be allowed?
6. Is a woman ever justified in killing her unborn baby?
7. Is a woman ever justified in having an abortion?
8. Is the state ever justified in interfering with a woman's right to choose what to do with her body?

Answers for all Quick Quizzes in this text are provided in the Student Manual. After doing the Quick Quizzes, consult the Student Manual to check your understanding of the material.

4. **Identify the alternate positions on the issue.** A *position* is a stand taken on an issue. It is an answer to the question posed. Once we have identified the issues, we try to identify the possible positions that might be taken on that issue. Some of these will be argued for by specific individuals in the controversy you are examining. However, often not all possible positions are defended. One of the dynamics of controversy is that positions tend to polarize and various intermediate positions disappear from the discussion. Often we can contribute to a controversy by identifying these **unexpressed positions** and developing arguments for them. Even if we don't use them in the final analysis, it will help us to be aware of other possible considerations.

5. **Identify the possible considerations for the positions.** *Considerations* are topics that would need to be taken into account in developing reasons for a position, and then in developing an argument for that position. A consideration is to a position as a topic is to an issue: It is an idea that could be developed into a reason in an argument but has not yet been developed. Considerations include both the stated and unstated reasons.

6. **Develop the possible considerations into arguments, for both the main arguments and the sub-arguments.** Develop complete arguments, supplying missing premises, testing the arguments for soundness, and, where necessary, defending weak premises. We want to find the best possible arguments for each position, to understand what is plausible about each of the positions.

7. **Identify the objections to the positions and arguments and the possible responses to those objections.** Often the best way of doing this is to use one position to help determine possible objections that might be made to the other positions on the issue. For example, in the controversy over the wearing of the hijab, I might use the positions of the defenders of the wearing of the hijab to develop challenges for those who want to restrict it. I should not confine myself to those positions, however.

   In considering possible objections, we should distinguish between

   a. **objections/challenges to specific arguments** — any challenge to a specific argument is simply that — a challenge to a specific argument. If a person's *case* (the set of arguments for a position) consists of three arguments, and you have challenged one, then the person still has two arguments supporting his or her position. Consider the strength of your challenges: A challenge that the opponent has not supported a claim is much weaker than the challenge that the claim is false.

   b. **objections to positions** — develop counterarguments that show why a conclusion is false or unacceptable. Making an objection to a position requires presenting arguments of your own and defending an alternate position.

QUICK QUIZ 10.2   Identifying Positions and Considerations

For each of the following topics

a. identify any possible positions; and
b. identify all possible considerations you can think of for each position, whether you agree with them or not.

1. Should violent or sexist video games be restricted or banned?
2. Should the government fund inexpensive daycare for all working parents?

10.4 DEVELOPING AN ISSUES MAP

One way of keeping track of the positions on and arguments about an issue is to draw an issues map. An *issues map* is simply a visual way of portraying the issues, positions, key considerations and concepts, and possible objections and responses. A variation of a mind map, it merges the techniques of mind mapping with those of argument analysis, and uses some of the notations for argument analysis.

There is no one correct way to draw an issues map. However, some are more elaborate or more insightful than others. The following are some general guidelines for constructing an issues map:

- Use unlined paper.
- Draw your map quickly, without stopping to judge correctness or completeness.
- Use words or phrases, not sentences.
- Print rather than write.
- Use colour to make associations.
- Use different shapes (circles, boxes, triangles) for different kinds of ideas — e.g., reasons, conclusions, objections.
- Use symbols, images, and pictures to help draw connections between items.
- Cross-link ideas.
- Look for relationships.
- Revise and redraw the map occasionally to see if new connections emerge.

The basic strategy for constructing an issues map is to start from the general and work toward the specific:

1. Identify the purpose, context, and audience for the analysis.
2. Identify the basic topic(s). Brainstorm various topics related to the overall topic.
3. Identify possible issues from the topics and select an issue that addresses the basic purpose. Put that in the centre of a blank (preferably unlined) page of paper. Draw a circle around it.
4. Brainstorm the positions, considerations (argument sketches), and key concepts. Add these to the map. Connect positions to the issues that they support. Identify and map any key concepts. Review the map to see if it suggests any additional connections, either of support or challenge. Draw lines connecting any of the parts of the diagram that are linked logically to one another.
5. Analyze for additional connections.
6. Elaborate on the considerations to create full arguments, using the techniques from earlier modules. Examine each position's arguments for similarities and differences. Are there points of agreement? Where are the specific points of disagreement? When developing a consideration for one position, consider how the defenders of other positions in the issue might either respond to that consideration or use it for their own purposes. Revise the arguments for the various positions *to make them as strong as possible.*
7. Further analysis. Examine the arguments to see what you can learn from them.
8. Select and defend your position. If necessary, further develop your arguments and sub-arguments.

You may have to redraw your issues map several times.

The more you know about a topic, the better an issues map you will be able to construct. There is no substitute for knowledge of a field. However, don't limit yourself to simply repeating what everyone else has said. Are there important considerations or positions that are not being addressed? Analyze the interests of those on the various sides of the issue and examine the issues map to help discover unexpressed considerations. Use your knowledge of the field and related fields to help identify further possible considerations.

10.5 CONSTRUCTING A SAMPLE ISSUES MAP

This sample issues map uses the *Huck Finn* dialogue in Module 1 of the Student Manual as the basis for analysis. Before continuing, reread the dialogue. For the purposes of this illustration, the analysis will be confined to the materials contained in that dialogue. The following is designed to demonstrate the use of the method described above, but it is not complete. Some of the steps, especially those illustrated in more detail elsewhere, simply identify what needs to be done without elaboration.

1. Analysis Purpose, Context, and Audience

The purpose of this issues map is (1) to illustrate how to do an issue analysis and (2) to understand the issue. Doing an issue analysis is like writing an essay for an instructor. Its **context purpose** (the reason for undertaking the task) is to produce for another a rendition of our thought process. However, this is not its only purpose. Just as our reason for taking a course goes beyond getting a good grade to gathering valuable information that we can use as we build our knowledge, we should undertake the illustration of an issues map to sort out our own positions and arguments on issues so we can make better decisions (this is called the **substantive purpose**). One of the common errors in writing university essays is focusing solely on the substantive purpose and ignoring the context purpose.

The specific context in our example is a dispute at the local school board over whether or not *The Adventures of Huckleberry Finn* should be taught in high school English classes. Some parents have objected to its study, arguing that it is racist. The specific dispute is part of a more general set of issues over what should be taught in schools and who should determine that. Even more generally, it relates to the issue of what the purpose of education is.

The **players** include the parents on both sides of the issue — for and against — the students, both in general and the discussants, C and D, teachers, the school board, and citizens of the community. Other possible players include provincial (or state) boards of education and the legal system.

Identifying the **interests** of the players requires a bit of speculation. The parents who support banning the book have interests in not promoting racism in the classroom and in not exposing their children and others to racist materials. The parents opposed to banning the book have concerns about curricula being dictated by interest groups with specific agendas; the best interests of all students; and the censorship of unpopular ideas. Students have an interest in getting a good education. Teachers may have a concern that their judgment and/or control of class content is being usurped and have an interest in maintaining control of their curricula. The school board's concern may be that what is taught in the classroom could promote racism; that interest groups could be trying to dictate course content; and that a public controversy that may affect their reelection or political futures could erupt. The citizens of the community have an interest because what is taught in the schools contributes to youths becoming good citizens. *Interests* represent underlying values and points of view. However, these underlying values are seldom explicitly stated as part of the arguments given.

The audience, of course, is who we do the analysis for. For this illustration, the audience is composed of readers of this text.

2. The Topics

The basic topic is teaching *The Adventures of Huckleberry Finn* in the high school classroom. Related topics include censorship, racism, use of language, ethics in teaching literature, authority in the classroom, and the purpose of high school education.

3. Possible Issues

We can generate a number of possible issues:

1. *Should we teach* The Adventures of Huckleberry Finn *in the high school classroom?* This is fairly broad and opens up the possibility of moving into areas and topics not dealt with in the original passage, such as a discussion of the literary merits or historical accuracy of the novel, without addressing the issues of censorship and banning.
2. *Should we restrict or censor the teaching of* The Adventures of Huckleberry Finn *in the high school classroom?* This is more precise than 1. It introduces the topic of censorship or restricting the study of the novel.
3. *Is* The Adventures of Huckleberry Finn *racist?* This is a sub-issue. It is one of the grounds for restricting the teaching of the novel.
4. *Should material that some consider racist be banned in the high school classroom?* This is the general principle behind 2.
5. *Should works of literature that some consider racist be banned in the high school classroom?* This reformulation of 4 limits the issue to works of literature because 4 could include historical materials.
6. *Should literature that is taught in the high school classroom be judged on ethical grounds before being allowed to be taught?* This formulation of the issue differs in that it focuses on ethical considerations.
7. *Who should determine what is taught in a high school English classroom?* This formulation differs in that it focuses on whose responsibility it should be to determine the curriculum for high school English. However, this could be too broad.
8. *On what grounds should we determine what is and is not taught in high school?* Far broader than 1, 2, 4, and 5, this asks for general criteria for curricula. Even if we narrow the scope to English literature courses, the topic is too broad. Identifying specific conditions for restricting a particular kind of literature narrows it. Examining the grounds for determining curricula might help develop some of the specific arguments on a narrower topic.

Each of these questions frames the issue in a different way through scope, focus, and language used. At this stage, consider different possible frames for the issue.

From these, let us select the second question as the basis for this illustration and analysis: *Should we restrict or censor the teaching of* The Adventures of Huckleberry Finn *in the high school classroom?*

We put the issue in the centre of a blank piece of paper.

Should we restrict or censor the teaching of Huckleberry Finn *in the high school classroom?*

4. Brainstorm and Map Considerations

The key positions on the selected topic include (1) We should restrict the teaching of *The Adventures of Huckleberry Finn* in the classroom (2) We should not restrict it (3) We should restrict it under certain conditions (4) We should ban it completely and (5) We should not ban it.

Considerations include (1) racist, (2) harmful, (3) offensive, (4) learn from it, and (5) teaching is not advocacy.

We add these to the diagram. (When working with an issues map, the lists tend to be derived from the map rather than generated and then placed on the map. This is the case with the materials that follow.)

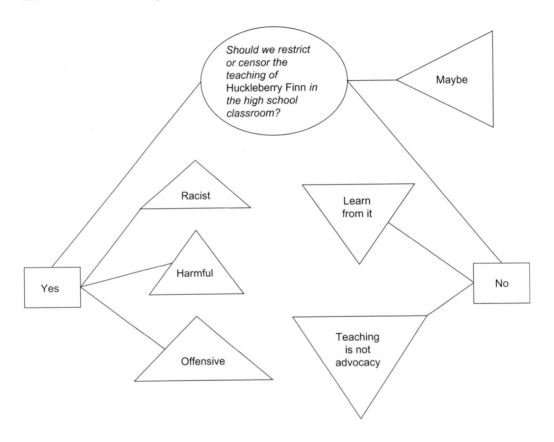

From this map, we identify the sub-issues: (1) Should we restrict something because it is racist? (2) Is *The Adventures of Huckleberry Finn* racist? (3) Should we restrict something because some parents find it offensive and hurtful? and (4) Should we restrict something because it causes harm?

There are three key positions and their main considerations are as follows:

1. Yes, restrict it under all conditions because it is racist, harmful, and offensive to some individuals and groups.
2. No, do not restrict it under any conditions because we can learn from it, and teaching a text is not the same as advocating what is in the text.

3. The restrict-under-certain-conditions position can be defended by a combination of the reasons in 1 and 2. What needs to be determined are the specific restrictive conditions.

Key concepts include (1) racist, (2) harmful, and (3) offensive.

5. Analyze for Additional Connections

The map suggests that the reasons offered for each position could also be framed as challenges to the other positions. For example, if the "yes" position argues for restricting on the basis of causing harm, harmfulness could count as a challenge against the "no" position. The "no restriction" position would have to show that there would be no harm, that the harm would not be serious, or that the harm would be outweighed by other, more important considerations.

Accordingly, the considerations offered for the "no" position could be used to challenge the reasons given for the "yes" position. For example, the defender of the no position could argue that even if *The Adventures of Huckleberry Finn* is racist, that is not sufficient grounds for not teaching it because through the book, we can learn about racism and its evils.

6. Elaborate the Considerations into Arguments

Including possible challenges and responses, develop each of the considerations into the best possible argument for the position. (Only one of the considerations will be developed for the purposes of illustration. A complete analysis would develop all of the considerations.)

A consideration for position 2 —"Do not restrict it under any conditions"— is that students can learn from it. The key point of the "learn from it" consideration is that despite material either (a) being racist or (b) possibly being thought of as racist by some, students can learn from it. Although (a) and (b) are similar, ideally, we should develop both arguments. Since the first is the stronger of the two, we will focus on it here.

For the sake of argument, this illustration will assume that *The Adventures of Huckleberry Finn* is racist. If it is not, this line of argument would be moot.

1.   We can learn from material that is racist.

2.   [We should not restrict materials that we can learn from. Or If we can learn from something, even if it is racist, we should not restrict its use in the classroom.]

∴ 3.   We should not restrict the use of materials, even those that some people may consider racist, as teaching tools.

The argument is valid (affirming the antecedent). Neither premise is obviously true; therefore, each needs defence.

Since the contents of the original dialogue do not provide any suggestions on how to defend either premise, I will need to develop my own reasons. Brainstorming conditions under which exposure to racist materials might be beneficial and could become part of a learning experience for students can help us develop reasons, which can then be turned into arguments.

I begin by generating a literary example — Shylock in *The Merchant of Venice* — and a historical example — Adolf Hitler's *Mein Kampf*. Analyzing these, I distinguish between different kinds of material called "racist"— materials that express racism, materials that reflect racism, and materials that advocate racism.

Thinking about the conditions under which each of these would be useful learning tools, I arrive at the consideration that they have some redeeming values:

- literary — Shakespeare;
- rhetorical — *Mein Kampf*;
- historical— understanding of why *Mein Kampf* and Hitler himself succeeded in persuading a nation to adopt a particular viewpoint;
- historical/sociological — understanding of the conditions under which racism develops and is sustained;
- recognition of different kinds of racism and analyses of them — for example, people may recognize racism directed toward one group (Jews, blacks) but not others (Muslims, Native Americans);
- recognition of how racism influences people;
- sensitization of students to different kinds of racist materials and recognition of the differences between racist and nonracist materials; and
- identification of emotional responses and knowledge of how to react analytically rather than simply emotionally to racist materials.

The material generated by this one consideration is varied and strong enough to be developed into many arguments. (In fact, we have enough for a decent five- to six-page paper.)

The most difficult argument to develop would involve addressing materials that advocate racism. A possible defence for claim 1 might be the following:

5. Students can learn from materials that desensitize them to potentially harmful and offensive materials.

4. Materials that advocate racist ideas are potentially harmful and offensive.

∴   1.   Students can learn from materials that advocate racist ideas.

Using the topics model, we can verify that this argument is valid. Premise 4 seems relatively unobjectionable. The weakest claim is 5 — that needs to be defended.

Objections to claim 1 include the following:

Obj. 1.1   Most, if not all, students will not learn from racist materials because they will be inflamed by the materials and this will prevent them from learning anything.

Obj. 1.2   Students will learn, but they will learn to be racist, and we do not want our students to become racist. Therefore, we should not teach racist materials in high schools.

Obj. 1.3   Students are not critical enough to deal with racist materials. Therefore, we should not teach racist materials.

Obj. 1.4   Teaching racist materials will contribute to the spread of racism, and the school should not do that. Therefore, racist materials should not be taught.

Note that these objections are to the conclusion, not to the reasons in the sub-argument. Nonetheless, they are the kinds of objections that a defence of claim 4 will have to forestall. We can reframe some of these objections to address 4.

Responses to objection 1.1:

Resp. 1.1a   The objection is based on an empirical claim—that students will become inflamed by the material and will not learn. What grounds are there for thinking that most, if not all, students will become inflamed? [This response simply turns the challenge back on the objector, which is not sufficient. Since the objection is not fully addressed, the reasoning behind Obj. 1.1 should be developed further. We could probe this, but we will not do that here.

Resp. 1.1b   There is another problem—the objector presupposes that becoming inflamed prevents learning. While it may in some cases, it may also facilitate learning by engaging the student and allowing the instructor to help the student explore why the material is objectionable. This can help turn an emotional response into a reasoned response and thereby facilitate learning.

In a complete analysis, we would work through all of the arguments, reasons, possible objections and responses, and possible formulations of the arguments to develop the best possible argument we can.

Important to working through objections and responses is identifying what we can learn from them. In a debate, we simply seek to refute our debating partner's arguments. In reasoned discourse, we seek to learn from the reasons and responses, to discover what we can about our own position and the various alternate positions.

One thing we may learn from this sample exchange is that there is a legitimate concern that using racist materials may unduly emotionally arouse students. This would call for caution in using such materials but would not necessarily be grounds for prohibiting their use. It might call for a qualification that such materials should be used only when other available materials would not accomplish the overall teaching goals of the curriculum. A response could be to show why it is a good thing that students learn to go beyond emotional responses to reasoned responses and how controversial material, including racist materials, can facilitate that.

Resp. 1.3a   The objection is that high school students are not critical enough to deal with racist materials. One way of responding would be to show that high school students are critical enough or can be taught to be critical enough in using such materials.

Resp. 1.3b   An alternate, and not necessarily incompatible, response would be to accept the objection and show that it can lead to a different conclusion. Students may not initially be critical enough to deal with racist materials, especially materials that arouse their emotions. However, a key function of education is to help students develop their critical thinking skills. One of the best ways of developing those skills is by exposing students to ideas and materials they do not accept as well as to ideas and materials they do accept and showing them how to be critical of both. [This would probably need some further defence.]

The two responses can be combined: Some students may have sufficiently developed critical thinking skills to deal with such materials, whereas others may not have. In either case, exposure to racist materials can help them develop these skills. This is an argument sketch that would need to be developed further if used in the final presentation.

The following pages contain a sample developed issue analysis with considerations, challenges, and responses.

Issue: Should we ban the teaching of racist materials in high school classes?

Concepts: racist: advocates racism
                                  expresses racism
                                  illustrates racism
                 ban: regulate, restrict, allow under certain conditions?
                 harmful: is offence harmful?

Scope: For whom? Grade nine, grade twelve? Does it make a difference?

Examples: *Mein Kampf*
                 Merchant of Venice (other literature?)
                 anti-black, anti-Catholic, KKK materials
                 Japanese anti-Chinese, anti-Korean materials WWII
                 Others?

Positions, Reasons, Challenges:

1. Yes, because

    1. Causes harm because
        Offends – Challenge – is that sufficient to ban?
        Upsets students – Challenge – need it? Evidence? Scope? Better handled with
                debriefing?
        Reinforces racist ideas – Challenge – need it; is that sufficient to ban?
        Maintains racism in society – Challenge – not discussing maintains prejudices;
                discussing exposes them
    2. Offensive in itself, but does not harm
    3. Supports racism (form of causing harm; treat as causing harm)

2. No, because

    1. Can learn from racist materials – Challenge – won't learn – Response – depends
                                on how taught
                                Challenge – students will become racist –
                                Response – depends on how taught
                                Challenge – students not critical enough to be
                                exposed to such materials – Response –
                                opportunity to teach how to be critical of such
                                materials
        Best way of teaching about racism is by exposing to such materials – Challenge
                – evidence?
        Use to analyze racism
        Teaching sensitizes students to racist materials – Challenge – does it?
        Enable students to respond not just react emotionally

    2. Teaching is not advocacy (response to challenge that using racist material in
        teaching is advocating racist ideas).

    3. Free speech – Challenge – limits to free speech in high school.

    4. Other things may end up being banned – unpopular ideas, things thought
        offensive or harmful — sex education, unpopular political opinions; "sanitized"
        history. May succumb to political and social pressure.

3. Under certain conditions (draws upon yes and no arguments) which include

    1. Minimize harm
    2. Well-trained teachers; not all teachers qualify
    3. Taught with sensitivity
    4. Clear purpose for material used.

This could be elaborated upon further.

7. Further Analysis

The issues map above generates a number of insights about the issue.

Any positions defended will have to qualify what is meant by "teaching racist materials" and probably limit the scope. What is appropriate for grade-twelve students may not be appropriate for grade-nine students. And not all students would be upset or harmed by exposure to racist materials. This will require a balance of considerations argument (see Module 12).

In the argument we've developed thus far, the intermediate positions will be developed from the extremes.

We should look for points on which there are agreement and disagreement. The points of agreement can be used to develop bridges between the positions; the points of disagreement can be used to sharpen the arguments.

8. Select and Defend Your Position

Now that we have a good map of the issue, the various positions, and arguments, we can more easily determine what our own position is and what we want to defend. If we were writing an essay, how much of this we could and would use would depend on the purpose and the length of the essay. Using all of the material, we could write a fairly extended (twenty-page) essay. If we had a shorter (four- to five-page) essay to write, we could select one or two key arguments and develop those. Such analyses usually give you something new and interesting to say on the issue.

10.6 DEVELOPING AN ISSUE ANALYSIS FROM A SET OF ARTICLES

We can use the basic model for developing an issue analysis to analyze the issue or issues laid out in a set of articles. Many of the issues we encounter are embedded in an extensive body of literature. The steps below will help you extract the issues from the materials you have:

1. **Read the texts you are analyzing, noting possible issues, considerations, and key concepts.** Are there any important distinctions made in the texts? How are the key concepts used? Are they used in the same way or differently by different authors? For example, in the pornography debates, one group of authors may use *pornography* to mean "sexually explicit representations," whereas another may use it to mean "portrayals of sex with explicit violence," and other authors may use it in yet different ways.
2. **Formulate in your own words the issues in the texts.** Many authors do not explicitly formulate the issue they are addressing, so read carefully for implicit claims.
3. **Identify the possible positions on these issues.** Dig beyond the positions actually stated and see if there are other possible positions that have not been identified. Which of those positions have already been stated or taken in the text(s) you have examined? Which positions have not been addressed? Why is that, do you think?
4. **Identify the main considerations offered by each author.** Can you think of additional considerations both for the stated positions and for the unstated ones?
5. **Identify the key concepts and do a brief conceptual analysis of them to see how the authors use the terms.** Do you agree with their use of the concepts?
6. **Draw an issues map incorporating the preceding steps.**
7. **Analyze the issues map.** Look for places of agreement and disagreement, similarities in types of considerations, ways to bring the different positions together, and ways to more clearly distinguish the disagreements.

8. **Identify and assess the key arguments that have been given.** Can you think of other arguments or considerations that could be developed into arguments? Assess the alternate positions with respect to one another. What elements of truth can you find in each position? How strong is each in relation to one another? Assess the alternate positions. Which has the strongest case? A *case* is the collective set of arguments and supporting evidence for a specific position. Can it be made stronger? Are there further challenges that could be made? This is not a matter of selecting the one whose conclusion or reasons you agree with. If the argument for the position is poor, then it is likely not the best case.

9. **Select a position that you want to explore and develop the possible considerations on that position into arguments.** Given the other positions and their considerations, what challenges might be made to your position? It is often easier to think of possible challenges to your own position by looking at it from another perspective. Trying to critique a position to which you are committed (even tentatively) is often difficult without knowing the alternatives and the contrasts. Simply defending a position and ignoring the challenges is doing only part of the job. How might you defend your position if challenged? Note that it is all right when developing a position (or presenting it in an argumentative essay) to acknowledge that there are objections for which you don't have a full answer.

10.7 PASSAGES FOR ISSUE ANALYSIS

Below are two sample passages on a topic. They will be the basis for developing an issue analysis. Before continuing on to Section 10.8, work through the passages using the steps above.

Euthanasia: No

Euthanasia is increasingly being discussed in our society. The Robert Latimer, Terri Schiavo, and Sue Rodriguez cases are only the most visible of a host of similar situations families and care givers are facing. Although we may be sympathetic to the circumstances of someone like Sue Rodriguez and wish her an easy death, that does not give us the right to kill her, nor does it give her the right to have someone help her die. Not only is euthanasia inherently wrong, it is also wrong on practical grounds.

Euthanasia is the intentional taking of the life of another person. Simply acceding to someone's desires not to have extraordinary life-extending treatment (often called "DNR," or a "do not resuscitate" order) is not euthanasia. In such a situation, the person is dying, and no one actively accelerates the process. However, in the case of euthanasia, someone intervenes to bring about the end of the person's life, usually through a lethal injection or some other means that defeats the disease process. According to this definition, there is no such thing as "passive" euthanasia. Euthanasia involves the killing of another person.

Euthanasia is inherently wrong for two reasons. It involves killing, and killing is always murder. All humans have a natural inclination to live. Every part of our body strives to survive. When disease invades the body, the body marshals its forces to fight the pathogens. Euthanasia violates this natural inclination to live. Ending one's own life goes against our nature and undermines our human dignity.

Euthanasia is also wrong for practical reasons. Death is irreversible and final. Not only is there the possibility of a mistaken diagnosis, but contemporary medicine is advancing rapidly. There is always the prospect of a cure that could bring someone back from the brink of death. Patients also recover from seemingly terminal diseases and diagnoses to the mystification of their physicians. Allowing euthanasia precludes the possibility of such miraculous cures. If we permit euthanasia, people might be tempted to abandon hope far too easily.

Finally, medical professionals are dedicated to the saving of lives, but the legalization of euthanasia would have a corruptive influence on their dedication. If involved in ending lives, doctors and nurses could easily adopt a less caring attitude, not only toward the severely or terminally ill but also toward their less ill patients, resulting in an overall decline of medical care.

Allowing terminally ill patients to authorize their deaths by euthanasia will lead to a slippery slope that would ultimately affect the killing of people not terminally ill but in constant pain and suffering, or others who are defined as "hopelessly ill." Once we make it acceptable to kill those who are hopelessly ill, it is but a short step to allow euthanasia for others who are not hopelessly ill. This is made easier by the appointing of proxies to make decisions for those who cannot make decisions for themselves and are not terminally ill. Once we open this floodgate, it will be a short step to legally killing individuals for all sorts of reasons.

Euthanasia: Yes

The debate over euthanasia comes down to one fundamental issue: whether or not an individual has a right to die in a time and manner of his or her choosing. The basic societal value of autonomy and the idea that adults are the most appropriate judges of what is best for them justify active euthanasia.

With medical breakthroughs, we can keep people alive biologically almost indefinitely. With the medical profession's commitment to maintain life, many individuals end up being kept alive long past the point at which they enjoy life or sometimes beyond the point at which they are even conscious of it. Many are in pain brought on by deadly diseases. Yet the prohibition of euthanasia prevents people from dying at a time and place of their choosing. Euthanasia is a matter of rights, and it is more humane than allowing people to suffer through the final stages of illness.

The right of autonomy is a fundamental value within Western society. As individuals, we are entitled to make choices about things that affect us and to act on those choices, as long as our doing so does not infringe on the rights of others. Autonomy is a core value because it permits people to live in accordance with their idea of a good life, makes them responsible for the lives they live, and encourages them to live their lives in ways they consider best for them and the kinds of persons they want to be.

My right to autonomy means I have a right to decide the time and place of my death, as long as it is within my power. Unlike what some of the opponents of euthanasia contend, my having a right to die does not mean that others have an obligation to help me die. However, someone who chooses to help me should not be held morally accountable.

A second core value is the idea of individual well-being. Individuals are best able to determine what will result in their own well-being. Pain and suffering do not contribute to well-being. Our ability to choose what's best for ourselves does have exceptions, such as mental illness (e.g., depression) and diminished decision-making capacity. I am not addressing those here.

A distinction is sometimes drawn between passive and active euthanasia. Passive euthanasia involves, at the request and direction of the patient, not taking extraordinary measures to extend life when it is at risk. It is a "letting die" whereby the individual is made as comfortable as possible and allowed to die. For example, not treating pneumonia but providing only pain relief would be an aspect of passive euthanasia. Active euthanasia involves taking active steps to help end someone's life. Administering a lethal injection is an example of active euthanasia.

Active euthanasia can be more humane than simply letting someone die. In some cases, no amount of medication will relieve an individual's intense pain and suffering. The pain simply overrides medical science's ability to control it. Allowing an individual to suffer for days, weeks, or months when he or she wants to die is not only inhumane, it deprives that person of their autonomy and imposes on them another's notion of well-being.

It might be argued that a miracle cure could be developed overnight or that the individual could have a miraculous recovery. Neither of these objections is realistic. It takes years to develop new drugs and treatments. Physicians usually know if there are any being tested that might offer some hope, and they can inform their patients before a decision is made. Miracle recoveries are extremely rare—not the common occurrence opponents suggest.

Denying individuals the option of active euthanasia is denying them their autonomy and their ability to dictate what is best for them and instead imposing someone else's notion of well-being on them.

10.8 A SAMPLE ISSUE ANALYSIS OF THE EUTHANASIA PASSAGES

Each of the passages above is relatively short; however, they will be sufficient to illustrate the method described in Section 10.6. Often we would work with more material.

1. **Read the texts, noting possible issues and considerations.** You can use the techniques for extended argument analysis in Module 7 to highlight and annotate the text.
2. **Identify the issues in the text.** The central issue in both texts is whether euthanasia is morally justified. One key distinction is made between active and passive euthanasia.

    If individuals do have a right to euthanasia, there are a number of possible related issues, including such things as the obligations of health-care providers and others. However, these are not central to the sanctioning of euthanasia. We might want to limit the scope more clearly to, for example, those with terminal illnesses, in the end stages of the illness, and suffering from pain that cannot be treated.
3. **Identify possible positions.** Possible positions include the following:
    a. Active euthanasia is morally justified.
    b. Active euthanasia is not morally justified.
    c. Active euthanasia is morally justified under certain conditions.
    d. Passive euthanasia is morally justified.
    e. Passive euthanasia is not morally justified.
    f. Passive euthanasia is morally justified under certain conditions.
    g. There is no moral difference between active and passive euthanasia.

    We could also substitute *moral* and *morally* with *legal* and *legally* in each of these positions. The "No" essay takes the position that active euthanasia is not morally justified and that there is no such thing as passive euthanasia. The "Yes" one takes the position that active euthanasia is morally justified under some conditions.
4. **Identify the main considerations.**

    "No" essay: a. inherently wrong:
    killing
    contrary to nature
    b. practical effects:
    abandon hope
    mistaken diagnosis
    spontaneous recovery

        c. decline in medical care
        d. extend euthanasia to others

"Yes" essay: a. right to die
        b. autonomy
        c. well-being
        d. more humane
        e. response to miracle cure and spontaneous recovery

Can you think of additional considerations both for the stated and unstated positions?

"No" essay: e. inherently wrong:
         cheapens the value we place on human life.
       f. practical effects:
         allowing euthanasia may lead to less research into some forms of
         illnesses, especially if individuals with those kinds of illness tend
         to elect euthanasia

"Yes" essay f. more efficient use of medical resources:
         rather than putting effort into those who want to end life, more
         time can be spent on others
       g. physician's obligation to relieve pain and suffering

5. **Identify the key concepts.** The key concepts are (1) active euthanasia, (2) passive euthanasia, and (3) autonomy. The conceptual analysis of how they are used in the text is not done here.
6. **Draw an issues map.**

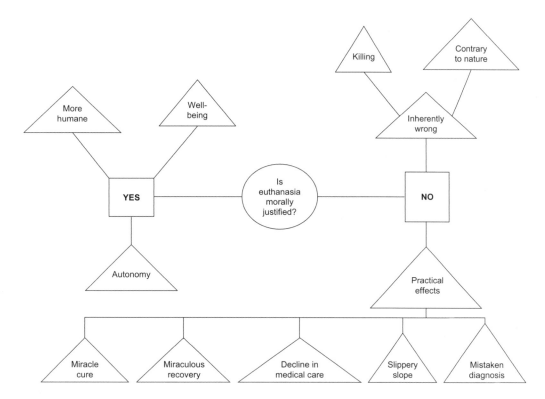

7. **Analyze the issues map.** The "No" side has two basic arguments, each with a number of sub-arguments. Both the "Yes" and "No" sides point to basic values — autonomy and well-being versus no killing and the preservation of life. One approach we can take in our analysis is to develop arguments about which of these should take precedence in this kind of situation. We could also examine whether different kinds of subjects — anencephalic infants, Alzheimer's patients in terminal stages, cancer patients in terminal stages — would make a difference to the argument.

8. **Develop and assess the arguments.** First, develop the main arguments for each position. Then assess those arguments using the tools of argument assessment, including possible challenges and responses. The assessments below are schematic and not fully developed. Where challenges and responses are available, they have been included.

"Euthanasia: No" Analyzed

The "Euthanasia: No" essay has two main lines of argument — the "inherently wrong" argument and the "practical effects argument." The "inherently wrong" line is supported by two sub-arguments; and the "practical effects," by five.

Euthanasia is inherently wrong:

1. **Euthanasia is killing:**

   1. Euthanasia involves killing.

   2. All killing is morally wrong.

      _____

   ∴ 3. Euthanasia is morally wrong.

   This is a valid argument, determined to be so by using the topics model (not shown here). The second premise is likely false. Counterexamples — self-defence, police, soldiers in wartime, some suicides — would be contentious but possible.

2. **Nature (or inclination to live):**

   4. All humans have an inclination to live.

   5. Euthanasia violates this natural inclination.

   A. [Anything that violates our natural inclination to live is morally wrong.]

      _____

   ∴ 3. Euthanasia is morally wrong.

   This is a valid argument, determined to be so by using the topics model (not shown here). Premises 4 and A are false. Premise 4 may beg the question. Reasons for this sub-argument do not establish the claim. Possible counterexample — suicide. That we have an inclination to live does not show that we will always choose to live or that violating that inclination to live is always morally wrong — for example, a parent sacrificing his or her life for a child; a soldier, for another soldier.

Practical effects:
3. Mistaken diagnosis:

6.   There is the possibility of a mistaken diagnosis, where someone thought to be terminally ill is not.

B.   [If there is the possibility of a mistaken diagnosis in such a case and it may result in someone dying unnecessarily, then euthanasia should not be allowed.]

∴ 3.   We should not allow euthanasia.

This is a valid argument that affirms the antecedent. Premise 6 is true, but patients can demand second and third independent opinions, thereby reducing the possibility of mistaken diagnoses. Premise B can be challenged. A response to this claim may be that the individual is choosing to die rather than taking a chance on living.

4. Miracle cure:

7.   There is always the possibility of a miraculous recovery.

C.   [If there is the possibility of a miraculous recovery, euthanasia should not be allowed.]

∴ 3.   Euthanasia should not be allowed.

This is a valid argument that affirms the antecedent. Premise 7 can be challenged: This is rare and simply does not happen in the end stages of most diseases (e.g., liver cancer).

5. Miraculous recovery:

8.   Some patients make a miraculous recovery from seemingly terminal illnesses.

D.   [If individuals might make a miraculous recovery from a terminal disease, then they should not be allowed to choose euthanasia.]

∴ 3.   Euthanasia should not be allowed.

This is a valid argument that affirms the antecedent. Premise 8 advances a claim of something that is extremely rare and can be challenged on those grounds.

6. Decline in medical care:

9.   Allowing euthanasia will lead health-care professionals to adopt a less caring attitude toward their patients.

E.   [Anything that leads health-care professionals to adopt a less caring attitude toward their patients should not be allowed.]

∴   3.   Euthanasia should not be allowed.

This is a valid argument, determined to be so by using the topics model (not shown here). Counterexample for E — palliative care and for-profit medicine could do the same.

7. Slippery slope:

10.   Allowing euthanasia for the terminally ill could easily lead to the killing of those not terminally ill.

F.   [Anything that could lead to the killing of those not terminally ill should not be allowed.]

∴   3.   Euthanasia should not be allowed.

This is a valid argument, determined to be so by using the topics model (not shown here). Premise 10 is a slippery slope fallacy.

"Euthanasia: Yes" Analyzed

The "Euthanasia: Yes" essay has four lines of argument — the "autonomy," "well-being," and "more humane" arguments, and the "miraculous cure/miraculous recovery" rebuttal.

1. Autonomy:

1.   Autonomy is a basic value (right) in Western society. (Sub-argument supports not diagrammed here.)

2.   Euthanasia is an exercise of autonomy.

A.   [No one has the right to prevent someone from exercising his or her right to autonomy.]

∴   3.   No one has the right to prevent someone from having euthanasia performed on them if they so choose.

This is a valid argument. However, all three premises can be challenged: 2. Even if autonomy is a basic value, it is not the only basic value. Find another basic value that conflicts and that may override — e.g., justice? 1. There are cases in which euthanasia may not be an exercise in autonomy; this will likely be rebutted by the defender of the argument by examples of cases where autonomy is not being exercised. A. See the possible objections to premise 1 and develop.

2. **Well-being:**

    4.   A core value of Western society is individual well-being.

    5.   Individuals are best able to determine what leads to their own well-being.

    B.   [If an individual determines that euthanasia is for his or her own well-being, then that individual should be able to act on that choice.]

∴ 6.   Each individual should be able to have euthanasia if he or she so chooses.

This is a valid argument. Premise 4 has the same problem as premise 1. It presents one core value but not necessarily the only overarching one. If in conflict with some other core value (or right, depending on how this is formulated), then this could be overridden. Premise 5 is not true under all conditions. Some individuals choose self-destructive behaviour — alcoholism, drug use, extremely risky behaviour, and other actions that shorten their lives. This could also be used to undermine B.

3. **More humane:**

    7.   Active euthanasia is more humane than passive euthanasia.

    Sub-argument:

    8.   It is more humane to relieve suffering than to stand by and allow it to continue.

    9.   Under certain conditions, active euthanasia relieves suffering, whereas passive euthanasia allows it to continue.

∴ 7.   Active euthanasia is more humane than allowing a person to continue to suffer in excruciating pain.

    C.   [If something is more humane, then it should be allowed.]

∴ 10. Active euthanasia should be allowed.

Both the main and sub-arguments are valid. Premise C might be challenged by trying to show that there are other values that override being humane. A challenger would need to create an argument to show that the injunction not to kill another overrides.

4. Miraculous cure/miraculous recovery rebuttal:

The argument that active euthanasia should not be allowed because some individuals may make a miraculous recovery or a miracle cure may suddenly be found is rebutted by the following claims:

Neither of these are realistic:

a. Cures take a long time to develop, and physicians are aware of treatments being developed.
b. Miraculous recoveries are rare.
c. Individuals can be given the relevant information and can then make their choices.

9. **Assess the alternate positions with respect to one another.** Of the arguments given, the position in favour of active euthanasia has made the strongest case. Each of the arguments for the "No" side has one or more serious defects, as given. Better sub-arguments might improve the "euthanasia is killing" or the "from nature" arguments, but there is no indication in the passages how this might be done. The arguments in the "pro-active euthanasia" position tend to be better arguments or are easier to correct. In addition, of the basic appeals (basic reasons) made in each of the two positions, those favouring active euthanasia appeal to fundamental values. The anti-euthanasia position appeals to the value that killing is wrong but has difficulty with counterexamples. Although the arguments raised in the pro-euthanasia paper have some weaknesses, these can be more easily addressed.

What such a comparative assessment does is evaluate, from the arguments presented, which side has made a stronger, more defensible case. This does not mean that it is the best position or the position that we would want to adopt. It does, however, assess which of the authors has made a stronger case for his or her position.

10. **Select a position and develop it.** You might decide to defend either of the positions above or to identify an alternate position that is not explored in the articles. The analysis of the issue and positions in the previous steps provides you with material. However, you should try to use that only as a basis for developing and going beyond what others have done. By developing sub-arguments and pursuing challenges and responses, you will be in a position to contribute further to the discussion. For more on developing your own arguments and turning them into prose, see Module 12.

MODULE SUMMARY

Issue analysis involves stepping back from the analysis of specific arguments and focusing on the issues, alternative positions on those issues, and considerations used in developing arguments for the positions. This module illustrates how to do an issue analysis on an issue of interest and on a body of literature. Issue analysis involves additional skills beyond those of argument analysis and evaluation. It involves argument analysis and evaluation and includes such skills as framing an issue; generating unstated positions, considerations, and arguments; drawing an issues map; and using the issues map to probe issues further. Much of the module has been devoted to illustrating two issue analyses — one of an issue of interest on which a person might wish to take a position and one on a body of literature.

KEY TERMS

case

considerations

context purpose

focus

framing of an issue

interests

issue

issue analysis

issues map

language

players

position

scope

substantive purpose

topic

unexpressed positions

ARGUMENTATION[1]

11.1 LEARNING OBJECTIVES

After completing this module, you should be able to

1. explain the difference between argumentation, persuasion, rational persuasion, debate, and other forms of dialogue that use argument;
2. explain the role of argument in each;
3. identify the three main skills in argumentation and the components of those skills;
4. use those skills in verbal argumentation;
5. identify and use the two components of listening in argumentation; and
6. engage effectively in an argument dialogue.

11.2 INTRODUCTION

Argumentation is the process of reasoning with reasoners — that is, of constructing arguments, presenting those arguments, challenging, and responding to those challenges in an ongoing dialogue. Although developing and challenging arguments are the core elements of argumentation, not all use of arguments in a discourse is argumentation. Arguments are used in a variety of other contexts, including such areas as persuasion, debate, and the law. Although the term *argumentation* is sometimes used to apply to all of these, there are some significant differences, the central ones being the aim or purpose of the discourse and the rules that govern that discourse.

Debate is an adversarial process in which opposing sides use arguments to defeat their opponents. The goal is not to reveal the truth about an issue but to establish who has given the better argument, thereby "winning." Debates often involve polarizing an issue and ignoring possibilities that would fall between the opposing viewpoints. A debater seeks out flaws in the opponent's position to show the weaknesses of that position and ultimately to defeat the opponent. To build a strong case, the debater must maintain his or her original position. Usually governed by fairly strict rules of process and turn-taking, debates focus entirely on the issue and ignore the person. Courtroom law shares many of the characteristics of debate.

Persuasion is the process of trying to win someone over to a particular point of view or to motivate a person to perform a particular act. Persuasion that is based purely on reasons and argument is **rational persuasion,** a form of argumentation. Most persuasion, however, uses other methods — appeals to emotion, desires, interests, threats of harm, or force. While arguments may be used, they are simply a means to an end. Persuasion is allied with marketing,

---

[1] I would like to thank Professor Michael Gilbert, York University, whose work on the practical aspects of argumentation, as described in his book *How to Win an Argument* (2nd ed, Toronto: McGraw-Hill Ryerson, 1996.) and his *Effective Dispute Manual*, (unpublished, Toronto, 1981.) has strongly influenced my ideas in this module.

rhetoric, and advertising. Typically, persuasion is one-sided — one person trying to persuade another. The persuader does not expose his position to critique and normally does not expect to have his opinion changed.

Argumentation is a cooperative, reciprocal process in which both sides state their positions, challenges the positions of each other, and have their own positions challenged. Issues are addressed and positions adopted and abandoned solely in terms of reasons. The aim is to discover the truth about an issue. Both sides explore the complexities of their own position and that of the other. Either side may change its position and the reasons for it in numerous ways and may become rationally persuaded by an argument partner. Argumentation results in reflection on and a better understanding of one's own position and that of an argument partner. Argumentation involves not simply providing justification for one's preexisting point of view but, rather, the examination, probing, and improving or modifying of it through reasoned discourse.

In practice, these, and other modes of discourse involving the use of arguments (e.g., negotiation, legal proceedings), can and do overlap and intermingle. Argument is used in various ways and for varying purposes, as are many of the skills of argumentation. We may start out in an argumentation and end up in a debate. Nonetheless, it is important to recognize the distinctions between the modes of discourse because both the aims and the rules of engagement in each differ. Although often not distinguished in the real world, understanding their differences can help us comprehend what is happening in any individual discourse and help us achieve our aims in it. It also helps us understand what pure argumentation can be like. The tools of argumentation are outlined in this module.

Argumentation is defined and distinguished from other forms of discourse both by its central aim and its constitutive rules. The central aim of argumentation is to find the truth about an issue through reasoned discourse. The **constitutive rules,** outlined in Module 1, define the practice of argumentation. Other forms of discourse — debate, persuasion, legal argument, and advertising — have different aims and correspondingly different constitutive rules.

In much of the analysis and evaluation of argument in previous modules, we have viewed arguments as static texts. Even when dealing with written arguments that might be part of an ongoing discussion — for example, a series of articles, letters, or memos — we have treated them as containing a series of discrete and static arguments. Yet in our daily lives, most of us encounter arguments as fluid and dynamic. They are a part of ongoing discussions and dialogues and develop through interaction with one or more others. Sometimes they emerge from discussions. In argumentation, more emphasis is placed on the challenges and responses to the challenges. This module examines the dynamic nature of argumentation and how to apply the skills developed in the preceding modules to it, with special emphasis on verbal argumentation.

11.3 THE DYNAMICS OF ARGUMENTATION

Verbal argumentation is free flowing and dynamic. Underlying the fluidity of the discussion, there are some core patterns that help define the key features of an ideal argumentation encounter. How these manifest themselves in a discussion will vary considerably. To be effective in any argumentation, there are three core tasks that must be addressed:

1. eliciting and identifying arguments;
2. clarifying meaning; and
3. evaluating arguments through challenging and responding to challenges.

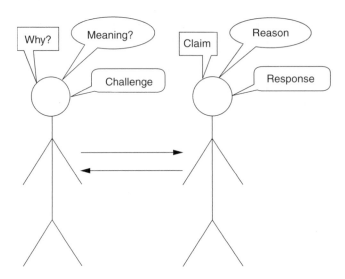

Each task uses a specific set of skills. How we use them and in what order vary between encounters.

The following terms, many of which were encountered in earlier modules, are used to identify the people, roles, and elements of the process:

arguer — any person involved in an argumentation; includes defender/presenter and challenger/listener/responder. Arguers are also called *argument partners.*

defender or *presenter* — the person presenting and defending an argument. This role may switch back and forth between the arguers in a discussion.

challenger or *listener* or *responder* — the person listening or responding to the presentation of an argument and raising challenges to that argument.

dialogue or *discussion* — the process of communication in which two arguers explore an issue or argument.

encounter — a specific interactive situation in which two arguers explore an issue or argument. An argument over a given issue may continue over a number of encounters at different times.

Although our formulations are based on two arguers, argumentation can include more than two. A single individual can also take the role of both arguers — presenter and challenger — and conduct a dialogue with him- or herself or with a text.

Before Starting

Ideally, before engaging in argumentation, we should answer for ourselves and our argument partner, "What's the point?" Although we often do not do this, thinking about the point of the encounter helps us clarify our desired outcome, which may be any of the following:

1. to explore an issue — yours or your argument partner's;
2. to present an argument and have your argument partner hear and understand it;
3. to present an argument and have your argument partner see that it is reasonable;
4. to present an argument and have your argument partner accept it; or
5. some other possible outcome related to the overall aim of argumentation.

The strategy adopted might vary depending on what outcome we want from the encounter. If we are simply exploring an issue with a friend and want to see what the respective positions commit each arguer to, then we might adopt a different strategy than if we are trying to persuade.

Often we simply assume the point from the context and leave the possible outcomes unexplored. However, if our argument partner presumes a different possible outcome, the two arguers may miscommunicate. If that happens, we can simply step back and clarify the point of the encounter and what outcomes each is looking for. If the outcomes are too discrepant or the two parties have quite different and incompatible aims, then the encounter may have to end.

Active Listening and Feedback

Argumentation is a form of interactive communication based on listening and responding. Listening involves two components — active listening and feedback.

Active listening is attending to what the other person is saying, making sense of it, and separating it from any interpretations or responses we may have to it. Often when we are engaged in dialogue and we suspect we disagree with someone, we listen for flaws, for what we can challenge and refute in the other person's argument — not to understand. Our listening is partial and selective. Giving our full attention and seeking to understand when we disagree is difficult. We naturally want to elaborate, challenge, add to, defend, or attack an idea — or change the topic.

Sometimes we fear that if we focus our full attention on the other, we will forget what we have to say. What often happens, however, is that when we give full attention to what the other person is saying, we gain a better understanding and, as a result, see stronger possible challenges. In argumentation, therefore, our first task is to understand what our argument partner is saying and the nature of his or her commitment to that. Only when we understand our argument partner's position fully can we effectively challenge him or her.

In active listening, we focus on two levels of communication — the content and the emotional and nonverbal component. We often deprive ourselves of valuable information by focusing solely on the content — the reasons, conclusions, challenges, and responses — and ignoring other aspects of communication. Listening to the emotional tone and nonverbal cues, such as body language and tone of voice, that accompany the content can provide us with information about the person's meaning and his or her investment in the issue. The way someone says, "That is not an important reason" may tell us how significant the reason is. Said forcefully, it may mean that the reason is, in fact, very important. Said diffidently, it may mean that it really is not important. My partner's shaking of the head while I give an argument may indicate disagreement even though he or she doesn't say anything. When people become emotional, it may mean that the issue is particularly important to them. If reticent or hesitant, they may not be sure of what they are saying or they may be disclosing something that is important but feel uncertain of how it will be taken. If diffident about what they are saying, they may be disengaged or simply repeating what others have said: They have no investment in the issue and we are not hearing reasons that are theirs. Context and knowledge of the other person are important in interpreting such cues.

Often when we present arguments verbally, we have not thought through the issue. We construct our ideas and develop our arguments as we speak; therefore, we may not express ourselves as correctly or precisely as we would like, searching for words and ideas concurrently. And sometimes our argument partners will not attend carefully to what they are saying. If both argument partners actively listen and paraphrase what they have heard, they can help each other formulate their arguments more accurately.

Providing feedback is paraphrasing for an argument partner our understanding of what he or she has said. In the paraphrase, we try to capture the core of the argument position, not simply repeat word for word what was said.

We have no way of knowing if our attempt to understand our partner is accurate unless we get feedback on our feedback. When giving feedback, we state our best hypothesis about what we think the other person's argument is. Good feedback may reflect both the content and the emotional element. If interpreting the emotional element, we do so by describing what we observe and then what we deduce the significance to be.

> As I understand it, your argument is . . .

> I noticed that when you talked about x, you became more animated, and I suspect that means that is a crucial consideration for you. Is that correct?

We have to be careful to distinguish what we hear and observe from our interpretations. We then confirm our interpretations with our argument partner, being careful not to anticipate his or her line of reasoning or adding things to what he or she has said. If we train ourselves to reflect back the other side's arguments before responding, we accomplish two things: First, we ensure that we have understood correctly before we raise our challenges. Second, we establish a certain amount of respect for our dispute partner. We show that we care enough to interpret his or her position correctly.

Listening actively and providing feedback has a further, equally important, function. It slows down the attack–response cycle, which can lead to a destructive escalation of conflict. When we don't listen actively and provide feedback, we tend to listen selectively for the criticisms of our own positions and the weaknesses of the other side's, often failing to see the strong points in the other side's position or to acknowledge the truly weak points in our own. By listening actively and representing the opposing arguments fairly and in their strongest light, we establish that we are concerned with pursuing the truth and not simply scoring points at the other side's expense. This helps establish rapport with our argument partner.

Feedback is simply a hypothesis about what the other side intended; it is not necessarily accurate. Our goal in giving feedback is to identify clearly our partner's ideas, claims, or arguments. If a partner does not agree with the feedback, we ask him or her to clarify. Some individuals may not pay close attention to what they themselves say and, therefore, may not realize what they have actually said. Rather than getting into a dispute about what was said, we grant them their intended meaning.

Provide feedback every few minutes in the initial stages of developing the skill. Don't try to remember a half hour's conversation and then summarize it. Once you have developed the skill, use feedback at crucial points in the conversation to formulate the central line of argument or point of dispute; to clarify when you or the other side seems confused or off track; to summarize points of agreement; to reiterate a main argument or point; or to transition from one point to another in a conversation.

Ask your partner to give feedback of his or her understanding of what you have said. Listen to the feedback and check it for accuracy. Do not simply verify everything you hear. Remember, whatever you agree to can and may be used against you later in the argument. It is always possible that your message has not come across to your partner as you intended it, or you may not be encoding your message in a way that can easily be understood. Rather than arguing over what you did or did not say or getting sidetracked on the issue of who is or is not listening, correct your argument partner's interpretation and focus on the content of the message that you intended him or her to receive.

Make sure that the claims or arguments are as clear and precise as you want. You will have to defend them.

Eliciting Arguments

Eliciting the arguments in a discussion involves identifying what the issue is, the arguers' positions on it, their reasons for their positions, and the structure of the argument. We do this by clarifying the issues and asking for reasons whenever our argument partner states a core position or a claim we want to examine. We use the components for identifying and portraying the structure of an argument developed in Module 2 and for identifying issues in Module 9.

Some of the questions we might use to elicit arguments include the following:

- "Why?"
- "What are your reasons for that?"
- "How would you support that?"
- "Can you give me another reason?"
- "What evidence do you have for your position?"
- "Do you have any other reasons?"

To illustrate:

A: I read in today's online *New York Times* that some U.S. states are requiring that doctors get the parents' consent when a minor tries to get an abortion or requests birth control. I think that's a great idea and should be the law in Canada.

B: Why should it be made the law in Canada?

A: Because parents have a responsibility for their children and should know when they are doing things like this.

B: So you are saying that we should make it the law that parents have the final say on issues such as birth control and abortion for their children because this is ultimately the parents' responsibility?

A: That's exactly what I am saying.

To help in this stage, paraphrase your understanding of the argument and ask for clarification and confirmation from your argument partner:

"So what you are saying is that . . . because . . ."

"As I understand it, your position is that . . . and your reasons for that position are . . ."

When structuring arguments verbally, use cue words to help identify reasons and conclusions. In the above dialogue, both A and B use cue words to help structure the argument.

When developing your understanding of the arguer's position, one good strategy is to continue probing. Identify the reasons for the reasons.

B: Why is it ultimately the parents' responsibility?

A: Because it's an issue of morals, and it's the parents' responsibility to instill morals in their children. Besides, the parents are financially responsible for their children.

B: So you're saying that because the parents are responsible for the morals and the financial support of their offspring, they should have the final say in issues such as birth control and abortion?

A: Yes.

B probes for further reasons. A introduces two reasons — morals and money. B could continue probing: "Why do you think it is an issue of morals?" "What does the financial issue have to do with whether or not parents should have a say in this?"

QUICK QUIZ 11.1   Probing Reasons

The Quick Quizzes in this module are designed to help develop your verbal argument skills, so they should be done reasonably quickly, without writing out various alternatives. After you have done them verbally, write them down. Then you can think about other possibilities.

For each of the brief arguments below, suggest three additional probes (questions) for reasons that B could use to find out more about A's argument. Do not challenge the argument.

1. A: I think we should have more bike lanes in the city because it will encourage more people to ride bikes, and it will reduce traffic.
   B: 1.
       2.
       3.

2. A: Downloading copyrighted music and videos from the Internet without paying for it should not be a crime. After all, it doesn't hurt anyone.
   B: 1.
       2.
       3.

3. A: I don't think we should allow genetically modified foods to be sold and put into the food chain. After all, we don't know its long-term effects.
   B: 1.
       2.
       3.

Answers for all Quick Quizzes in this text are provided in the Student Manual. After doing the Quick Quizzes, consult the Student Manual to check your understanding of the material.

Clarifying Meaning

The second task in argumentation is to clarify the meaning of terms and claims, including implications, presuppositions, and assumptions. Before we can develop a critique, we must know not only what our argument partner is saying but also what the intended meaning of his or her central claims and concepts are. Some of the things we can do to clarify include

- ask for examples to illustrate concepts;
- do a conceptual analysis on contentious and unclear concepts;
- check the scope of claims (all, some, a few), especially if not specified;
- ask our partner to clarify terms; and
- test with implications of the use of the term.

Continuing the parental consent dialogue from above:

B: What do you mean by children—people aged thirteen, sixteen, eighteen, twenty-one? (*request for scope*)

A: As long as someone is living in their parents' house, the parents should know and their approval should be sought.

B: Even if they are old enough to vote or join the military? (*testing the implication*)

A: Yes, if they live at home.

B: What about if they legally move out at sixteen?

A: Yes. They are still minors.

B: So you're saying that regardless of age, as long as a child is a minor or lives at home, then parents should have the right to determine whether their child uses birth control or has an abortion? (*restates giving the criteria*)

A: Yes.

B: What if the "child" is twenty-five or even twenty-eight and hasn't left home because he or she is in school? (*testing the implication*)

A: I would put an upper age limit of twenty-one.

B: Why then?

B could also probe the concept of "parents having responsibility for their children" and what that entails.

Thus far, B is simply eliciting A's position and reasons. Had B started to challenge, issued a judgment ("That's absurd!"), or counterargued, B would be arguing against a position he or she did not yet understand.

QUICK QUIZ 11.2   Clarifying Meaning

For each of the brief exchanges below, identify a concept or claim that might need to be clarified and provide B with three questions that would probe for meaning of that concept.

1. A: I think pornography exploits women.
   Concept:
   B: 1.
      2.
      3.

(continued)

2. A: Some video games are sexist and encourage violence against women.
   Concept:
   B: 1.
       2.
       3.

3. A: Violent video games cause harm.
   Concept:
   B: 1.
       2.
       3.

Evaluating

Evaluation includes testing and assessing both the truth of the claims and the logic of the argument. To evaluate, we address two basic questions:

- Do the premises adequately support the conclusion?
- Are the premises true?

Before evaluating the claims, however, it is useful to identify the unstated and implicit assumptions. In dialogues, arguers often do not give full arguments, and the defender usually gives one reason or several independent reasons. As active listeners, we search for missing links that will make the arguments work.

> A: We should ban the use of cell phones when driving.
>
> B: Why?
>
> A: Because using them while driving can cause accidents.

Often the arguer is unaware of the implicit reason needed to make the argument valid. Someone skilled in argumentation can help with this through probing.

> B: Why do you think they cause accidents?

Usually, as in this case, the reason given is the one the arguer considers the least contentious. People not trained in argument don't always realize that they have omitted part of the argument on which their conclusion rests. If we want to be effective in helping our argument partners probe their arguments, we need to be able to supply the implicit premises.

Identifying the unstated reasons can give us more room for exploring and challenging an argument.

Identifying Unstated Reasons

What we want to be able to do in verbal argument, thinking on our feet, is to connect the stated premise to the conclusion. We can use one of four methods for doing this: the topics model; recognizing argument patterns, particularly conditions; a shortcut method; and the counterexample. Consider the above argument about cell phones. We can supply the implicit premise:

> A.   [We should ban anything that is likely to cause car accidents.]
>
> 1.   Using cell phones while driving causes accidents.
>
> ———————————————————————————
>
> ∴   2.   Ban cell phone use while driving.

We can use one of these four models to generate the missing premise and, from that, the challenge to it.

1. The **topics model,** introduced in Module 4, involves asking two questions of the conclusion to find the missing premise:

   - Under what conditions?
   - Does x meet those conditions?

   The stated premise will answer one of these questions. By finding the answer to the other, which we can infer from the stated premise, we can supply the implicit premise. In the example above, the questions would be

   - Under what conditions should we ban something?
   - Does that apply to using cell phones while driving?

   The answer to the first question is not given but is implied by the answer to the second question, which is given — using cell phones while driving causes accidents. This gives us the implicit premise: If something is likely to cause car accidents, we should ban it. This is a general claim, and we can challenge it with a counterexample.

2. The **conditional model** uses the stated reason and the conclusion. From them, we construct a conditional argument that affirms the antecedent. Once we have identified the conditional, we can generalize it.

   For the above example, we can construct the following conditional claim:

   > If using cell phones while driving causes car accidents, then we should ban their use.

   We can generalize this to

   > If something causes car accidents, then we should ban it.

   > OR

   > Anything that causes car accidents should be banned.

   We can then use a counterexample to challenge this.

3. The **shortcut method** builds on the implicit pattern in the two preceding methods. The argument can be stated as follows:

   > Using cell phones while driving causes accidents.
   >
   > ———————————————————————————
   >
   > ∴   Ban cell phone use while driving.

The purposes of supplying an implicit premise are to help make the argument valid and to identify what assumptions the arguer is making in giving the argument. What both the preceding methods do is recognize that the terms in the conclusion must be reflected in the premises and connected together. In this argument, the two terms in the conclusion are

ban

cell phone use while driving

The stated reason talks about

using cell phones while driving

causing accidents

For the argument to work, we need a premise that connects the two unconnected terms. That is, we have to say something about banning things (the conditions under which we would ban something) and causing accidents:

We should ban things that cause car accidents.

In many arguments with one reason and a conclusion, there will be a total of three terms used, one of which will be repeated. In this example, "cell phone use" is the term that appears in both the reason and the conclusion. What we want to do is connect the two terms that are not yet connected — things that should be banned and things that cause car accidents. That will give us an implicit premise.

<u>Using cell phones while driving causes accidents</u>.
      1   2

∴   <u>Ban the use of cell phones while driving</u>.
      3   1

Each separate term has been underlined and numbered to help us see the connections.

What this method does is identify the common term (1) and connect the remaining two terms (2 and 3) to create the missing premise, as follows:

<u>We should ban things that cause car accidents</u>.
      3   2

While this does not work in all cases and does not guarantee a valid argument in all cases, it often does provide a useful way of generating a hypothesis about the connection between the stated reason and the conclusion. By formulating this connection for ourselves about our argument partner's potential assumptions, we can then formulate a counterexample to further probe his or her argument.

4. The ***counterexample*** is an even simpler method. With this method, we move straight to a counterexample from the argument without formulating the implicit premise. The argument is

> Using cell phones while driving causes accidents.

> ∴   We should ban the use of cell phones while driving.

We identify the specific term that occurs in both the reason and the conclusion, substitute another term that might be relevant, and pose it as a counterexample to see if the person wants to ban that as well. The specific term that occurs in both the premise and the conclusion is "cell phones." What we want to do is find something done while driving that may cause accidents but that the person would not want to ban — eating, having kids in the car, listening to the radio. In effect, we simply substitute another term for the one in the reason and pose that as a counterexample to our argument partner:

> B: So we should ban taking excited kids to hockey practice because they might distract the driver and cause accidents?

All counterexamples are based on the ***principle of similar cases*** — likes should be treated alike and when they aren't, we must justify the difference of treatment. This is basic to all reasoning. If the arguer is going to reject the counterexample of driving excited kids to hockey practice as a cause of accidents, then he or she must provide a relevant reason for treating them differently.

Each of these methods provides a way of generating a missing premise and generating a challenge for the argument. Once we have generated the implicit premise, we can then evaluate and challenge the argument.

QUICK QUIZ 11.3   Generating Counterexamples

For each of the brief exchanges below, without writing out the argument, generate a counterexample verbally.

1. A: I think we should have more bike lanes in the city because it will encourage more people to ride bikes and it will reduce traffic.
   B:

2. A: Downloading copyrighted music and videos from the Internet without paying for it should not be a crime. After all, it doesn't hurt anyone.
   B:

3. A: I don't think we should allow genetically modified foods to be sold and put into the food chain. After all, we don't know their long-term effects.
   B:

Argument Challenges and Responses

Once the responder has an understanding of the argument, he or she can try to determine what the person is committed to, whether the premises support the conclusion, and whether the premises are true. The primary way of doing this is through the issuing of challenges to a partner's arguments, and then responding by developing further challenges.

This chart lists some of the main types of possible challenges and responses:

	Challenges		Responses
1.	to meaning	1.	clarify; define terms; give examples to illustrate
2.	to truth of claims	2.	show why true; provide evidence or additional reasons to support claim; provide supporting arguments; find a new reason if the claim is false; give plausibility arguments. If the claim is not or cannot be defended, "accept for the sake of argument" and explore other elements of the argument
3.	counterexamples	3.	counterexample does not apply because . . .; embrace consequences; modify position; modify argument
4.	implications	4.	embrace implication; show implication does not apply
5.	fallacies	5.	if correctable, fix; if not, present new argument; if a mistake, apologize
6.	other considerations	6.	discuss; define

Below we will expand on each of these methods of challenging and responding. (Much of this draws on material in previous modules.)

Meaning

Challenges to meaning can include

- simply asking for a clarification ("What do you mean by . . .?");
- requesting an example;
- challenging the term's use (i.e., that it is not being used in a regular or normal sense);
- stating that a term or claim is ambiguous;
- stating that a term or claim is too broad; or
- stating that a term or claim is too narrow.

For more on clarifying meaning, including challenging, see Module 2.

Possible ways of responding include defining the term, giving a paradigm instance, or engaging in a conceptual analysis of the term. If the argument hinges on the meaning of a term, then the technique of conceptual analysis will be the basis for the dialogue. See the dialogue on *immigrant* in Module 9.

> A: Pornography exploits women.
>
> B: What do you mean by exploits?
>
> A: Takes advantage of.
>
> B: But many things take advantage that I wouldn't want to call "exploitation." My employer takes advantage of my goodwill by asking me to work overtime. I wouldn't normally say that he is exploiting me.
>
> A: I would. That's the way I define the term.

B could either continue exploring the meaning of *exploit* and whether this is an adequate account of the meaning or accept it "for the sake of argument" and probe in other directions. Note that B has provided a counterexample for the definition A proposes for *exploits*. When B offers an example in which B would not use the term, A claims that is precisely what A means by *exploits*. The argument partners need to distinguish the different kinds of definitions being used and not get caught in an essentialist argument over a reportive or stipulative definition.

QUICK QUIZ 11.4   Challenging Meaning

For each of the brief exchanges below, without writing out the argument, generate a challenge for the meaning and give an appropriate response. Use a different kind of challenge for each of the examples.

1. A: We should be allowed to use torture against terrorists to get them to inform us about future terrorist attacks.
   B: *Meaning challenge:*
   A: *Response to the challenge:*
   Kind of challenge:

2. A: Downloading songs from the Net is not theft.
   B: *Meaning challenge:*
   A: *Response to the challenge:*
   Kind of challenge:

3. A: Sexual harassment is the misuse of power by a man against a woman.
   B: *Meaning challenge:*
   A: *Response to the challenge:*
   Kind of challenge:

False

One of the most obvious challenges to an argument is to show that a reason is false or likely false.

> A: Tommy Douglas was the greatest Canadian because he was one of the
>   greatest prime ministers this country ever had.

> B: He was never prime minister; he was the premier of Saskatchewan.

If we are defending a position and a basic reason is false, then we need a new argument. Perhaps the person arguing about Tommy Douglas has confused Douglas with someone who *was* prime minister. In some cases, even though a reason is false, we do not necessarily have to abandon the position. We may have other, more defensible reasons for the conclusion.

These include all challenges based on "How do you know?" "What is your source?" "What is your evidence?" and the resulting discussions.

A challenger does not have to show that the claims are false but merely unsupported or inadequately supported.

> A: We need to take tougher measures against marijuana grow-houses.
>   There are more and more of them all the time, and they cause serious
>   problems for those who live near them.

> B: I heard on the news the other night that the number of grow-houses
>   has actually decreased by about 25% over the past two years.

A is basing part of his claim for tougher measures on the increase in the number of grow-houses. B has challenged that argument with other evidence.

> A: That is not what I understood. The news media have been making a
>   big issue of this for the past few weeks.

> B: They also have been making a big issue of the murder rate increasing,
>   but it has actually gone down somewhat from what it was ten years ago.

> A: We'll have to agree to disagree on this until we can get some further
>   evidence.

> B: Do you have other arguments for developing tougher measures against
>   grow-houses?

The material introduced in Module 4 on assessing various kinds of claims can be used to challenge the truth/acceptability of a claim. If an arguer is making a causal claim, we can examine whether all of the criteria for a causal claim have been met. If the person is advancing a normative claim, we can probe for the criteria being used to make the judgment and challenge whether that criteria is appropriate or the best available in this case. If the person is advancing a claim based on authority, we can use the criteria for an appropriate appeal to authority to determine whether the claim is acceptable.

In some cases, a factual premise may be called into question but not shown to be false. The defender can either continue the line of reasoning "for the sake of argument" to see where it leads and whether there are other difficulties with it, or he or she can offer other reasons to support the position without necessarily conceding that the line is fatally flawed.

For each of the brief exchanges below, without writing out the argument, generate a challenge for the truth of a key claim and give an appropriate response.

1. A: Marijuana should be legalized for medical purposes because it is more effective in treating some conditions than other forms of treatment are.
   B:
   A:

2. A: I think we should look into the hiring practices of professional schools. Men tend to get far more places than women do.
   B:
   A:

3. A: We should ban *The Adventures of Huckleberry Finn* from high school libraries because it promotes racism by using the offensive n-word throughout.
   B:
   A:

Counterexamples

This text has introduced two kinds of counterexamples — one for claims and one for inferences. Both can be used in argumentation. Claim counterexamples are discussed more fully in Module 6.

A *claim counterexample* is a *specific instance* that is designed to counter (show the limitations or falsity of) a claim or a generalization.

> A: We should ban drivers from using cell phones because cell phone use can cause accidents.
>
> B: Cabdrivers and some truckers use cell phones instead of radios. Should we ban them from using them?

A claim counterexample has two components: a stem and an application. The **stem** is the term that shows up in the claim we are trying to counterexample and in the conclusion. The **application** is the specific case to which the stem is being applied. It usually shows up in the conclusion. In the above, the missing premise is "We should ban anything that can cause car accidents." The stem is "things we should ban." The application in the original claim is "things that cause accidents."

The original example was applied to the specific case of cell phones. In generating a counterexample, we replace the specific application in the original argument with another application (i.e., another example) and see if our argument partner would accept or reject the new claim. In this argument, the challenger replaces "all drivers" with a specific application — cabdrivers and some truckers. B might have used "some police officers" or other possibilities. B could also go beyond various kinds of cell phone users since the claim being challenged is "We should ban anything that causes car accidents." In other words, the counterexample retains the stem and substitutes another application to test whether or not the defender would accept the conclusion.

Original argument:

> [Ban anything that causes accidents.]   (*implicit premise*)
>
> Using cell phones while driving causes accidents.

> ∴   We should ban the use of cell phones while driving.

In this argument, the implicit premise is a general claim. The stem is "things that we should ban." It is applied to the specific case of "drivers who use cell phones" to arrive at the consequence — ban drivers from using cell phones.

> B: Cabdrivers and some truckers use cell phones instead of radios. Should we ban them from using them?

The arguer can respond to a counterexample in one of three possible ways:

1. The arguer can **accept the new application and embrace the consequences.** This involves accepting that the general principle applies to the new example and accepting the consequences.

> A: Sure, ban the cabdrivers' and truckers' use as well. They are some of the worst offenders.

A has accepted the counterexample as relevant and embraced its consequences. This tells the challenger that A is committed to some of the consequences of his general claim. B could test with other counterexamples, both of types of cell phone users and of other kinds of things that can cause accidents.

> B: And you'd want to ban people from eating or drinking coffee while driving as well? They can cause accidents.

B has now provided counterexamples of other things that may cause accidents but which A may or may not want to ban.

2. **The arguer can reject the new example as irrelevant.** Since it is not the same kind of thing, the two cases can be treated differently.

> B: How about the police? They use both radios and cell phones while driving. And that can cause accidents.
>
> A: No, that's not what I am talking about.
>
> B: Why not? (asking for a relevant difference)
>
> A: They need cell phones for work, and using the cell phone while driving is part of their work. (*supplies a relevant difference*) I'm concerned about all of those people who don't need to use a cell phone while driving, those for whom it is a distraction from their driving. (*expands on the difference and in so doing, qualifies his original reason*)

In this case, A rejects the counterexample. When A does not give a reason, B asks the difference between the situation where the general claim applies and the one where it doesn't. Often, the response will open up new areas to probe. In this case, A supplies new information that qualifies the original argument — the conclusion is now not to ban all drivers from using cell phones but all drivers who unnecessarily use cell phones. This change requires a modification to the missing premise as well because it has to include this qualification. B could now use counterexamples to test other exceptions and to challenge the modified argument.

The challenger can also compare the stance taken with the original version of the argument and the later one. What is the difference between a cabdriver and a policeman? Why is A willing to ban one but not the other? Again, the principle of similar cases comes into play.

3. The arguer can **accept the new application as relevant but not want to apply it to the stem.** The arguer may acknowledge the counterexample's relevance but not accept it in relation to the conclusion (i.e., does not embrace the conclusion). In this case, the defender accepts the counterexample as relevant and accepts the consequences. In order to continue the argument, A must modify his original argument in some important way. Instead of the previous response, A could have given a different one:

> B: How about the police? They use both radios and cell phones while driving. And that can cause accidents.

> A: You're right. I guess we'd have to ban the police from using radios, but that would make their jobs much more difficult. And I don't want to do that.

A has accepted the counterexample as relevant and sees that it would lead him to a conclusion he does not want to accept. If he is going to sustain his argument, he is going to have to find some way of modifying either the reason or the conclusion so that it will ban what he wants banned and not ban such things as police use of radios and cell phones. A specific counterexample or a set of counterexamples can lead A to realize that the position as stated is untenable; however, that does not mean that the underlying consideration needs to be abandoned.

> B: Let's reformulate. You want to cut down the number of accidents on the roads and highways. You see things that take drivers' attention from the road as contributing to accidents—and many drivers' use of cell phones as a major thing that does this.

> A: Yeah.

> B: So can we reformulate the argument to capture that? What is the difference between, say, the police and a regular citizen?

B has started the reformulation process to try to capture the core of what A was trying to get at. By helping A reformulate, B, as well as A, can gain a deeper understanding of how a good argument might work.

Inference counterexamples are used to challenge the inference in an argument by showing that the premises do not support the conclusion. This is achieved by providing an argument counterexample — a parallel argument that has the same structure with clearly acceptable premises and a clearly false conclusion — thereby demonstrating that the structure of the original argument can lead to a false conclusion.

B: How do you know that using cell phones causes accidents?

A: How do you know it doesn't?

B: That's the same as arguing that because I don't know that the earth is flat, it must be flat.

The inference is if one does not know something, then it must be true — the fallacy of appeal to ignorance. The method that B uses to show that it is unacceptable is an inference counterexample.

There are a number of possible responses the presenter can make, depending on the circumstances. He or she can show that there is not a parallel between the two argument forms, provide another reason, or in some other way modify the argument.

QUICK QUIZ 11.6   Stem and Application

In each of the following claims, identify the stem and the application. Provide an alternate application to generate a counterexample.

1. *The Adventures of Huckleberry Finn* is racist because it uses the n-word over 200 times. And anything that uses the n-word is racist.
   Stem:
   Application:
   New application:
   Counterexample:

2. It is legitimate to use torture on terrorists because they threaten national security. And it is legitimate to use torture on anyone who threatens national security.
   Stem:
   Application:
   New application:
   Counterexample:

3. UFOs exist. Many people have seen them.
   (This claim does not contain the general claim that must be inferred.)
   Stem:
   Application:
   New application:
   Counterexample:

QUICK QUIZ 11.7   Challenging and Responding to Counterexamples

For each of the brief exchanges below, without writing out the argument, generate a counterexample and give an appropriate response. Then identify the kind of counterexample (claim, inference) and the kind of response you would use.

1. A: Marijuana should be legalized for medical purposes because it is more effective than some other treatments.
   B:
   A:
   Kind of counterexample:
   Kind of response:

2. A: Astrology must be true because my friend claimed that it worked for her.
   B:
   A:
   Kind of counterexample:
   Kind of response:

3. A: You can't trust philosophers. My intro philosophy prof misled us on her grading scheme.
   B:
   A:
   Kind of counterexample:
   Kind of response:

Implications

An implication is an unstated claim that follows from another (stated) claim in the argument. Usually, we draw implications from the conclusion and use those to show that accepting the conclusion commits the arguer to something else, preferably something unacceptable. However, implications can be drawn from any claim in the argument.

> B: If the purpose of banning cell phone use by drivers is to cut down on accidents, then wouldn't we have to have some very effective means of ensuring that drivers don't use cell phones or that a significant number are caught when they do use them?
>
> A: Yes.
>
> B: So wouldn't that require more policing or some other way of monitoring when people use cell phones while driving?
>
> A: I suppose so.
>
> B: And wouldn't that be rather costly in terms of policing?
>
> A: I suppose so.

Identifying a possible consequence of banning cell phone use while driving, B is trying to get A to commit to the fact that taking this action would require increased policing and increased costs. B is looking for an implication that A would not accept and that might lead A to change his or her argument.

The defender has a number of possible responses. The defender can

- **embrace the implications,** as in the example above;
- **challenge the inference**—"That doesn't follow"—in which case A will be asked to explain why not:

"I don't see that that follows. Police can enforce the law like they do with seat belts. That law didn't require more police, just more enforcement."

- **change his or her position.**

QUICK QUIZ 11.8   Challenging and Responding to Implications
_____

For each of the brief exchanges below, without writing out the argument, generate a challenge for the implication and give an appropriate response.

1. A: We should introduce more bike lanes because they will reduce car traffic downtown.
   B:
   A:

2. A: We should increase tuition in order to increase the quality of education.
   B:
   A:

3. A: If we require students to take logic, then they will improve their reasoning, and that is a good thing. Therefore, we should require students to take logic.
   B:
   A:

Fallacies and Other Dirty Tricks

A *dirty trick* is any tactic in an argumentation that gives an unfair advantage to one side. In order to work, the rules of argumentation must be followed by the argument partner who is not using the dirty trick. If all sides in an argumentation used them, the aims of argumentation could not be achieved.

If our argument partner commits a fallacy, we can't be certain that he or she intends to deceive or mislead. The following strategy helps prevent escalation while correcting the error:

1. Identify/recognize the fallacy.
2. Neutralize the fallacy.
3. When argument partners persist in using fallacies, raise the issue with them — let them know that you are aware a fallacy has been committed but don't accuse them of any intentional wrongdoing.
4. If necessary, confront argument partners about the tactics they are using and their aims in the encounter. If they are persistent in using faulty reasoning, it may be that they don't know better and need to be educated, or it may be that they are engaged in some kind of interaction other than argumentation. If that is the case, then you need to decide whether to continue, what you want to accomplish by continuing, and what your other options are. Sometimes it is better to stop the interaction than to continue in one that is self-defeating. A presenter can reply to a charge of fallacy by

- showing that, although the argument may look like a fallacy, it is not one;
- fixing the fallacy if it can be fixed (a false cause fallacy or a faulty appeal to authority might be correctable under certain conditions);
- modifying or changing the argument, including giving a new reason; or
- apologizing.

In addition to the fallacies identified in Module 7, several other common dirty tricks and fallacies occur in verbal argument.

A common tactic is **labelling.** This happens when a dispute partner dismisses an argument or position by providing a name or label rather than giving reasons for challenging the position.

> That's just a typical feminist (liberal, conservative) position.

Labels are commonly used to short-circuit the reasoning process. Defenders often end up responding to the label and arguing about the label rather than addressing the arguments. Labelling may fall under the category of the *ad hominem* or poisoning the well fallacy. Sometimes, however, it is best to recognize it simply as "labelling" and deal with it in that way. The easiest response is to refocus on the argument:

> I don't care what you want to call it. What specifically is wrong with the argument?

If an argument partner persists, we can raise the issue and, if that fails, confront him or her about the tactics used. We raise an issue by identifying what is occurring.

> You are simply labelling my position, not giving a reasoned challenge.

Here we have verbalized what our argument partner is doing. In many cases, simply identifying what our argument partner has done will lead him or her to recognize it is not a legitimate move and to then modify the method of argumentation.

If an argument partner does not modify the method of argumentation and persists in using dirty tricks, we can directly confront him or her. We do this by identifying the move, pointing out the effect (e.g., by showing how it violates the constitutive rules or thwarts the common aim in argumentation), and directly asking our argument partner if this is how he or she wants to interact. If we find our goals in the argumentation are not aligned, we have the option of walking away.

> You continue to label my position without giving reasons. This doesn't address my argument. I could do the same and we would get nowhere in this discussion. We would simply call each other names. (*identifies the behaviour and shows the consequences if both engage in it*) Is this how you want to proceed? (*confronts the individual by suggesting a possible alternate rule for proceeding*) If so, then there is no chance of rational persuasion. (*identifies the common aim and the consequences of continuing with such tactics*) And if that is the case, then I am not willing to continue. (*points out that you are willing to engage in one activity—argumentation and rational persuasion—but not others, especially when that activity puts you at a disadvantage. Your option is to walk away.*)

Disrupting, although not a fallacy, can interfere with argumentation. Disrupting occurs when an argument partner repeatedly interrupts what we are saying by interjecting or changing the topic. We can deal with a **disrupter** by leading him or her back to the main topic. If the person persists, we can raise and negotiate the issue, as outlined above. If necessary, we can confront the disrupter.

Identify the dirty trick/fallacy if one is committed and suggest a strategy for handling it.

1. Your argument partner says the following in response to your argument in defence of gay marriage:
   A: You're arguing for gay marriage? Are you homosexual or something?
   B:

2. B has quoted Rush Limbaugh's argument that executing Saddam Hussein was a mistake.
   A: You are using Rush Limbaugh as an authority. Don't you know he's just an apologist for a right-wing conservative viewpoint?
   B:

3. B has been arguing for not teaching creationist theory in biology classes.
   A: That is what's wrong with society today. No one wants to take religion seriously.
   B:

4. B has given an argument for increasing existing taxes and using the increase to pay down the national debt.
   A. Garbage!
   B.

Other Considerations

The raising of other considerations builds on the topics model and introduces into argumentation the broader aspects of issue analysis. In much argumentation, the focus is on specific arguments. However, arguments are about issues. They are developed to help us in taking stands on issues. Focusing solely on arguments can blind us to the underlying issues and the concerns that give rise to those issues. Specific arguments — even good ones — can sometimes miss the point of an issue or not adequately address an issue. And they may not address the relevant considerations of other positions on the issue. The raising of "other considerations" allows us to step back to see how the specific arguments fit into the overall context. It takes us away from the specific arguments to focus on the underlying issues and considerations. In so doing, it enables us to step back and examine what exactly is at issue and how best to approach it, so that we can better formulate our arguments. It includes such tasks as

1. **Formulating or reformulating the issue.** This can require stepping back from the specific argument, looking for the underlying considerations and motivations, and reframing the issue in terms of deeper, related, or other issues. Sometimes we start an argument without seeing the connections or broader issues or recognizing the factors that motivate an individual to advance a particular argument. As we continue in the dialogue, we discover that we are not getting at the central issue or that there is something else going on. Formulating or reformulating the issue helps us reassess the issue as a whole.

   In the *Adventures of Huckleberry Finn* dialogue (Module 1 exercises), the two argument partners might realize that looking at the more basic issue of what the purpose of education is and what should be taught in the schools might enable them to address the specific issue of *Huck Finn* a bit better. Or they might reformulate the issue as one of who should determine what is taught in high school.

2. **Framing and reframing.** Often we can gain a different understanding of an issue by framing or reframing it — i.e., putting it in a different context — or by expanding or contracting the scope or focus of the issue.

Playful reframing of the issues can help the argument partners explore new dimensions of the issue. Reframing the *Huck Finn* dialogue as a matter of freedom of speech, community values, or racial tolerance might bring out considerations not yet examined:

"How might the teaching of *The Adventures of Huckleberry Finn* be seen as an issue of racial tolerance rather than one of racism? What kind of argument might we develop for that?"

"What kind of argument could we give if we were going to argue this as a freedom of speech issue? Freedom of speech for whom? How would freedom of speech justify teaching (or not teaching) this?"

3. **Identifying other considerations.** This includes asking an argument partner for additional considerations. This can involve looking for additional unstated reasons, and possible objections and responses, including reasons that that argument partner does not advance.

"What other reasons do you have for this?"

"What are some of the common objections that you have heard to this position?"

"How have others defended this position?"

4. **Comparing other perspectives and positions.** Identifying alternate perspectives and positions on the issue can give us further insight into the issue. Comparing similarities and differences with different perspectives and positions may give us insight into why our argument partner holds a particular position and why he or she appeals to certain considerations.

"What might this issue look like from the perspective of the parents?"

"What kind of arguments do the teachers raise on this issue?"

5. **Looking at underlying concerns.** This includes looking at legitimate concerns expressed by our argument partner, elaborating on those concerns, and then exploring how the elaborations can be addressed.

"It seems that your basic concern is that individuals who are black or of colour not feel threatened or denigrated by the language used in the classroom. Is there a way that we might teach *Huck Finn* without allowing that to happen? Can we explore that a bit?"

11.4 A SAMPLE ARGUMENT DIALOGUE

Joe: *Did you see that—there's another person driving and trying to talk on a cell phone! That shouldn't be allowed!*

Angela: *You sound really upset by that.*

Angela reflects back Joe's feelings about the issue. She is listening to both his content and emotional level.

Joe: *I am! Did you hear about that case in Fredericton where a driver on a cell phone crossed the line and crashed head-on into an oncoming car? It was a completely avoidable death. The driver died, along with two of her kids, and she killed the other driver. The family loses a mother. The other family loses a son.*

Angela: *That sounds horrible! You sound really upset about it.*

Joe: *I am.*

Angela: *So do you think we should ban cell phone use in cars?*

Angela identifies a possible conclusion and suggests it to Joe.

Joe: *Of course.*

Angela: *Why, exactly?*

Angela probes for reasons.

Joe: *Because it is unsafe. You can't do two things at once.*

Angela: *So you think that we should ban cell phone use for drivers because talking on them while driving is unsafe. And they are unsafe because you can't safely do two things at the same time?*

Angela identifies and reflects back the argument. Note that it is a complex argument.

Joe: *That's right.*

Angela is now faced with which way to take the discussion:

1.   She can probe the grounds for banning:

- *Why ban rather than do something else?*

- *How unsafe does something have to be to justify banning it?*

2.   She can probe the scope:

- *all cell phones?*

- *some kinds of cell phones—handheld vs. hands-free?*

- *some users?*

3.   She can challenge the truth of the stated reason.

4.   She can formulate and challenge the missing premise.

Angela: *But there are lots of things that are unsafe—for example, having kids in the car and being distracted by their antics. Taking a bunch of rowdy 10-year-olds to a hockey practice. Should we ban parents from taking their kids to hockey games?*

Angela has formulated a missing premise—we should ban anything that makes driving unsafe—and challenged that with a counterexample.

Joe: *Of course not.*

Angela: *Why not? How are they different?*

Joe rejects the counterexample; Angela asks for a reason using the principle of similar cases.

Joe: *I don't know. . . . Because you have to drive your kids around. You don't have to talk on a cell phone.*

Angela: *So let me get this straight. Your argument is that we should ban things that are unsafe to do when driving a car, so long as they are not necessary.*

Angela restates the argument.

Joe: *Yeah. That's what I am saying.*

Angela: *How is driving kids to hockey practice necessary and talking on a cell phone not necessary?*

Angela challenges Joe's response and asks for a relevant difference.

Joe: *You know what I mean.*

Angela: *I'm not sure I do.*

Joe: *Well, kids have to get to hockey practice, but no one has to use a cell phone while driving.*

Angela: *But isn't a carful of unruly kids as distracting and as potentially dangerous as talking on a cell phone?*

Joe: *No, it's not.*

Angela: *Why not?*

Joe: *It just isn't.*

Angela senses this is becoming unproductive. She has hit a point at which Joe doesn't have a reason or isn't willing to give a reason. She could keep pushing, but that might end the discussion. She chooses another line of reasoning.

Angela: *Let's leave that for a moment. You said that using a cell phone while driving is unsafe. How do you know that?*

Joe: *Well, it's just common sense. You have to dial and then focus on your conversation while driving. Your attention is split.*

Angela: *Lots of things that seem to be common sense turn out to be wrong— it was once common sense that the earth was flat. Have there been any studies?*

Joe: *Yeah, I read a long article in a weekend newspaper awhile back that various academic studies and studies by insurance bureaus showed that drivers who regularly used cell phones were four times as likely to be involved in injury-causing accidents than drivers who didn't use cell phones.*

Angela: *Sounds impressive. Do you know who did the studies?*

Joe: *No, but they were reported in* The Globe and Mail, *so I assume they are reliable.*

Angela: *I think I can accept that.*

Joe: *So you see I'm right.*

Angela: *Let's take this a bit further. You say that we should ban drivers from using cell phones while they are driving because cell phones are unsafe. And we agree that studies reported in* The Globe and Mail *have shown that they are unsafe.*

Angela restates and summarizes the argument to this point.

Joe: *That's what I said.*

Angela: *But why ban all cell phone use in cars?*

Joe: *Because it can lead to accidents.*

Angela: *That's not quite what I mean. Lots of things can lead to accidents. Why is banning the best solution?*

Angela returns to the missing premise.

Joe: *What else are we going to do?*

Joe tries to turn the argument around by asking Angela to defend the alternative.

Angela: *I'm not the one who wants to ban cell phones. You are. Why is banning them the appropriate response? Why not just fine those who are using cell phones and are involved in accidents?*

Despite her attempt not to get drawn in, Angela does offer an alternative.

Joe: That doesn't change people's behaviour and prevent the accidents in the first place. Look, you wouldn't want your son to be injured or killed by someone not paying attention because they were on a cell phone, would you?

Joe has not answered Angela's request for a reason. Rather than address that, he challenges her alternative. Joe introduces a personal consideration that could sidetrack the discussion.

Angela: No, I wouldn't want him to be hurt. However, I am not sure that banning all cell phones in cars is justified. Let me rephrase your argument. Rather than offer incentives for people not to use cell phones, you want to prevent the harm by punishing them after the fact. And this means banning cell phone use by drivers?

Angela recasts Joe's response as an argument.

Joe: Yeah. Look. I see too many people driving, using cell phones, and not paying attention. The studies show that such people are far more likely to be involved in accidents than those who don't use cell phones while driving. I just want to stop some of the carnage on the roads. This seems reasonable and doesn't seriously infringe on anyone's rights or cause further harm. It just seems like the right thing to do.

Angela: You know, I do tend to agree with you on cutting the carnage. I'm just not sure that banning cell phones is the best way of doing that. Let's think about it and continue our talk at lunch tomorrow.

Joe: Sure.

This is a fairly typical example of an argumentation dialogue. Joe and Angela have probed issues and positions, considered some arguments, made some "mistakes," and learned about one another's arguments and positions. There is no one right way of pursuing an argumentation dialogue.

Now, let us explore the various things we can do that will undermine the goal of argumentation.

11.5 ESCALATION AND DE-ESCALATION

Argumentation is an ongoing process. It involves not only the giving and challenging of arguments but the personal and interactive elements between people. As such, one of the things that can happen is *escalation* — the intensification of the disagreement between two people. This occurs when what starts out as a disagreement over an issue is taken personally, emotions become heated, and there is an increase in hostility between the parties.

In the early stages of escalation, communication becomes more guarded; one or both parties become increasingly defensive. This results in distorted listening, where each side starts listening only for what supports his or her position and undermines the other's, ignoring positive information about the other's position. The argument may stray off the original issue and into other issues. The discussion tends to polarize around two opposing views, the middle ground and alternatives overlooked. The ability to see the merits of the other side gets lost, often resulting in cognitive rigidity — the tendency to misinterpret the other side or to see only those things that support one's own position. Each side is likely to become increasingly anxious. A marked increase in hostility between the argument partners may lead to the two sides reaching the point that it is impossible to communicate with the other.

De-escalation is the reduction of tensions between the parties, which allows them to reestablish a relationship and return to the original issues.

If you find yourself engaged in a dialogue that is escalating, stop the process. Take a timeout to figure out what is going on. Make a decision about whether the discussion is worth continuing. Look for strengths in the other side's position and acknowledge the weaknesses in your own. If and when you resume, begin by reaffirming the process and the point of the discussion. Try paraphrasing the other side's position with an emphasis on its strengths. This will help establish rapport. If heightened emotions were part of the escalation, acknowledge those and probe them. Identify commonalities at the start, rather than differences.

Try reversing positions. Defend the other side's position; ask your argument partner to present your position as strongly as possible. At further signs of escalation, stop the process and invite your argument partner to reflect on what is happening and how you can prevent a further recurrence of escalation.

11.6 ARGUMENTATION IN ACADEMIC, PUBLIC AND PERSONAL LIFE: TOLERANCE AND ENGAGEMENT

Argument and argumentation enter into our lives in many ways. They are tools for exploring what we believe and what we should do, and for assessing the evidence and reasoning for our beliefs and the decisions we make about what to do. We use these in a variety of contexts — in academic, public, and personal life.

Much of academic inquiry revolves around controversies and disputes or inquiry. Inquiry is often undertaken to resolve controversy and disputes: *How old is the earth? Is light composed of particles or fields of force? Did Shakespeare write Macbeth? What is the best form of corporate governance?*

Such academic inquiries and controversies are carried out in the context of a community of inquirers and against a background of shared knowledge and expectations. The members of that community of inquirers (whether in English literature, philosophy, biology, women's studies, sociology, or any of the academic disciplines) are expected to be familiar with the background or context of the controversy or inquiry. That is, they are expected to know and address the relevant evidence, arguments, positions, and issues within that controversy, including the relevant contributions and challenges within it (and sometimes the surrounding materials and fields). Part of what is involved in establishing competence within a field is learning the issues, controversies, and state of knowledge within that discipline. As a student, you are in the process of learning the geography of the field you are studying.

An academic issue, then, is set against a background context of claims, arguments, evidence, other related issues, and an ongoing discussion about these by the community of inquirers. A key defining feature of academic discourse is the commonly shared goal of the pursuit of truth. This acts as a guideline and constraining factor on the discourse. Academics do not knowingly introduce claims and evidence that are faulty, false, or shoddy. Doing so would mislead and take away from the pursuit of truth and lead to being discredited within the field. In this, academic discourse shares a common feature with argumentation.

The situation is somewhat different with personal and public discourse. Some personal argumentation involves a specific issue in the here and now — "Should we have Thai or Indian for supper?" That specific issue has reasons relevant to it but, as it is given, is not a complex issue. I am simply trying to find out what I should do. There may be no broader implications or issues. The focus of the discussion in personal discourse may be "What should I do?" "What should I believe?" "What should I major in?" "What do I believe about abortion?" and so on. My personal values and goals are an integral part of my reasoning about these issues.[2]

On the other hand, some of the personal issues we take stands on — "Should gay marriage be legalized?" "Should the state relax privacy laws?" "Should *The Adventures of Huckleberry Finn* be banned?" "Is abortion immoral?" — are a combination of public issues and personal ones. We are wondering what we believe and/or should personally do about such issues. Our reasoning has gone beyond the personal to a public forum, intersecting with the reasoning — the argumentation — going on within a community of disputants. To enter into that, I need to address the issues and considerations being raised by that community of inquirers. My focus is no longer what I believe, what I should do, but how do I contribute to this ongoing discussion.

Although my personal beliefs and values come into play in helping me determine what position I will take, these issues that are being debated in a public forum are similar in structure to academic ones. A community of people are engaging in discourse about them. However, there is often a more loosely defined set of positions, arguments, considerations, and evidence on these issues. Unlike the situation in the academic world, no one has to demonstrate competence or show an understanding of the background arguments in order to participate in the discussion. Sometimes the arguers engaging in the controversy have additional agendas — social, political, economic, or personal. In some cases, individual participants may be committed neither to discovering the truth about the issues nor to the rules of argumentation but may have instead a different aim in their discourse. As individuals, we have to wade through all of this extraneous material to identify and assess the issues, arguments, positions, and, eventually, to take our own stand.

If our goal is to engage in argumentation, then we seek the truth about the issue, with the idea that it will guide us in our stand and our actions. Ideally, we want to base our beliefs and actions on the best available reasoning, argument, and evidence. If we want to know what treatment we should undertake for cancer, we don't simply select the first argument that comes along or the first piece of reasoning that strikes our fancy. Rather, we examine the various alternatives and the evidence for them and make our decision based on our assessment of the evidence. Insofar as we want to base our beliefs and decisions on the best available evidence, we will tend to use the principles of argumentation — those shared with academic discourse — to develop our own beliefs and stands on issues. And that will involve using some of the features of academic argumentation — looking for the best available arguments and evidence, critically examining the arguments of others, presenting our arguments for critical evaluation by others, responding to critical evaluation, and holding our beliefs provisionally.

But why should we do this? Why should we be rational? Why should we not, as many do, simply use arguments to defend and state our positions and ignore the principles of argumentation? Ultimately, this is a choice we make about who we are and will become, and how we

---

[2] I am not claiming that personal decisions and reasoning is, should be, or can only be "merely" personal or subjective. I am claiming that often in engaging in such reasoning, we take into account our basic values and preferences. That does not mean that we don't consider the various arguments and considerations available in the broader public sphere. Part of becoming a skilled critical thinker is going beyond personal opinion and developing our positions and arguments in light of the broader reasoning on an issue. For some issues — "Which restaurant should I go to?" — there may be no broader controversy. For others — "What do I believe about abortion?" — there will be a broader discourse and our reasoning will need to take that into consideration.

engage with others and the world — to base our choices and beliefs on evidence based on reasoning rather than simply letting our surroundings condition us.

Who we are and what we will become are influenced very strongly by what we do and what we believe. When we simply unreflectively respond to the beliefs of those around us, we are allowing our past experience to condition our present and future. Reflecting on and thinking about our ideas and actions, challenging, probing, looking for reasons, and examining the basis of our reasons and choices enable us to make choices about how we should live our lives and how we should relate to others. In so doing, we become more autonomous and get outside of the little island that is our self and, by engaging with others and the world, develop our self.

But there is a stronger reason. We live in a world of plurality and difference. A central issue in our lives is how we as individuals and as members of a community and a society should deal with the diversity within and outside of our own groups and between groups. Mere tolerance is not enough, for tolerance simply recognizes differences without seeking to engage or bridge those differences. It gives us little or no common ground. Argumentation is a way of bridging differences, of understanding, and of possibly effecting rational persuasion. Argumentation and critical reasoning in general are ways of becoming, of engaging with the world and with others, of sharing, of recognizing, of respecting and probing differences and similarities, of discovery and inquiry, and of commitment. Reason will not always help us bridge differences, but it will give us a better understanding of those differences. And with that, we can make more informed decisions about how to address them.

MODULE SUMMARY

Argumentation is the process of reasoning, using the techniques of argument and issue analysis, in interaction with other arguers. The dynamics of argumentation involve listening, eliciting arguments, clarifying meaning, evaluating arguments, and interacting with an argument partner through a process of probing, challenge, and response. Over time, the arguments develop, and individuals may be rationally persuaded to change their positions or reasons.

KEY TERMS

active listening

application

arguer

argument partners

argumentation

challenger or listener or responder

claim counterexample

conditional model

constitutive rules

counterexample

debate

de-escalation

defender or presenter

dialogue or discussion

dirty trick

disrupter

encounter

escalation

inference counterexamples

labelling

persuasion

principle of similar cases

providing feedback

rational persuasion

shortcut method

stem

topics model

WRITTEN ARGUMENTATION

12.1 LEARNING OBJECTIVES

After completing this module, you should be able to

1. explain the stages of writing;
2. identify the audience and purpose for writing a specific argument essay;
3. analyze an assignment for the requirements and criteria;
4. identify and be able to use several strategies for generating ideas and arguments;
5. clarify and refine a thesis;
6. develop an argument to support that thesis;
7. make a case for a position;
8. develop a balance of considerations argument;
9. construct an argument outline for an essay;
10. construct a one-paragraph argument for an essay;
11. transform an argument or a case into reader-based prose; and
12. revise and edit for coherence and clarity.

12.2 INTRODUCTION

Often, while in school, we are asked to produce an ***argument essay*** — an essay whose focus is the presentation and defence of one or more arguments for a position. For example, we might be required to write an essay for a humanities class on the role of education in Mary Shelley's novel *Frankenstein*. Simply developing a position and then producing an argument for that position is sufficient for this context.

Sometimes we are called on to produce an ***argumentation essay.*** Although not a widely used term, it identifies a type of essay that is broader than an argument essay. In an argumentation essay, we not only present a position and arguments for that position but we implicitly or explicitly engage with the positions and arguments of others. Our essay is part of an ongoing dialogue. This is true whether or not the others in the dialogue read and respond. We write the argumentation essay with the intention of contributing to a discussion. This means that we try to build on the discussion as we understand it to this point. We represent the arguments of others fairly; we challenge their arguments and positions; we anticipate and respond to their objections. We put ourselves into the place of a discussant in a dialogue as we compose and present the essay.

In both argument and argumentation essays, we construct arguments with the intention of presenting them to an audience. To do this, we use the basic skills of developing good arguments and responding to challenges. The central difference between argument and argumentation essays is that the argument essay tends to stand alone. It does not acknowledge other positions or arguments on the issue. The issue might even be unique to the essay. Sometimes the argument essay is the author's way of working through his or her own issue, and the audience is limited to whoever happens to be interested in that author's particular issue. An argumentation essay, by contrast, is concerned, either implicitly or explicitly, with an issue on which other arguers have contributed and for which there is an audience. The author may explicitly mention and use other authors as foils in developing his or her own position, or he or she may write on an issue of concern to others and address implicitly the positions and considerations of others, even though specific others may not be known; that is, the author addresses an ongoing dialogue, real or potential. An argumentation essay may initiate a dialogue by posing an issue of concern, taking a stand, and presenting a case on an issue. Whether others read and respond to it is not the point. It is framed as a contribution to a dialogue on a particular issue of concern to others.

Because of this difference, the demands on the two are different. The criteria for an argument essay to be good revolve around whether it has presented an argument that is sound, has sufficient supporting evidence, and so on. The demands on an argumentation essay are more stringent. Not only must it satisfy the criteria for a good argument essay, it must also meet the conditions for good argumentation: It must engage with the issue and alternate positions on the issue, address challenges, and contribute something new to the ongoing dialogue. Being able to write a good argument essay is a prerequisite to engaging in written argumentation.

To write any essay, we undertake two distinct processes — composing ideas and translating those ideas into *reader-based prose.* We sometimes move back and forth between these functions. The composing process consists of determining our purpose for writing, identifying our potential audience, generating ideas, developing those ideas into an argument, and making a case. Translating ideas into reader-based prose involves transforming the argument from a complex, multidimensional structure into a more linear presentation, which means organizing the argument to fit the structure of the essay and providing elements that will make it easier for a reader to follow the logic of the argument and understand the claims and arguments being made. It also includes the revising and editing process.

The primary purpose of this module is to help the reader develop an argument and transform that into reader-based prose.

12.3 THE COMPOSING PROCESS: CONSTRUCTING AN ARGUMENT

Composing an argument essay is a process of developing an idea and an argument, writing, evaluating, editing, and then rewriting, sometimes a number of times. Often we do not know precisely what we want to say until we have written and rewritten our ideas several times. Through writing, we can discover new ways of framing an issue, new positions, new considerations, and new ways of expanding arguments. Like any skill, writing and composing improves with practice and deteriorates with lack of use.

We begin an argument essay by identifying and refining a conclusion, for which we will develop an argument. Before we start, however, we need to ascertain the essay's purpose and its intended audience.

What Is the Purpose?

Why are we writing this particular essay? We can have different reasons for writing an essay — as part of an assignment, as a response to an article in the paper, to persuade someone of a position, to explore an issue, to present an alternate point of view, or to probe where a particular point of view leads. Different purposes can affect how thoroughly we pursue an issue, what we can assume, and what we need to develop. Even if we are "simply" constructing an essay for an assignment, we should seek personal reasons for writing the essay — something we can learn from the exercise. Often, if we have a personal interest, we create better arguments and write better papers.

Who Is the Audience?

All writing is for an audience. Different audiences have different requirements — different things that can be assumed, different things they need to know to be able to follow the argument, different reasons for reading the finished paper, and different assumptions, values, and attitudes toward the issue.

By identifying the audience, we also identify the context in which we are writing. Writing an assignment for a course is different than writing to work out a position on an issue, and that is different from writing a letter to the editor. An informal communication with a colleague or friend usually does not require footnotes and citations; a paper submitted for a course or publication does. In writing an essay for an instructor, the point might not be simply to generate a good argument for a position but also to demonstrate certain skills and to work with certain materials. Such requirements set constraints and focus our purpose for writing the paper.

Analyzing an Assignment

When giving an assignment, instructors often provide students with guidelines that offer direction for the finished paper.

Start by reading the entire assignment. Annotate it, identifying the requirements (e.g., the kind and purpose of the assignment) and constraints (e.g., formatting, due date, length, submission criteria), and raising questions about what is being asked of you (e.g., scope, formality). Make a list of what you need to do to complete the assignment successfully. Check this list frequently.

1. **What is the point of this piece of writing?** Why are we constructing and presenting an argument on this topic? Obviously, one reason is that it is an assignment and we need to complete it to pass the course. However, that does not get at why we are being asked to write about this particular subject. What are the various possible purposes the instructor has for assigning this paper? Not identifying the instructor's underlying purpose for the assignment — demonstrating certain skills, using a particular mode of analysis — may prevent us from earning a good mark.

2. **Who is the audience?** Although the instructor is the one who will be reading the assignment, the audience may be presumed, for the purpose of the assignment, to be the other students in the class, other students who have not taken this class, or some other group. The instructor may have a certain audience in mind in giving the assignment. Find out.

3. **What is the context?** In the case of an assignment, one context is that of the course. Are we expected to demonstrate knowledge (concepts, categories, approaches) and skills learned in the course? Is there a wider context? If we are analyzing a contemporary controversy, how much of that controversy are we supposed to address?

4. **Are there any special considerations or constraints for the argument?** How long is the paper supposed to be? How much outside literature are we expected to cite? What is the format or style? How is the paper to be submitted?

QUICK QUIZ 12.1   Analyzing an Assignment

Use the questions above to analyze the following assignments. Where answers are not clear, identify the questions you would have to ask the instructor.

1. One-page argument assignment for a first-year critical reasoning course:

   Read the attached passage, "The Terri Schiavo Case," and write a one-page (one paragraph) argument on a central moral or policy issue arising from the case as it is presented here. I want to see how you develop your own reasoning on this. Do not simply repeat the arguments in the passage. Your essay will be assessed on how well you frame an interesting and central issue, how well you develop and defend your argument, and the how original your argument is. The use of outside materials is discouraged; however, if you use such material, it must be cited appropriately.

   Do an argument analysis and critique of your own paper and submit that as an appendix.

   Since your papers will be marked and returned electronically and will be used for electronic peer review, you must use the following formatting conventions: The paper should be formatted in Microsoft Word or Rich Text Format (not WordPerfect), using an easy-to-read font (e.g., Arial) in 12-point type, black, and flush left.

   Due at midnight, Pacific Standard Time, March 26, 2007, via e-mail.

2. Assignment for a second-year English literature course (the class has spent the past three weeks analyzing Mary Shelley's *Frankenstein*):

   Write an essay on the role of education in Mary Shelley's *Frankenstein*. The essay should be ten pages and focus only on the primary source (the novel itself).

   The paper should use MLA format, cite all material appropriately, and include a bibliography.

   The essay is due in class on October 1, at the beginning of class. Late papers will be marked down in accordance with the course policies.

3. Assignment for a third-year sociology course analyzing ethnicity and race:

   Examine the websites given for the Canadian, Irish, and Indian censuses. Find and identify their respective definitions of ethnicity and the questions used in the most recent census to measure ethnicity. Compare and contrast these definitions and relate them to the lectures on ethnicity. What conclusions can you draw about the categories used to identify ethnicity in the respective censuses? Relate to David's discussion of ethnicity.

   Length: 4 pages
   Due: In class March 2, at the beginning of class.

Answers for all Quick Quizzes in this text are provided in the Student Manual. After doing the Quick Quizzes, consult the Student Manual to check your understanding of the material.

12.4 GENERATING IDEAS

Having identified the purpose for writing, we next have to define the issue and start generating ideas about it. This may take a number of attempts. Producing an interesting thesis and argument worth defending may require analysis and research or some thought about the question. Simply selecting the first or second idea that comes to mind is likely to result in a fairly trite theory or one that half the class will adopt.

Our starting point will depend on the nature of the writing project. For a critical analysis, we need to start by doing an extended analysis of the text or argument. If we are developing our own argument on an issue, we will usually start by trying to define clearly and precisely the issue we are investigating, exploring the alternate possible positions, the key concepts, and various ways of formulating the issue. A research project will involve gathering, organizing, and analyzing the appropriate information.

Whatever the kind of project, at some point, we need to generate the core idea. The point of writing an argument paper is not simply to repeat what someone else has said but to contribute something to the discussion — to find a point of view and support that with arguments. Even when using considerations that others have used, we try to develop those considerations in an original or different way.

When research is involved, we do not simply read and report the materials unprocessed. We need to analyze, organize, and assess that information. What positions have not been given? What other arguments are possible? Which arguments give the most support? Are there undeveloped considerations?

For some projects, we can apply a particular method or mode of analysis, such as conceptual analysis, discussed in Module 9, or issue analysis, discussed in Module 10, or a model from a particular discipline to help generate ideas. This section introduces additional ways of producing and developing arguments.

Brainstorming and *free-writing* are two common methods. In **brainstorming,** we set a period of time and generate everything we can on the topic without censoring, evaluating, or criticizing. In free-writing, we write for a given period of time — five, ten, fifteen minutes — on the topic without editing or constraining what we are saying. With both, once we have come up with some material, we then edit and analyze what we have produced to see if we can find something useful.

Brainteasers

Brainteasers[1] can help expand our thinking. To illustrate how they are used, we will imagine the following situation: The provincial government is proposing to raise tuition fees for university students. You have been assigned to write an argument essay on this.

1. **Get beyond the obvious.** Go beyond your first (and second and third) idea. Original ideas are rarely the ones that initially enter our minds. Look for what is not obvious, and do not censor yourself. Write down any idea you have. Even try the opposite of what comes to mind.

    On the issue of tuition increase, some of the first ideas that you may have are that raising tuition fees will put a greater burden on lower-income students–that some students might not be able to finish their programs; or that faculty and student-faculty contact hours can be increased. From these, we can generate opposing considerations: Raising tuition fees might benefit lower-income students who can get grants and disadvantage middle- and upper-income students who can't; it might encourage students to finish their programs sooner; not raising fees might force universities and faculties to be more efficient in their delivery of programs.

2. **Good ideas are often complex.** Develop competing ideas that challenge your initial ones. Put your initial ideas on trial by examining alternatives to them. Working through competing ideas and testing each with details and possible support often lead to a more complex truth. There may be both benefits and disadvantages to raising tuition fees. Explore them all. Which are likely to outweigh the others?

3. **Use your senses.** List sensory details about your topic. Look for anything unusual or forgotten. Recall specific relative cases or scenarios that have sensory material to work from and write down any ideas that emerge from this. Sensory details draw us into the topic and

[1] Bauman, M. Garrett, and Clifford M. Werier. *Ideas and Details: A Guide to Writing for Canadians.* Toronto: Harcourt Brace Canada, 1996.

provide sharper details. I conjure up images of students eating Kraft Dinner (already pushed to the limits); students driving expensive cars (can afford higher tuition); a student working long hours at a low-paying job (work to afford university); vacant arts classes and overfull economics and business classes (differences in student demand); and a small seminar room where students are questioning the instructor and one another (engaged students in a philosophy class).

4. **Examine the topic from alternate viewpoints** — different individual points of view, perspectives, disciplines, and positions. Look for the missing viewpoints. Probe each, trying to see the issue as others would. What truth would each see in the issue? This will often lead to more honest and sophisticated ideas. Good ideas stand up to such critique; poor ones fade. Consider the "tuition increase" issue from the point of view of faculty, the administration, parents, and employers as well as students.

5. **Identify and challenge stereotypes, unquestioned ideas, and slogans.** These all prevent honest, imaginative thinking by encouraging us to think in accepted, ordinary patterns. List the "common truths" or obvious statements about your subject. These are positions you will take if you want a substandard paper. Now find **exceptions and qualifications** to the items in this list. Generate as many as possible. After you have attacked the obvious, the unquestioned, the stereotypical, the taken-for-granted, you can more honestly decide what you really think, and you will likely have plenty of material for an outline or draft. Attack stereotypes by looking at the range of variation within them. Challenge the stereotype that students are rich (or poor) by looking at the differences among students — consider the different kinds of students there are and how tuition increases might affect each.

6. **Develop classifications for your topic.** Classifying breaks a subject into categories and places individuals or things into each of the categories. Identify possible categories and subcategories for your topic. Look for interesting, vivid, fresh classifications. Classifications help us see patterns and interconnections. Various classifications might produce different insights — working students, nonworking students, full-time and part-time students, mature students, and direct-entry students, students in different programs, majors, and faculties.

7. **Develop comparisons and contrasts.** Compare this topic with another. Compare allocation of funding for higher education versus that for lower education, education versus health funding, funding in private schools versus that in universities, and accountability in higher education versus that in lower education.

8. **Create metaphors.** A metaphor is a special comparison between things in different categories. Metaphors stir the imagination and help in visualization. Find and explore the ideas behind metaphors. The metaphor can be the backbone of an essay or simply help you create details that will add sparkle to the paper. For example, we can use the metaphor of students as sponges versus students as curious cats.

9. **List examples.** List all of the specific examples you can think of. An example is a single, concrete instance, never a generality: my friend Pia, a single mother, who is going to university and taking a liberal arts program; Ambreen in my anthro class, who is working two jobs to afford school; Liam in the nursing program, a new Canadian and the first in his family to go to university. Analyze your examples.

10. **Make "bug" lists.** What really bugs me about *x* is [insert list of complaints]. This may help formulate a problem that you can use as the basis for the paper. What bugs me about government is . . .; about students is . . .; about education is . . .

11. **Ask questions.** Ask all the hard questions you want answered. What is important to know about this topic? Ask the journalist's questions — who, what, when, where, why, how? Get beyond these. Try to answer the questions with all the ideas and details you can. Use some of the *brainteasers* above to help answer these questions.

At various stages through the composing process, we should ask ourselves what we don't know and what we need to know to develop a better understanding of the issue, to be able to take a stand on the issue, to develop an argument, or to make a case. This is not just a matter of saying, "I need more information" but of identifying the kind of material we need and how having it would advance our understanding of the project. Sometimes it is useful to identify, before undertaking a project, everything that we don't know about the topic. Taking a stand too soon on an issue can often lock us into a position and stop us from looking at other positions or challenges. The art of ignorance can leave us more flexible in considering alternatives. For our sample paper, some things we might not know and might need to answer before continuing include the following:

1. What percentage of the cost of education is paid by tuition fees and what percentage by government grants?
2. What are the government's reasons for wanting to raise tuition fees?
3. What will the increased tuition fees be used for?
4. If the fees are not raised, what effect will there be on students and on universities?

12. **Use humour and fantasy.** Think of all kinds of fantasy situations for your topic and look for the humorous side to them. Reverse the normal rules of reality (e.g., tax employers to pay for upgrading the critical skills program). Break a social, scientific, or mathematical law related to your topic and imagine the results (e.g., treat higher education as being universally accessible as it is in some other countries). Create a new rule or law and imagine its results (e.g., charging politicians for every bad decision they make that costs taxpayers money).

13. **Vary your thinking style** — verbal, visual, written. If you normally think in words, try thinking in terms of images, diagrams, or sounds. What ideas does a triumphal march, a funeral dirge, the Rolling Stones' "You Can't Always Get What You Want" bring to mind?

These are just examples of possible ways you can use brainteasers to illuminate a topic. The more of these brainteasers you use, the better prepared you will be for writing your paper. Your ideas will be better developed, more resistant to attack, and more original.

QUICK QUIZ 12.2   Using Brainteasers

Use brainteasers to develop ideas on the following topics:

1. Should downloading copyrighted music and videos from the Internet without paying for them be legal?
2. Should marijuana be legalized?
3. What critical skills, as opposed to discipline-specific skills, should a student learn in university?

12.5 DEVELOPING THE ARGUMENT

At some point, we need to stop generating ideas and develop a thesis. This requires us to examine our various materials, formulate a central idea that we want to develop, and express that in a thesis statement. Completing the following sentences can help us start to develop a thesis:

• What I really want to say is . . .
• The most gripping part of my topic is . . .
• The key question about my topic a reader would want answered is . . .
• What interests me most about my topic is . . .

Before developing the argument, we must develop a strong thesis, and then reasons to support that thesis. If some of our reasons are weak, we must provide support for them as well as address whatever possible challenges we can imagine.

What Is a Thesis?

A *thesis* is the conclusion of an argument. In the context of an essay, it is the main point to be made. Without a thesis, the essay is little more than a tangle of sentences and paragraphs. The thesis unifies the paragraphs and essay. Essential in both the development and evaluation of the arguments in an essay, the thesis provides the writer a focus for selecting material to support his or her argument. An unclear or nonexistent thesis makes it difficult for readers to determine what the author is claiming and how the evidence supports the claim.

A good thesis should satisfy the following criteria:

- It is a **substantive assertion or claim,** not a statement of a process or intent. That is, a thesis takes a stand on an issue. "I am going to investigate the role of education in *Frankenstein*" is a statement of intent; it does not state a position. A substantive thesis would be "*Frankenstein* shows that technical knowledge without moral guidance and a connection to a social community is not really a product of education." This makes a claim, an assertion, about knowledge and education. It also needs to be defended; it is not obvious.

- It is **controversial, interesting, and/or original.** The thesis "*Frankenstein* shows that science can lead to disastrous consequences" is not particularly original. Get beneath the obviousness of that claim. What is it about science that can lead to this? Is it science or something else that can produce this outcome? That it is controversial means that it needs to be defended.

- It is often **complex or complicated.** Good ideas are often complicated and/or qualified. The claim "*Frankenstein* shows that science can lead to disastrous consequences" is overly general. It suggests a very narrow or shallow way of seeing the topic, not acknowledging the subtleties of the issue. "Although Mary Shelley appears to condemn scientific inquiry in *Frankenstein*, her main target is not scientific knowledge but human ambition." This thesis takes a deeper and more interesting slant on the topic.

- It serves as the **central idea of a unified composition.** The thesis is the main point of the paper; it can be treated as the conclusion of an argument, with the body of the essay the support for that conclusion.

- It is
  - **clear;**
  - **precise;** and
  - **adequately limited in scope for the space allotted.** (This often means a topic is qualified or narrowed to an appropriate point. We cannot write a ten-page essay on everything in the novel *Frankenstein*. We can, however, write quite a good essay of that length on the role of education in the novel.)

QUICK QUIZ 12.3   Evaluating a Thesis

Examine the following proposed theses for a three-page argument essay on whether the government should crack down on street racing. Identify how each does or does not fit the criteria of a good thesis. Suggest what could be done to improve the ones that do not fit the criteria. Are the theses as stated likely to be interesting to an audience of students who have been discussing the issue for two weeks? Explain.

1. Street racing is dangerous.
2. The government should ban street racing.
3. Anyone caught engaging in street racing should have his or her car confiscated and face a minimum of two years in jail.
4. Although street racing can sometimes be dangerous, it would be futile to attempt a ban on all street racing.
5. A more effective approach to dealing with street racing than further banning an already illegal activity would be educating and imposing curfews on younger drivers.

Developing and Refining a Thesis

Make an assertion about your topic and write it down. Use the criteria on page x to start refining your thesis. There are two parts to refining a thesis: (1) developing clarity and precision and (2) identifying the ideas that need to be supported.

In developing clarity and precision, examine your proposed thesis. What exactly does it say? Look at each term you've used. Does the statement capture exactly what you mean, what you want to say? Could it be phrased more precisely? Consider this thesis from an essay on Mary Shelley's novel *Frankenstein*:

> Mary Shelley believed that education was detrimental to mankind.

To refine the thesis, isolate each term in the statement — every noun, adjective, and adverb — and make it more precise by asking who, what, when, where, why, how, how much/many, how do we know this, et cetera. The sample thesis above contains a number of terms — *Shelley, believed, education, detrimental, mankind.* By applying the questions to each of the terms and phrases in this statement, we get the following:

Shelley:	The reader knows who Mary Shelley is, presumably. If perhaps not, we can explain. Is there something about her personal circumstances that is relevant here? What were her views on education, on science? How did that affect her writing of the book?
believed:	Did she actually believe this, or is this something that she simply expresses as one of the themes in her novel? How do we know what Shelley's real beliefs are? Perhaps this needs to be better phrased.
education:	All education, some education, certain types of education? Is it the education or how that education is used that is the problem? What kind of education, what aspect of education are we referring to here? Education is a big topic. Do we really want to say all education? Qualifying terms, phrases, and claims often leads to a more defendable thesis.
detrimental:	How is it detrimental? Detrimental is an abstract term. Is there a more precise word that could be used here? Is

"detriment" inherent in education? If so, how? Or is it
somehow an accidental feature?

to mankind: To all mankind? Some? Only a few?

To make this into a more defensible thesis, we would minimally need to qualify what
Shelley means by education, how it is detrimental, and whether it is detrimental in the same
way to everyone.

The government is considering raising tuition fees next year. Consider the following as a
thesis for a 650-word argument essay for an opinion piece for the student newspaper.

Tuition fees should not be raised.

As a thesis for a two-page argument essay, this has several problems. It uses the passive rather
than active voice. A better thesis would specify the agent — who is raising the fees — making
the sentence active. In most provinces, the government sets the range of permissible increases,
and the individual universities and colleges work within that. Further, this does not specify
whose tuition fees are in question — universities', colleges', College of General and Professional
Educations' in Quebec, undergraduate programs', or graduate and professional programs'. Nor
does it specify the time frame — next year, the next three years, indefinitely.

A better thesis would be the following:

The provincial government should not raise undergraduate and graduate
tuition fees in the province for the next three years.

The more qualified or limited in scope a claim is, the easier it is to defend. For example,
we can more easily defend the claim that rock music that is crude and offensive should be censored than we can that all rock music should be censored.

QUICK QUIZ 12.4   Refining a Thesis

For each of the following possible theses, identify what needs to be established. Where possible,
make it a better thesis using the information in the previous section. Where it already is a good
thesis, show how it meets the criteria for a good thesis.

The assignment is to write a two-page argument paper that is to be used as the basis for
further discussion of the issue. The students have been studying the specific topic for three
weeks.

1. For a first-year sociology course: Criminal behaviour is more a product of the individual's
   specific interactions with his or her peer group than of general social norms.
2. For a second-year urban planning course: We should ban cars in the city.
3. For a first-year course on genetics and society: Although the knowledge gained from genetics
   promises major gains in agriculture, medicine, and forensics, it also poses serious threats to
   individual privacy and well-being.
4. For a second-year computer ethics course: Maintaining the privacy of individuals is an
   important concern for those delivering computer services, and every company should have
   and follow a privacy policy.

Developing the Argument

We now need to develop the reasons to support the thesis. We can do this by using the brain-teasers in Section 12.4 above and formulating reasons from those; by using the issues model, outlined in Module 10, to develop considerations and turn them into reasons; or by using the topics model, outlined in Module 4, to identify the topics in the conclusion and then develop reasons to support those topics by generating answers to the topics questions.

The following uses the topics model on the tuition example in the preceding section to illustrate the process. We can identify three topics for the revised tuition thesis:

- the provincial government
- should not raise undergraduate and graduate tuition fees
- for the next three years

We can generate the following questions:

Q1: Under what conditions should someone not raise undergraduate and graduate tuition fees?

Q2: Does this apply to the government?

Q3: Why three years?

Using the brainstorming method, I can generate possible answers for each of the three questions:

Q1: 1. Raising tuition fees makes it more difficult for existing students to complete their degrees.
2. It makes it more costly for incoming students.
3. It may restrict future students, especially students from low-income families, from going to university.
4. It may mean that more students take on more debt to complete their degrees.
5. It may mean that students move away from the liberal arts and toward "more practical" degrees such as science, economics, and business.

Q2: 6a. The provincial government has obligations to encourage students to complete their degrees.
6b. It is in the government's and province's economic interests for students to complete their degrees.
7. The government has both social policy (social justice) and economic interests in encouraging more students to attend university.
8. The government has a social policy interest in encouraging more students from lower-income families to attend university.
9. Not only the government but society has an interest in minimizing the debt students take on as a result of university education.
10. A greater focus on "more practical" degrees will likely mean less development of some of the core critical skills and attitudes that we expect students to attain in university.

Q3: 11. Three years allows time to do a better assessment of university funding.

Once we have a set of reasons, we need to select the ones that are most important or interesting and most relevant to our intended audience. Reasons 1 through 4 are commonly given when governments suggest raising tuition fees. The audience is likely to know these. Unless we have something new or interesting to add to the argument, we are likely to rehash old considerations. Reason 5 is more interesting and not as familiar. Although we can mention the other reasons if there is space, developing 5 would likely lead to new considerations on the argument.

Developing the other part of the argument, reasons 6 through 10, might also shed new light on the issue. Or to develop a more original approach to the argument, we could select one of reasons 1 through 4 and then work on developing the reasons in Q2.

We could have used other methods for generating the reasons. What is important is that we generate a sufficient number to be able to select from among them those that are best for our purposes in the paper we are writing.

Next, we should make the argument sound. If it is a deductive argument, we try to make it cogent; if inductive, we try to make it as strong as possible.

1.   The government's raising tuition fees will likely result in students moving away from the liberal arts and toward "more practical" degrees such as science, economics, and business.

2.   This is undesirable.

∴   3.   The government should not raise tuition fees.

Claim 1 could be turned into a conditional, in which case the argument is valid — affirming the antecedent. Once we know that the conclusion is adequately supported by the premises, we should check each premise to see if it is acceptable. If any is likely to be challenged or not obvious, we either provide support for that premise through sub-arguments or rewrite the premise to make it more defensible.

The first premise in the argument seems plausible, although we may want to develop a sub-argument to support it. Premise 2 in this argument is weak: It doesn't say why 1 is undesirable. To strengthen it, there are two possible reasons we could include:

4.   Having fewer students taking liberal arts courses would weaken the liberal arts programs and leave undeveloped the core critical skills they are designed to teach. Fewer students mean fewer faculty members and fewer courses. As a result, there would be less opportunity for all students to gain the skills taught in liberal arts courses.

5.   Professional programs have extensive course requirements that allow for few electives outside their major requirements. As a result, students will have less opportunity to gain the skills taught in liberal arts courses.

We could develop each of these into a sub-argument to support 2. We examine each to see if either is obvious and likely to be accepted by the audience or if they need further defence. (Since we are illustrating the basic strategy for writing an essay rather than developing the details of the essay, we will not do that here.)

Before writing up the argument, we should consider possible challenges and responses to it. The following two objections could be raised to 4 and 5. Both claims 4 and 5 presuppose that the liberal arts currently provide critical skills. Objections might be raised:

6.   The liberal arts do not provide these skills now.

7.   Liberal arts courses are not the only or best place to acquire these skills.

These claims would then need to be elaborated upon and responded to. Claims 8 and 9, as yet undefined, will stand as the responses to 6 and 7, respectively.

In dealing with objections and challenges, it is important to note that we often do not have conclusive responses. It is better, both from an argumentation point of view and psychologically, to acknowledge a legitimate objection and admit that we don't have a conclusive response than to ignore it or try to present a partial or inconclusive response. From an argumentation point of view, if we are trying to arrive at the truth about an issue, presenting an argument as though it were stronger than it is defeats the basic purpose. Psychologically, presenting a weak response or argument as strong undermines our credibility as an arguer in the eyes of our argument partner.

A Sketch of the "No Tuition Increase" Argument

Using the numbers from above, the arrow diagram of our argument would look like this:

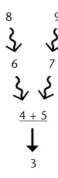

The One-Paragraph Argument

Having developed a thesis, we need to organize the argument. One way to do this is by developing an outline. However, outlines can be sketchy and more topic oriented than argument oriented. We end up with a set of sub-topics but the connections between these are not clear.

An alternative method is to develop a ***one-paragraph argument.*** In writing a one-paragraph argument for our essay, we start with our thesis statement, which we develop into a paragraph outlining the main points of the argument we are going to make in the paper. Every claim in the paragraph must support the thesis. This paragraph then serves as the basis for the outline of the paper. Each of the sentences can, in turn, act as a topic sentence for one or more paragraphs in the paper.

Using the sample thesis and the questions we formulated above, a one-paragraph argument might look something like this:

> The provincial government should not raise undergraduate and graduate tuition fees in the province for the next three years. Increased tuition fees will likely result in students moving away from the liberal arts and toward "more practical" degrees such as science, economics, and business. This is undesirable because it would weaken the liberal arts programs and leave undeveloped the core critical skills, such as critical reading, reasoning, and writing, on which all programs, including professional ones, rely. To the objection that liberal arts courses are not the only or best options for acquiring such skills, I respond that liberal arts programs are currently the only ones systematically developing such skills, whereas other programs have no incentives to teach such skills systematically.

Ideally, the thesis should be the first sentence of the paragraph. We can then identify what minimally needs to be shown to establish our thesis and reassess each statement in the one-paragraph argument to determine whether it actually contributes to the argument. If we find a claim that does not contribute to clarifying, defending, or supporting the thesis, then we drop that statement. If we find a gap — something that needs to be established to support the thesis and that is not established in the one-paragraph argument — then we need to add to the argument. The goal is to produce, in one paragraph, a conclusion (the thesis) and the basic reasons that support that conclusion. Developing our paragraph from a properly constructed argument structure ensures that the one-paragraph argument contains all that is necessary and only what is necessary.

Once we have a good one-paragraph argument, we can develop it into an outline for the essay. The paragraph's remaining sentences become the topic sentences for the body of the essay. We can use the same method to develop the rest of the essay's paragraphs.

The advantage of this method is that it forces the writer to develop an argument and test that argument early on. The one-paragraph argument serves as an abstract of the logic of the paper and enables the writer to develop an overall view of it early in the writing process.

QUICK QUIZ 12.5   The One-Paragraph Argument

In each of the following one-paragraph arguments, identify the thesis and then determine which claims are relevant and which are not relevant to establishing it. Rewrite the passage to organize the claims while eliminating the irrelevant claims.

1. Although marijuana can be used for some medical conditions, it should not be legalized either for medical or recreational use. Marijuana has been used to relieve the nausea that accompanies chemotherapy, for example. It should not be used for medical use because there are other, more effective treatments. Many people claim that marijuana helps them relax and that it is not harmful. But marijuana has proven harmful effects. Moreover, it is an addictive drug. Legalizing it for medical purposes would be allowing the use of a dangerous drug when more effective drugs are available. For similar reasons, it should not be legalized for recreational purposes: It has harmful effects and is addictive.

2. University courses should consist of fewer lectures and make available the information delivered in lectures through materials such as iPod videocasts. Most students have iPods, and video iPods are not expensive. Downloading iPod videos is easy. Many students can't attend class regularly because they have jobs and other commitments. One survey says that over half of all students work at least fifteen hours a week. Some have family commitments as well. Many lecturers are boring. One professor I had simply read from the assigned text. Lectures being available in video format would help ESL students who often need to hear a lecture several times to get its full meaning. Many students are ESL students.

12.6 MAKING A CASE

The preceding sections help us develop an argument on an issue. However, an argument, even a good one, is not necessarily a case for a position. An argument presents one set of related reasons for a position we are defending. A **case for a position** is a set of arguments and sub-arguments, and the responses to the main challenges, structured to show that the position is superior to other positions. A lawyer can make an argument on a particular issue in a trial; however, to win the case, the lawyer must show that his or her arguments outweigh those presented by the other side. While both attorneys may have some good individual arguments, their goal is to try to show that they have made a better *case* — that their collection of evidence and arguments as a whole prevails over those of the other side.

Thus far, we have made an argument for not increasing tuition, but we have not yet made a case. To turn our argument into a case, we would have to introduce further reasons for our position, challenge the other side's, and show that the considerations for our position outweigh those for the other side.

Imagine that a couple is discussing where to go for a winter vacation. They engage in the following discussion:

Richard:	I think we should take our winter vacation in Jamaica. I need to go somewhere quiet and would really like some good food.
Chris:	I would really like to go somewhere I can do some shopping, and the shopping isn't that great in Jamaica.
Richard:	I agree, but I do like the food there.
Chris:	The last time we were there, it wasn't all that quiet. How about St. Maarten? It's quiet. There are wonderful secluded beaches. The food is great—French and Dutch. And I can go shopping.
Richard:	Sounds better than Jamaica. Let's look into it.

Richard makes the argument for taking a winter vacation in Jamaica. Chris partially counters that argument and makes a case for St. Maarten that challenges one of Richard's reasons for going to Jamaica and incorporates his other concerns.

The Balance of Considerations Argument

The ***balance of considerations argument*** is a special type of case-making argument where good reasons exist for several sides of an issue. A balance of considerations argument acknowledges and addresses the various legitimate considerations on both sides of the argument. Additionally, it shows that, given these various considerations, one side is better than the other.

Using a balance of considerations argument on the issue of whether the government should raise tuition would require us not just to provide reasons for not raising tuition but also to address the reasons the government has for raising it. Then we would need to argue that, even though there are some strong arguments for the government's position, the considerations against it outweigh those for it. We have explored considerations against raising tuition. Now, we will explore those for raising tuition:

- Universities could hire more faculty or not cut existing members.
- Universities could maintain or lower faculty–student ratios, thereby improving teaching quality.

- Universities could increase facilities, including access to libraries and computers.
- Universities need such increases simply to maintain existing staff and services.

These are good and relevant considerations. To show why the "no tuition increase" considerations outweigh these, we could explain how these goals could be achieved without a tuition increase or argue that the underlying interests behind the "no tuition increase" arguments outweigh the considerations for the other position.

Many papers written for an academic audience call for a balance of considerations argument. Whether we were analyzing human origins, the role of genes versus environment in explaining behaviour, the causes of the increase in school violence, whether Pluto should be classified as a planet, or almost any academic issue, there are competing considerations and theories that we would need to address. The same is true for social, ethical, and policy issues, where competing values and principles are invoked.

Whether we give an argument, make a case, or give a balance of considerations argument depends on the context, our audience, and what we are trying to accomplish.

QUICK QUIZ 12.6   The Balance of Considerations Argument

For each of the following issues, identify the alternate positions and competing considerations. Identify possible overriding considerations that would weigh the argument toward one side or the other.

1. Should parents be allowed to spank their children?
2. Should the government ban cell phone use while driving?

12.7 DEVELOPING READER-BASED PROSE

Knowing the Reader

Once we have developed an argument or a case, we need to turn it into reader-based prose, which means we will have to accomplish two things: (1) address the audience and their interests and (2) present the arguments clearly and with signposts so that the audience can follow.

Although in developing an argument, we ideally start out thinking of the potential audience, we often lose sight of that. In turning our arguments into reader-based prose, we should review our purposes and the audience and refine our arguments accordingly.

To successfully address the reader, we must identify the reader's knowledge (including both concepts and facts), attitudes, viewpoints, interests, and needs regarding the issue, as well as our purpose in addressing the reader in this essay.

If a reader is not likely to know certain concepts or have certain information, then we have to introduce and explain those concepts and provide the relevant information with supporting documentation.

If we are presenting the argument on tuition developed above to a general audience, we may need to explain the skills taught in liberal arts courses and why they are not likely to be taught in professional courses. If our audience is composed primarily of university faculty, we may not need to explain that.

We should also make a reasonable assessment of the readers' attitudes and viewpoints. This does not mean we simply write so that our argument agrees with them but that we consider the readers' viewpoints when constructing and presenting our arguments. In a secular context, we would not use religious-based arguments. If arguments are going to seriously challenge a reader's perspective, it is best to look for and start with areas of agreement before moving to the more controversial areas.

In presenting the "no tuition increase" argument to members of the government who are in favour of raising tuition fees, we would likely start with points on which we agree — for example, that developing certain skills found in the liberal arts is an important part of a university education. Then we would move to the more contentious part of the argument. Having agreed thus far, readers are more likely to hear us out on the other premises.

Turning Arguments into Reader-Based Prose

Prose is simply ordinary speech or writing. It can be contrasted with poetry and visuals such as argument diagrams. The challenge of putting arguments into prose is transforming our complex, multifaceted, and sometimes visual representations of arguments into a linear form. Arguments contain many different parts — some more important than others: reasons, main conclusions, intermediate conclusions, objections, responses, issues, definitions, and examples. In prose, we can present only one idea at a time.

If we were to transcribe a simple argument as it is given, we would likely end up with some fairly deadly prose.

1. If the government raises tuition fees, students will likely study for "more practical" degrees such as science, economics, and business.

2. Having students take "more practical" degrees such as science, economics, and business is undesirable.

∴ 3. The government should not raise tuition fees.

becomes the following:

If the government raises tuition fees, students will likely take "more practical" degrees such as science, economics, and business. Students taking "more practical" degrees such as science, economics, and business is undesirable. Therefore, the government should not raise tuition fees.

This contains redundancies and is not very fluid. To turn the argument into more fluid prose, we often have to reorder the claims, supply cue words, and eliminate redundancies:

The government should not raise tuition fees. If it does, students will likely choose to study toward "more practical" degrees such as science, economics, and business. This would be undesirable because it would undermine the liberal arts programs and would result in many students not learning the critical skills that the liberal arts teach.

QUICK QUIZ 12.7   Turning a Simple Argument into Prose

Rewrite each of the following arguments into a fluid prose paragraph that clearly displays the structure of the argument.

1. Background: Tara has submitted an expense form for reimbursement for attending a conference and entertaining a dozen clients and coworker Eli at an expensive dinner.
   1. Eli claims he was not at the dinner.
   2. Eli claims that he did not see Tara at any of the sessions at the conference, including the plenary session.
   3. Eli did see her at the reception and the evening banquet.
   4. Eli claims that at the time of the dinner for which Tara is claiming expenses, he was with another company client.
   5. He has offered to supply the name of the client to his manager.
   6. Eli is trustworthy.

   ∴   7. Tara has falsified her expense account.

      8. If someone has falsified expenses, he or she has stolen from the company.

   ∴   9. Tara has stolen from the company.

      10. If someone steals from the company, he or she should be fired.

   ∴   11. Tara should be fired.

2.   1. If a reorganization results in an increase in morale, greater productivity, and more profits, with no serious detrimental effects, then it is a success.
      2. The reorganization of the ACME bolt company resulted in an increase in morale.
      3. The reorganization of the ACME bolt company resulted in greater productivity.
      4. The reorganization of the ACME bolt company had no serious detrimental effects.
      5. The reorganization of the ACME bolt company had no serious detrimental effects.

   ∴   6. The reorganization of the ACME bolt company was a success.

3.   1. Arguers who persistently misuse the principles of logic, quote evidence they know to be false, and use refuted arguments are either grossly deficient in reasoning skills or are not interested in argumentation.
      2. The supporters of intelligent design[2] persistently misuse the principles of logic, quote evidence they know to be false, and refute arguments.

   ∴   4. The supporters of intelligent design are either grossly deficient in reasoning skills or are not interested in argumentation.

      5. The supporters of intelligent design are not grossly deficient in reasoning skills.

   ∴   6. The supporters of intelligent design are not interested in argumentation.

[2] Supporters of intelligent design are individuals who believe that evolution cannot explain the observed complexity of nature; that the complexity of nature must be explained by appeal to the theory that nature was intelligently designed; and that this can be determined through scientific means.

Turning Complex Arguments into Prose

We can use the same techniques — reordering claims, supplying cue words, and eliminating redundancies — to transform more complex arguments with multiple lines of argument into prose. We then have to develop the connections and flow between the lines of argument. This will be discussed next.

The Structure of the Essay

Argument essays typically have three components, each with a different function: an introduction, a body, and a conclusion.

The *introduction* gives the reader an overall road map of how we are going to develop the paper. It opens the essay, introduces the reader to the topic, defines the issue, states the thesis, and identifies the main lines of argument and, perhaps, the main challenges and responses to the argument. For a very short paper or presentation, we may omit some of these. Minimally, the introduction should identify the conclusion and the main lines of development. Ideally, the introduction should be written twice — once to serve as a guideline before writing the rest of the paper and a second time to be refined and sharpened after having written the paper. Since the introduction is the first impression the reader will get out of the paper, it should be the best written part of it, grabbing the reader's interest and giving him or her a reason to continue reading the paper.

The **body** of the essay builds the argument for the thesis by developing each of the lines of reasoning. The order of presentation of the arguments should allow the reader to move through the paper fluidly, following the logic of the arguments.

The body should contain only material that either directly supports the thesis or illustrates and clarifies it. Unless background material, historical origins of the issue, discussion of various authors, or parallel issues are directly related to the argument, they should be omitted.

Start with your strongest argument. Generally, readers notice and best remember what comes first and what comes last. This is true for the overall essay and for paragraphs within the essay. Putting the weakest argument first draws attention to it and makes the reader expect more weak arguments. Burying the strongest argument in the middle of the paper is likely to result in it being ignored. As mentioned earlier, the argument we start with should be one that the reader is likely to agree with, thereby establishing a climate of agreement. We then move to the more contentious and controversial arguments.

The *conclusion* not only provides a summary of the argument but takes the reader back to the broader issues and their implications. The introduction framed and established a broader context for the issue, and the paper has added something to the discussion of it. The conclusion should identify what the paper has contributed and suggest where one could go from there, perhaps stating the limits of the discussion, specific research or arguments that could be pursued, or possible further lines of inquiry based on the arguments of the paper. These should be specific — not "More research needs to be done."

Placing Definitions and Objections

Where definitions and objections are placed within the essay depends on how they function in an argument. If a definition is central to understanding the issue, then we may put an abbreviated form of it in the introduction of the essay or in the first paragraph of the body of the paper, depending on how that affects the flow of the essay. If the term being defined comes later in the argument, then the definition normally follows the first use of the term. If it is placed before it, the reader will not know why the term is being defined and likely will not remember the term's meaning by the time it needs to be applied.

Objections and responses to objections are normally placed after the argument or premise that is being objected to. In exceptional cases, we might start with an objection to a position or argument, address the objection, and then develop our own argument. As with most rules of writing, if there are good reasons for breaking them, they can and should be broken.

Making Connections: Paragraphs

In addition to its overall structure, the essay should have an internal logic or structure. This internal structure is built on the paragraphs and transitions between paragraphs.

Each paragraph within the body of the essay develops one argument or one objection and response, or, in longer papers, one premise within an argument. If the paper is quite long and the argument involved, an argument may require two or more paragraphs.

Paragraphs have an internal structure. Each develops one point, which should be stated as a single claim either at the beginning or end of the paragraph. This helps the reader who would skim through the essay and makes it easier for the careful reader to follow the logic of the argument. In an argument essay, if the paragraph contains an entire argument, its topic sentence will be the conclusion and the rest of the paragraph will develop that argument and support the key claim.

One way of testing the coherence of a paragraph is to identify the topic sentence and then examine each sentence to see how it relates to the topic sentence. If it does not support it or provide an illustration, the statement is probably irrelevant and should be cut. See "Turning Arguments into Reader-Based Prose" above for more about topic sentences.

Use *signposts* to guide your reader through the paper. These are transition devices that let the reader know the flow of the essay. For example, if an argument structure has three sub-arguments, we might start the second sub-argument with "My second argument is . . ." Alternatively, if we have named the arguments, we can say, for example, "The main conclusion of the 'harm to children' argument is . . . This is supported by . . ." Other signposts might include "An objection to this position is . . ." or "In response to this . . ."

12.8 REVISING AND EDITING

Revising focuses on the big issues — the logic, coherence, clarity, and flow of the paper. Editing focuses on making sentence-level changes, such as correcting spelling and grammar, altering word choice, and sentence flow. Good writers revise and edit in two separate steps.

Revising for Coherence: Paragraphs and Whole Texts

After writing an essay, put it aside and focus on something else for awhile before revising. Distancing yourself somewhat from your work allows you to come at it with fresh eyes.

If possible, have a peer review the paper. Peer reviewers provide concrete feedback about what works and what does not work. Also, offer to be a peer reviewer for others. Critically examining the work of others helps sharpen your own perceptions and writing.

Read the paper aloud at least once, noting where it sounds stilted or doesn't flow. If possible, tape your reading and listen to it, or have another person read the paper while you listen. This exercise often helps you identify awkwardness, slips of logic, and gaps in the paper.

Look at the whole text for coherence. Construct an outline, précis, or one-paragraph argument of the essay. Start with the thesis statement. Then go through the text paragraph by paragraph, selecting the topic sentence — the main point — in each. Examine the argument using the suggestions for constructing a one-paragraph essay in Section 12.5. See if the argument flows clearly from one point to the next. If not, reorder and rewrite the paragraphs, or, if possible, introduce transitions. If there are sentences that don't contribute to the argument, reexamine them and revise so they do or cut them.

Examine the overall essay to see if you have included enough signposts for the reader. Not simply logical cue words, signposts signal to the reader where he or she is in an essay and where major changes of direction occur. They are also used to clearly indicate when you are presenting your own position and when you are presenting an alternate position or a challenge to the position you are defending.

Now look at each paragraph individually, starting with its topic sentence. Examine each sentence in the paragraph in the same way you examined the sentences of the one-paragraph argument. How does each relate to the topic sentence? What does it contribute to the overall argument? If it does not contribute to the argument or serve to illustrate a point in the argument, rewrite it so it does or cut it.

Revising for Clarity and Style: The Sentence Level

Both when writing and when revising the paper, we should strive to make the text — each sentence, transitions, and the overall organization — as clear as possible. A clearer style requires using the active rather than the passive voice; using concrete nouns and descriptive verbs rather than prepositional phrases, adjectives, and adverbs; and eliminating unnecessary words and redundancies. Richard Lanham in *Revising Prose* (5th ed. Englewood Cliffs, N.J.: Prentice Hall, 2006.) has proposed a "paramedic method" for turning sick and weak prose into more robust prose. The following expands on his method:

- **Identify and circle the prepositions in a passage.** Extensive use of prepositional phrases takes attention away from the subject and verb and deadens prose. Prepositions include *after, before, in, on, at, to, apart from, above, from, by, beside, over, among, through, around,* and *between.* One prepositional phrase is fine. Sometimes two in a row is unavoidable. More than that suggests that the sentence lacks focus. Replace prepositions or prepositional phrases with stronger verbs and nouns.

    Before: After considering the objections in light of the relevant information and for the purposes mentioned, we conclude that additional research is needed for the purpose of resolving the issue.

    The prepositional phrases make the text sluggish. Rewriting to eliminate them and using an active voice in place of *is needed*, we get the following:

    After: To respond to the relevant objections and resolve the issue, we need further research.

- **Circle forms of the verb *be***—*is, are, was, were, will be, seems to be,* etc. Forms of *be* often signal the passive voice and, even when the sentence is not passive, they are weak verbs. Note, however, that *be* verbs help form the progressive tense (e.g., *are writing*) and are necessary in this construction.

    Before: There are some situations in which arguments are not persuasive.

    After: Sometimes arguments do not persuade.

    In the first sentence, the main action falls in the subordinate clause ("in which . . ."), not in the main clause. Not only is the revision shorter but it focuses the reader's attention on the action.

- **In each sentence, identify what action is occurring.** Often the action has been turned into a prepositional phrase with no agent in sight. Who (or what) is acting? (See the preceding example.)
- **Put the action into a simple, active verb form, preferably with a human subject.** This technique helps when you find your prose confusing or hard to follow. It is based on the principle that the actor in a sentence should serve as the subject of a sentence, and the action should be in the sentence's verbs.

Before: A situation has arisen in which the raising of tuition has been proposed by the province and to which students and parents are opposed.

After: The province has proposed raising tuition fees. Students and their parents are opposed.

Before: This essay is in need of a stronger thesis.

After: This essay needs a stronger thesis. (*eliminating three words—two prepositions—results in a stronger statement*)

Before: There is much discussion among students about the proposed tuition increase.

This sentence uses a *be* verb, relies on an abstract term (*discussion*) that hides the action, and buries the subject of the action (students) in a prepositional phrase.

After: Students are discussing the proposed tuition increase.

The rewrite replaces the passive voice, in which we don't know who the actor is, with the active voice and changes the weak *is* to a stronger verb.

Before: In this essay, I show why tuition increases should not be implemented by the provincial government.

After: This essay examines why the provincial government should not implement tuition increases.

- **Rewrite nominalizations as verbs or adjectives.** A *nominalization* is a noun that replaces a verb or adjective. For example, instead of *organization*, use *organize*, which forces you to identify the actor. When nominalizations are used, actors are often hidden in prepositional phrases. Fewer nominalizations make our language clearer.

Before: The intention of the province is to proceed with the implementation of the proposal with the utmost haste. (*eighteen words*)

After: The province intends to implement the proposal quickly. (*eight words*)

The revision turns nominalizations into actions and eliminates unnecessary prepositional phrases.

- **Use simpler, more concrete terms, rather than abstract ones.** Using plain language makes your writing clearer and easier to read. In each of the following, the first term is a nominalization, the second a somewhat abstract verb, and the third a plainer and more concrete verb.

assertion, assert, say

am cognizant of, have knowledge of, know

demonstration of, demonstrate, show

discourse, conversation, converse, talk

initiative, initiate, start

modification, modify, change

- **Eliminate needless introductory words.** We often start sentences with preambles that contribute little to the content. The following are some common examples of unnecessary wordiness:

The question as to whether . . .

The reason why is that . . .

Owing to the fact that . . .

On the basis of . . .

In regard to . . .

It is the opinion of the author that . . .

The point of this is that . . .

These can often be rewritten or eliminated altogether.

Before: The question as to whether the province should raise tuition fees is not easy to answer.

After: Whether the province should raise tuition fees is not an easy question to answer.

Sometimes, other words within a sentence do little work and can be eliminated.

QUICK QUIZ 12.8   *Making Prose Clearer*

Revise each of the following sentences to make the statements clearer and more forceful.

1. The issue of importance noted by this writer is the extent of control that groups of parents should have over what is being taught in the schools. (From a student essay on the *Huck Finn* dialogue, used with permission.)
2. According to this writer, it is imperative that in light of the issue that we are considering, it should be given further thought.
3. There has been a modification to the expectation about the release date of the proposed new edition of the software.
4. In this essay, the reasons why tuition increases by the provincial government should not be implemented will be examined.
5. The crossing of the blue line is an action engaged in by a player acting in the capacity of a forward.

Editing

Finally, edit the paper for grammar, spelling, subject–verb agreement, correct use of words (*there, their*), and formatting.

Title Your Essay

A well-chosen title helps frame the essay, telling the reader what it is about. "The Tuition Essay," "Project #1," or "Tuition in University" tells the reader little about the content or position of the essay. Use your imagination to devise a title. This, your thesis, and your opening paragraph convey to the reader your basic argument. Weakness in any or all of these undermines the effort that you put into your essay. More descriptive titles might be "No to Tuition Increase," "Tuition: A Loss of Critical Skills," "More Tuition, Less Liberal Arts." These tell more precisely what the paper is about.

MODULE SUMMARY

Written argumentation involves not just putting an argument into written form but doing so while attending to our purpose for writing; the audience and the context of presentation; and the other arguers on the issue. Although we are not directly talking with these arguers in written argumentation, we are addressing them and the intended audience. We need to present opponents' arguments fairly while contributing to the ongoing discussion with our paper. The two processes central to written argument are composing, which includes developing an argument, and turning that argument into reader-based prose. In composing, we develop a position and the considerations that support that position, then turn those into reasons. We can develop reasons by using the issue model, using the topics model, brainstorming and editing, or doing research. We have to make these arguments as sound as possible and are expected to contribute something new to the ongoing dialogue. Our resulting arguments often have multiple lines of argument with numerous sub-arguments. Sometimes we have to make a case rather than simply develop an argument for a position. With complicated issues, we often need to develop a balance of considerations argument.

The challenge of presenting these complex, nonlinear arguments in a sequential form that the reader can understand and follow is the main task of producing reader-based prose. For simple arguments, we work from the formal structure of the arguments we have produced, eliminate the redundancies, order the claims, and provide cue words. For complex, multilinear arguments, on the essay level, we connect the various arguments, provide signposts, and develop a coherent, integrated structure. On the paragraph level, we write a coherent paragraph in which all of the claims support the topic sentence. On the sentence level, we write clear sentences.

Once we have produced an essay, we need to revise for logic, coherence, clarity, and flow; edit for grammar, spelling, agreement, and word choice; and provide a good descriptive title for the essay.

Congratulations! You have made your contribution to the ongoing process we call argumentation.

KEY TERMS

argument essay	free-writing
argumentation essay	introduction
balance of considerations argument	nominalization
body	one-paragraph argument
brainstorming	reader-based prose
brainteasers	signposts
case for a position	thesis
conclusion	

INDEX